W9-ATY-393

DEADLY CONSEQUENCES

DEADLY CONSEQUENCES

HOW COWARDS ARE PUSHING WOMEN INTO COMBAT

ROBERT L. MAGINNIS

REGNERY
Publishing, Inc.

An Eagle Publishing Company • Washington, DC

Copyright © 2013 by Robert L. Maginnis

All rights reserved. No part of this publication may be reproduced or transmitted in any form or by any means electronic or mechanical, including photocopy, recording, or any information storage and retrieval system now known or to be invented, without permission in writing from the publisher, except by a reviewer who wishes to quote brief passages in connection with a review written for inclusion in a magazine, newspaper, broadcast, or on a website.

Cataloging-in-Publication data on file with the Library of Congress
ISBN 978-1-62157-190-2

Published in the United States by
Regnery Publishing, Inc.
One Massachusetts Avenue NW
Washington, DC 20001
www.Regnery.com

Manufactured in the United States of America

10 9 8 7 6 5 4 3 2 1

Books are available in quantity for promotional or premium use. Write to Director of Special Sales, Regnery Publishing, Inc., One Massachusetts Avenue NW, Washington, DC 20001, for information on discounts and terms, or call (202) 216-0600.

Distributed to the trade by
Perseus Distribution
250 West 57th Street
New York, NY 10107

*This is dedicated to
my children and grandchildren.*

CONTENTS

INTRODUCTION ix

CHAPTER 1   How We Got Here 1

CHAPTER 2   Why Put Women in Combat? 43

CHAPTER 3   Myths about Women in Combat 55

CHAPTER 4   The Risks of Putting Women in Ground Combat 97

CHAPTER 5   What Should We Do? 163

CONCLUSION   What Kind of Country Are We? 193

ACKNOWLEDGMENTS 197

NOTES 199

INDEX 229

INTRODUCTION

The Obama administration has set a deliberate course to change the very nature of the United States military. On January 24, 2013, just before stepping down as secretary of defense, Leon Panetta ended the exclusion of women from direct ground combat. If implemented as planned by 2016, this policy will erode the military's warrior culture and its ability to defend America. The commander in chief's decision to assign women to direct ground combat units is contradicted by science, all empirical data, the experiences of other nations, and common sense. It is immoral and un-American.

Our senior generals are showing moral cowardice in the face of the enemy by failing to speak out against an ideological initiative that will harm readiness and troop morale.

Congress is derelict in its duty to establish the laws and policies that govern the military. It is kowtowing to radical feminists and accepting the mass media's illogical formulation of the issue as one of "equal rights."

The naïve American public has suspended critical thought, sharing in the government's blame by blindly acquiescing in this violence against women in the name of equal opportunity.

Putting women in combat will seriously weaken our fighting force, discourage males who are already abandoning the all-volunteer force, encourage sexual improprieties that erode unit cohesion, inflict physical and psychological injury on young women fooled into serving in combat, and ensure that eighteen-year-old females will be subject to the draft just like men.

America is being deceived by the highest levels of its government. We must end this insanity or we will reap the whirlwind.

CHAPTER 1

HOW WE GOT HERE

Most of the supporters of putting women in direct ground combat have no idea what they're really proposing. The generals, however, *do* know, and they are bowing to political pressure anyway. The Joint Chiefs of Staff compliantly provided their unanimous recommendation that the combat exclusion be lifted. Their chairman, General Martin E. Dempsey, looking not entirely comfortable, sat beside the secretary of defense as the new policy was proclaimed and recited the approved words of approbation. If anyone was going to object to this radical change in military practice, it wasn't going to be the top brass. That wasn't always the case.

General Robert H. Barrow, the twenty-seventh commandant of the Marine Corps, shocked the Senate Armed Services Committee in 1991 with his frank testimony about women in combat.[1] Any discussion of the issue, he told the senators, "should not be about women's rights, equal opportunity, career assignments for enhancement purposes for selection to higher rank. It is about, most assuredly, is about … combat effectiveness, combat readiness, winning the next conflict." General Barrow fought in World War II, Korea, and Vietnam. Looking back on his forty-one years of service, he "found nowhere for women in the ground combat element."

Barrow dismissed the arguments in favor of women in combat as "strange." Combat, he said, is a lot more than "getting shot at, or even getting killed by being shot at.… Combat is finding and closing with and killing or capturing the enemy. It's killing! And it's done in an environment that is often as difficult as you can possibly imagine; extremes of climate, brutality, death, dying. It's uncivilized and women can't do it. Nor should they be even thought of as doing it."

"I just cannot imagine why we are engaged in this debate about the possibility even of pushing women down into the ground combat part of our profession," Barrow said. Then he asked, "Who wants them to be an infantryman? The hard-line feminists do.… They have their agenda and it doesn't have anything to do with national security."

"It doesn't work," to which he added, "Please, Congress of the United States, you keep this responsibility. You draw the line. Don't pass it to DOD [Department of Defense]. Don't pass it to the executive branch, because they come and go. You have some continuity and you would put it in law; they put it in policy. The policy can change at a whim."

"We all believe in civilian control of the military, but sometimes that authority is abusive and coercive," Barrow warned. "And it's done over there [at the Pentagon] quietly; you don't necessarily know about it. When people in the civilian hierarchy of the Pentagon push on the military, the uniformed military do things not because it's the right thing but because they [civilians in control] can do it. They make them do it.… They change the policy to fit the pressure!"

The pressure, from radical feminists and craven politicians, never let up. Unless Congress quickly heeds General Barrow's plea to intervene, the disastrous policy of putting women in direct-fire, close combat will become a reality. In the pages that follow, I examine that policy from every angle, offering abundant firsthand observations by service members, from privates to generals and flag officers— men and women who put a human face on this contentious and critical issue.

First, I examine how America came to consider pushing women into direct ground combat. We arrived at this point partially because of the pressure, which General Barrow described, on senior uniformed military leadership to acquiesce to the whims of a bankrupt political class. Those politicians are pressured in turn by radical feminists and an ideologically driven media, who are enabled by a complacent public that is ignorant of military matters, especially the demands of combat.

Second, I consider eight arguments that have been made for putting women in combat, none of which holds up.

Third, feminists and the media promote a number of myths about women, men, and combat to advance their agenda at the expense of our national security. I scrutinize and puncture each of these myths.

Fourth, I explain the dangers of sexualizing our ground combat units. Specifically, I consider the lessons learned from past experiments in mixing the sexes and suggest a better approach if the Pentagon insists on this reckless policy. Ending the exclusion of women from combat has major implications for the all-volunteer force that we have enjoyed since the Vietnam War, and I explain why this change is almost certain to lead to including women in conscription.

I conclude with a plan of action. The hour is late, but there is still an opportunity for an awakened nation to forestall this historic error.

"I'm Amanda"

The incremental process by which the United States military decided to put women into direct-fire, close ground combat assignments has been deceitful. It is the work of political leaders who naïvely treat ground combat as an equal-opportunity issue and of military commanders who know better but are afraid to speak the truth about its adverse effects on readiness.

Immediately after the Pentagon lifted the combat exclusion for women in January 2013, members of the Washington political class rushed to demonstrate their support for the latest example of President Obama's social engineering. Democrats fell in line with their president, and a Republican critic of the scheme could hardly be found.

Then the politically correct generals rallied behind their commander in chief, uttering the same nonsense about equal opportunity. The chairman of the Joint Chiefs of Staff told his conversion story to a receptive press. Shortly after taking command of the Army's First Armored Division in June 2003, as he was preparing for one of his first trips outside his Baghdad headquarters, General Dempsey had paused to introduce himself to the crew of his Humvee. "I slapped the turret gunner on the leg and I said, 'Who are you?' And she leaned down and said, 'I'm Amanda,' and I said, 'Ah, OK.'"[2]

"So, female turret-gunner protecting division commander. It's from that point on that I realized something had changed, and it was time to do something about it," Dempsey said. Even though his two daughters served in the Army during wartime, the chairman's "I'm Amanda" moment was apparently the first time he had thought about the issue of women in combat.[3]

There is no question American women have served the nation honorably throughout its history. Their military service increased substantially in the mid-1970s, and today they account for 15 percent of the armed forces, serving in most military jobs.[4] In this chapter, I will examine that history of service and the incremental changes in the laws and regulations governing women's service over the past hundred years. I will also address the political engine behind those changes, especially the feminist movement, which enjoys the support of the entertainment and news media. Promoting women as groin-kicking, karate divas and wannabe special-ops killers, they have desensitized Americans to violence against women. National polls now show that three-quarters of the population support sending women as gladiators into the most violent environment known to man—direct ground combat.

Only a couple of decades ago, the idea of putting women at the point of the spear would have been ridiculed. Men who proposed such a thing would have been "accused of cowardice for even considering that women take their place on the battlefield," says Colonel Valerie O'Rear, a twenty-three-year U.S. Air Force veteran. "But once a little ground is gained, even if it doesn't enjoy complete public support at the time, the public becomes desensitized, and the action normalized. Once normalization occurs, another step is taken toward the previously unthinkable."

Cowardice of Silence

Our armed forces are now led by senior flag and general officers who act more like skilled and obedient politicians than authentic military officers. They have an uncanny sense of which way the political winds are blowing and immediately correct their heading accordingly, while ignoring the consequences for operational readiness, the mission, and the safety and morale of our troops.

Such is the case with the support of the chairman of the Joint Chiefs of Staff for lifting the ban on women in combat units. More principled officers, with a sense of honor, would recognize the hypocrisy of this intellectually corrupt policy, resign in protest, and go public with their views. There have been no such resignations, however, and it is plain that the country's senior military leadership is guilty of the cowardice of silence.

Americans are resigned to political leaders pushing political agendas for political reasons, but when it comes to national security, they want their military leaders to remain above politics. The military must focus on the realities of war and avoid the muck of partisan politics. Yet the service chiefs have endorsed President Obama's latest attempt at social engineering like agreeable bobblehead dolls, betraying the same lack of principled leadership with which they greeted the new policy on homosexuals in the military in 2010.

It is disturbing to watch our top generals, who have decades of experience—some in combat zones—and who know the demands of ground combat, endorse this radical policy shift. Yet that is what they have done.

Sitting next to Secretary of Defense Leon Panetta at the Pentagon press conference on January 24, 2013, General Dempsey said:

> Today we are acting to expand the opportunities for women to serve in the United States Armed Forces and to better align our policies with the experiences we have had over the past decade of war.... Ultimately, we're acting to strengthen the joint force....
>
> We'll also integrate women in a way that enhances opportunity for everyone. This means setting clear standards of performance for all occupations based on what it actually takes to do the job.

The chairman of the Joint Chiefs sounds more like a diversity officer at a university than the nation's top military officer. What's most disconcerting is that General Dempsey and the service chiefs have a choice, but they continue to acquiesce in this radical and misdirected feminist crusade. Dempsey could resign rather than endorse the president's radical policy. He would still collect his $180,000 annual pension. The general's conduct implies that he agrees that putting women in combat is a good idea.

Why have the Joint Chiefs of Staff followed in lockstep behind Obama when the evidence is overwhelmingly against this policy?

Dempsey and the service chiefs are in their positions "because they agreed to support these policies," according to retired Lieutenant General Jerry Boykin, the former commander of the U.S. Army's Delta Force and deputy undersecretary of defense for intelligence under President George W. Bush. "They have shown lack of courage to stand up to the administration when it is clear the policies do not enhance readiness."[5] The secretary of defense probably looked at Dempsey, Boykin believes, and said something like, "This is the new policy, and I expect everyone to endorse it."

Heather Mac Donald of the Manhattan Institute agrees that the Pentagon brass acted like cowards, suggesting that "the feminine infrastructure in the Pentagon is more than [Dempsey] can withstand." His endorsement of the policy is another "triumph of radical feminists and cowardice of males to stand up to female victimology."[6]

Of course the Joint Chiefs of Staff are appointed by the president, but they are expected, Boykin explains, "to represent the best interest of the military, not the administration." But Dempsey appears to be representing the administration and not the military. If a general is at odds with the administration, the White House has two choices, says Boykin. The president can "let him continue or remove him," but very few generals turn in their stars in protest, even when the stakes are high.

General Harold K. Johnson, the Army chief of staff from 1964 to 1968, was heavily involved in the policy debates about the escalation of the Vietnam War in 1964. He felt strongly that President Lyndon B. Johnson should declare a national emergency, call up the reserves, fight a decisive war, and quickly withdraw. A combat veteran of World War II who spent three years as a prisoner of war and was awarded the Distinguished Service Cross, General Johnson decided to go to the White House and confront LBJ about the decision not to call up the reserves. Getting out of his car, however, he had second thoughts and left without expressing his strong disagreement with the president.

Years later, General Johnson spoke at the Army Command and General Staff College, where he explained his objections to President Johnson's "graduated response" in Vietnam. "He told us that his worse regret was not resigning as Army Chief of Staff and [then] fighting the Vietnam limited war strategy in the political arena," recalls retired Marine Brigadier General William Weise, an exchange staff college instructor at the time. We will never know what might have happened if General Johnson had resigned rather than retreating. Perhaps the president would not have escalated a war that lasted another decade, cost 58,282 young American lives, and ended disastrously for both our South Vietnamese allies and America's reputation abroad.

General Boykin's own standards are rigorous. "I think a general officer who objects [to a policy] must put the country above his own career. This [decision about women in combat] is about the future of America and not about them." Such resignations are the exception, and General Ronald Fogleman's was one of them. He stepped down as the Air Force chief of staff in 1997, citing "a variety of reasons," but mostly differences with President Clinton over the failure to defend against a terrorist attack that killed nineteen U.S. servicemen in Saudi Arabia. "I do not want the institution to suffer and I am afraid it will if I am seen as a divisive force and not a team player," said this honorable man in a written statement.[7]

General Carl Mundy, the thirtieth commandant of the Marine Corps (1991–1995), led the other service chiefs in opposition to allowing open homosexuals in the military during President Clinton's first term. "I never got threatened with getting thrown out," General Mundy insists. There were calls from retired officers for Mundy to resign in protest over the issue, but he explains, "You can't abandon troops on the battlefield." He predicted—incorrectly, as it turned out—that "this too will pass," and "these guys will not be here that long," and we just need to "gut it out."[8]

General officers know, of course, that the president can fire them for disobedience or if they publicly disagree. Abraham Lincoln sacked General George McClellan for refusing to attack Confederate forces. Lyndon Johnson fired General Curtis LeMay of the Air Force for criticizing the White House for not carpet bombing North Vietnam's cities. The most famous presidential dismissal was that of General Douglas MacArthur for public criticism of Harry Truman's conduct of the Korean War. MacArthur wanted to attack China, which had sent troops to back North Korea, and lashed out at Truman, declaring, "There is no substitute for victory." Truman's refusal to expand the war into China, he insisted, imposed "an enormous handicap, without precedent in military history."[9]

More recently, Jimmy Carter unceremoniously sacked General John K. Singlaub in 1977 for criticizing Carter's promise to remove all U.S. troops from the Korean peninsula. Before a final decision had been reached, Singlaub expressed his grave concerns publicly. Carter swiftly recalled Singlaub, humiliated him, and forced him to retire.[10]

President Obama has sacked a few generals himself, no doubt capturing the attention of today's general officer corps and chilling future resistance. Obama relieved General Stanley McChrystal of his duties for appearing to disagree publicly with the president about troop levels in Afghanistan. The general also made improvident comments about the administration to a *Rolling Stone* reporter. The general, claimed Obama, had undermined "the civilian control of the military that is at the core of our democratic system."[11] Another target of Obama's displeasure was General James "Mad Dog" Mattis, the head of U.S. Central Command. The White House was unhappy with Mattis's advice about Iran, Afghanistan, and the Arab Spring, and with the general's uncomfortable lines of questioning. He stepped down in March 2013, five months early, one of the few generals willing to speak his mind.

The U.S. military serves as the commander in chief's instrument to defend the country by combating actual or perceived threats to national security. He has the right to select officers who will faithfully execute his orders, remain tight-lipped, and accept responsibility for their failures. Nevertheless, the country deserves principled military commanders who are prepared to stand up to foolhardy political leadership, even at the cost of their careers. The chiefs of staff who have lined up with President Obama on the question of women in combat apparently don't believe this standard applies to them. "We are all cowards sometimes," says a retired Marine general with substantial Capitol Hill experience. Dempsey "just caved to political pressure."[12]

Sometimes generals must ask Congress for help, as General Mundy did when the Marine Corps faced a 25-percent cut in manpower in the early 1990s. He took to heart the advice given him by the former Marine commandant General Lou Wilson: "Never forget, the Marine Corps would have never come to be and never continue to exist without the will of Congress." General Mundy briefed congressional staffers about the effect of the threatened cuts. When the news of his briefing hit the front page of the *Washington Post* the next morning, Mundy concluded, "I'm going to be dog meat."[13] He called the military aide to Secretary of Defense Dick Cheney: "I need to see the Secretary." Mundy met with Cheney that afternoon and explained, "We can't take the Marine Corps down that far. I'm not the guy to do it." Cheney was gracious with the general and called a meeting of all the chiefs. With the help of the chairman, General Colin Powell, the Corps ended up with 174,000 Marines rather than the 150,000 initially threatened.

Leadership like General Mundy's is rare today. In 2011, the Center for Army Leadership's annual survey drew responses from over 16,800 uniformed and civilian leaders in the Army, with a margin of error within +/− 0.7 percent. Three-quarters (74 percent) of active-duty leaders said the Army is not going in the right direction in part because the top leaders—that is, general officers—are ineffective and focused on the wrong priorities. Political correctness—a form of psychological command and control whose purpose is the imposition of uniformity in thought, speech, and behavior—has become a powerful force in the military. The leadership survey identified it as a reason that the Army is not headed in the right direction—top officers bow to "politically correct solutions" to appease policy makers or to "play politics."[14]

A survey of all active-duty generals' and flag officers' views about political correctness would be useful, but it is unlikely in today's environment; a survey of retired general and flag officers, however, is the next best thing. One such survey was conducted in 1992 for the Presidential Commission on the Assignment of Women in the Armed

Forces. More than half of those officers responded. Three-quarters (78 percent) opposed ground combat service for women, and 90 percent opposed women in the infantry.[15] The numbers were higher among retired Army and Marine Corps officers. The retired Marine general with Capitol Hill experience whom I quoted earlier believes that if the survey were conducted today, the results would be much the same.[16]

Generals like Dempsey feel they "must fall in line with this administration" or "risk their jobs," says Paul Vallely, a retired Army major general and chairman of Stand Up America. Their willingness to put their careers ahead of their country, says Vallely, "is evidence of the degradation of the senior officer corps."[17] If generals disagree with Obama's decision, he says, they "should stand up and be counted like a warrior. They must cling to the values and traditions of the service…. They need to stand up and state the truth."

General Boykin's sad conclusion is that the service chiefs have displayed "a lack of moral courage" on the issue of women in combat. These officers should think about the "future of America and not about themselves" when facing such explosive issues.

Women at War

Women's wartime service is to be celebrated and appreciated. Women have been warriors, heroines, adventurers, scouts, partisans, revolutionaries, nurses, and camp followers. Their contributions are a matter of historical record across the world.[18]

Boudicca, queen of the Iceni, led an uprising against the Romans in Britain.[19] Zenobia, queen of the East, tried to bring Syria, western Asia, and Egypt under her command.[20] She wore military garb and accompanied her troops, but there is slim evidence she actually physically fought.

Joan of Arc, the simple, illiterate daughter of a French plowman, played a pivotal military role in ending the Hundred Years' War (1337–1453). Queen Isabella of Spain is credited with the development of artillery, the modern use of infantry, and engineers. Kit Welsh, Hannah Snell (alias James Grey), and Trooper Mary were all famous English female fighters.[21]

Women constituted one-fourth of the Russian revolutionary movement. They were frontline combatants in Cuba and the Philippines, and the old Mexican armies also employed female combatants.[22]

Thousands of women actively fought the Germans in World War II. Yugoslavian women trained and fought with men. By the end of the war, twenty-five thousand had died in battle, and another forty thousand had been wounded. Italian women resisted the Germans. French, Hungarian, and Czechoslovakian women fought alongside men.[23]

Russian women served in all ground combat positions during World War II. The German invasion required that men and women of all ages defend their homeland. Women were drafted and trained and eventually became sharpshooters, machine gunners, automatic riflemen, mortarmen, and more. They were engineers, technicians, radio operators, turret gunners, drivers, and mechanics. Thousands served in the infantry and command positions. Wartime exigency, however, did not become postwar normality. Women in combat units were quickly demobilized, and the Russians have never appointed women to combat units since. National survival was the driving force for their use, and that all changed with the defeat of Germany.[24]

Approximately a hundred thousand British women were drafted during World War II for military or national service duties. Many of these female soldiers were assigned to antiaircraft and searchlight batteries throughout England.[25]

During World War II, thousands of women joined, and sometimes led, units of the French liberation forces. These women participated in raids and sabotage missions; they also acted as couriers and spies. They often used weapons. French women also served in noncombat positions in Vietnam during the French Indochina War.[26]

Israeli women fought to the death at the beginning of their nation's War of Independence (1947–1949). Their combat roles were eliminated when it was discovered that the Arabs fought more fiercely to destroy units containing women. Since 1948, women drafted into the Israeli army have served as regulars, but they receive separate basic training, and their combat training is mostly defensive.[27] The Israelis have no plans to use women in frontline, combat arms.

Canada has abolished laws barring women from combat, and Canadian women can now serve as infantry soldiers. "Combat Related Employment for Women (CREW) trials began in the mid-1980s," but only one of the eighty women initially recruited for the infantry successfully completed the training program. Other women were more successful, and now women serve in artillery and armor units.[28]

American women have a limited military service history because of national policies and because there has not been a war on American soil since the Civil War. Though their service opportunities have been limited, their commitment and ability should not be discounted. During the Revolutionary War, women performed the traditional duties of cooking, sewing, and nursing. Some, like Mary Hays McCauley, also served as soldiers along with their husbands. She earned the nickname "Molly Pitcher" by carrying water to her husband and other artillerymen. When her husband fell wounded at the Battle of Monmouth, she took his place.[29] General George Washington picked Ann Simpson David to carry messages. She slipped through British lines, carrying secret orders stashed in sacks of grain throughout eastern Pennsylvania.[30] Mad Ann Bailey was a scout, spy, and messenger, as well as an expert shot and skilled horsewoman. Sarah Fulton delivered dispatches through enemy lines. Deborah Sampson Gannett, from Plymouth, Massachusetts, was one of the first American female soldiers. Disguising herself, she enlisted as Robert Shurtleff and served for seventeen months. When she was wounded, she avoided detection by the doctors by removing the shot from her own thigh.[31]

American women served in the War of 1812 and in the Mexican War. Elizabeth C. Newcom disguised herself in men's clothing and joined the Army at Fort Leavenworth, Kansas. She was discharged ten months later when her sex was discovered, but Congress recognized her service by paying her with both land and money. Mary Marshall and Mary Allen served as nurses aboard Commodore Stephen Decatur's ship, the *United States*.[32]

Numerous women served in traditional roles—and some in nontraditional roles—on both sides of the Civil War. Again, some women disguised themselves as men in order to enlist and fight. Sarah Edmonds served as a male nurse but later became a Union spy, infiltrating Confederate lines eleven times in 1862 and 1863.[33] Sally Tompkins ran a military hospital in Richmond and was the only woman to receive an officer's commission in the Confederate Army.[34]

Dr. Mary Edwards Walker volunteered to care for wounded servicemen in the Union Army and was later appointed the Army's first female surgeon. She followed the battles, working as a volunteer surgeon at Manassas and Fredericksburg, Virginia. She was captured in April 1864 after making a wrong turn while visiting units. In 1865, Walker became the first woman awarded the Medal of Honor,[35] but for "distinguished service," not heroism. The Army removed her name (and about nine hundred others) from the Medal of Honor

Roll in 1917, when Congress established that the Medal of Honor was to be awarded only for gallantry in an engagement with the enemy, not for distinguished service.[36] President Jimmy Carter, bowing to protests from feminists, restored Walker's medal in 1977.[37]

Twenty-one thousand American military nurses saw active duty in the First World War. Other women filled nonmilitary jobs at munitions factories, aviation plants, the American Red Cross, and the United Service Organizations and took other jobs vacated by men who were off at war. General John J. Pershing, the commander of the American Expeditionary Force, sought to employ women in Army clerical and telephone jobs. At his request, 223 civilian contract women known as "Hello Girls" were sent to England and France to meet this need.[38]

In World War II, 350,000 women served in the U.S. military, mostly as nurses. They served in administrative, medical, and communication jobs, and some in direct support of combat units. Lieutenant General Mark Clark's V Corps advance party included female communication specialists.[39]

Women shed their blood for their country in that war. Of the eight thousand women who served in the European theater, seventeen received the Purple Heart, and sixteen nurses were killed.[40] Others were prisoners of war. In the Pacific, sixty-six Army nurses were captured in the Philippines in 1942. They cared for sick American prisoners at the Santo Tomas camp until freed in February 1945.[41] Women constituted 2.3 percent of the twelve million U.S. service personnel at the end of June 1945, and nearly 1,600 were decorated for meritorious service and bravery during the war.[42]

More than 540 American women deployed to Korea in 1950, serving as nurses, stenographers, aides, and interpreters.[43] The number of females in war-zone service soared to eleven thousand during the Vietnam War. The names of eight of them—all Army nurses—are engraved in the somber black granite of "the Wall," the Vietnam Veterans Memorial in Washington, D.C.[44] Up to seven hundred WACs were consistently stationed at Long Binh, Vietnam, during the war. Overprotected and locked up at night, they were given no weapons and no offensive combat training. Many feared that they would be easy prey if overrun by the enemy in a locked-up camp.

Approximately two hundred Army women participated in the Grenada relief expedition in 1983, but they were not welcomed by many of their male counterparts. For example, four military policewomen were mistakenly sent to the island with their unit only to be sent right back to Fort Bragg, North Carolina, because fighting continued. Women were permitted on the island only after hostilities ceased.[45]

On December 20, 1989, approximately 803 Army women participated in Operation Just Cause in Panama. They served in combat service and support roles, not in actual combat. Two female pilots ferried infantrymen in Black Hawk helicopters into "hot" areas. Captain Linda Bray, whose military police unit liberated a dog kennel, became the first woman to lead American soldiers in combat. She eventually left the Army after her unit's actions were wildly exaggerated in press reports to make it appear as if she had been in direct combat.[46] A slight, five-foot, one-inch, 105-pound woman, Bray explained the physical toll she paid for her service. "I carried too much weight. I always felt pressure in the military. *You don't have very much weight in your rucksack. Why don't you carry a little more?* I kept adding more until my hips broke. I can't run, jump. I can't even go grocery shopping without having to sit down because it hurts," she explained.[47]

Over 7 percent of American forces in Operation Desert Storm were women. They were assigned to most units, and a few of those units spearheaded the attack on Iraq. Women served in Riyadh, Saudi Arabia, with the joint staff and in southern Iraq with forward combat support and combat service support forces. They filled upward of 25 percent of the combat service support jobs, the people who supported General H. Norman Schwarzkopf's "Hail Mary" maneuver.

More than 283,000 women have served in operations in Iraq and Afghanistan since 2001; as I write, 154 have died in service and over 964 have been wounded. They account for more than 11 percent of our forces in the theater of operation. Even though they are excluded from ground combat, many have been exposed to direct fire while serving in support roles, such as military police, helicopter pilots, and truck drivers. Women have served heroically.[48]

In 2005, Leigh Ann Hester became the first female soldier to receive the Silver Star for exceptional valor in close-quarters combat in Iraq. Monica Lin Brown, serving in Afghanistan, received the Silver Star in 2008 for protecting with her own body soldiers wounded by a roadside bomb and running through gunfire to save their lives.

Many American women have served honorably in combat over the last century. A tiny number of them served in combat units under subterfuge, while most provided support to the frontline soldiers in other valued capacities. But only the Stalin-era Soviets—under the pressure of a war for national survival—have ever placed women in direct frontline combat on a large scale. They abandoned this experiment for reasons that will become obvious.

Women's Road to Combat

American women are being pushed into combat through a deliberate "incrementalist" strategy orchestrated by radical feminists and abetted by self-serving politicians and politically correct senior military officers. The strategy is succeeding because of cultural shifts and weak national leadership. Not so long ago, however, leaders resisted the idea of women serving in the military, and women in combat were simply unthinkable.

In 1908, Congress established the Navy Nurse Corps.[49] During World War I, the War Department opposed further expansion of the female role in the American Expeditionary Force. A memorandum from the department regarding proposed legislation read:

> The enlistment of women in the military forces of the United States has never been seriously contemplated and such enlistment is considered unwise and highly undesirable.... The action provided for in this bill is not only unwise, but exceedingly ill-advised.[50]

In spite of these objections, the secretary of the Navy allowed women to perform clerical duties in the Marine Corps and Navy beginning in 1918. But major changes in the role of women in the armed forces did not begin until late 1939 with an Army General Staff study that recommended a "quasi-military female organization." The Women's Army Auxiliary Corps (WAAC), established in May 1942, provided female accountants, cooks, draftsmen, telephone operators, chauffeurs, librarians, postal clerks, and other support personnel. The name was shortened in July to Women's Army Corps (WAC). Women were trained as noncombatants (with limited weapons training for a few) and served in all overseas theaters of war.[51]

Soon the other services followed suit. The same year, the Navy formed Women Accepted for Volunteer Emergency Service (WAVES) to fill administrative, medical, and communication jobs. The Coast Guard set up SPARS (for *semper paratus*—"always ready," the Coast

Guard motto), and the Marine Corps staffed its headquarters with its new Women's Reserve.

In 1942, Nancy Harkness Love helped organize twenty-five female pilots into the Women's Auxiliary Ferrying Squadron (WAFS), located at New Castle Army Air Base in Delaware. Their mission was to deliver planes from the factory to military bases. The WAFS grew to forty women before merging into the Women Air Force Service Pilots (WASPs).[52]

The WASPs were disbanded in 1944. A letter of notification from General Henry H. Arnold states, "When we needed you, you came through and have served most commendably under very difficult circumstances … but now the war situation has changed and the time has come when your volunteered services are no longer needed. The situation is that if you continue in service, you will be replacing instead of releasing our young men. I know the WASP wouldn't want that…. I want you to know that I appreciate your war service and that the AAF [Army Air Force] will miss you…."[53]

In 1946, the U.S. Army chief of staff, General Dwight D. Eisenhower, directed the preparation of legislation to make the WACs a permanent part of the Army. The next year this draft legislation was combined with the WAVES and Women Marines bill as well as a section on women for the Air Force. President Truman signed the Women's Armed Services Integration Act on June 12, 1948.[54]

Once women had been given permanent legal status, the services began issuing them regular officer appointments and enlisting them from the ages of eighteen to thirty-five, but women were limited to 2 percent of the total armed forces. That limitation was lifted in 1967, allowing the female force to grow. Women could now attain flag rank and more fully participate in the military services. Constraints on the full participation of women, however, continued.[55]

The Women's Armed Services Integration Act of 1948 included combat exclusions for women and made it unlawful for female pilots to fly combat missions regardless of their capability, training, or time in service.[56] Thirty years later, in 1978, Congress codified restrictions on women in the Navy and Marine Corps. Title 10, Section 6015, of the U.S. Code provided: "Women may not be assigned to duty on vessels or in aircraft that are engaged in combat missions nor may they be assigned to other than temporary duty on vessels of the Navy except hospital ships, transports, and vessels of a similar classification not expected to be assigned to combat missions."[57] Similar legislation (Section 8549) barred women in the Air Force from duty on aircraft engaged in combat missions.

Women in the Army were never excluded from combat by statute, so in 1983 that service developed the direct combat probability coding (DCPC) system to govern the assignment of women. Every military occupational specialty or area of concentration in the Army was evaluated on the basis of the duties it entailed, the unit's mission, tactical doctrine, and battlefield location. Positions were then coded according to the probability of engagement in direct combat.[58]

In February 1988, the Department of Defense adopted the "risk rule," a standard for evaluating positions and units across the services from which the military could exclude women. Such exclusions extended to noncombat units or missions if the risk of exposure to direct combat, hostile fire, or capture was equal to or greater than the risk in the combat units they supported. Each service used the risk rule to evaluate all positions to decide whether to open or close them to women.[59] Citing the implied congressional intent to exclude women from combat in Sections 6015 and 8549, the Army applied the risk rule to exclude women from routine engagement in direct-fire, close ground combat.

After the adoption of the risk rule, two events caused the Pentagon to weaken its protection of servicewomen. The first was the invasion of Panama in January 1990, an operation that included substantial numbers of women. The major media's coverage of the action was designed to influence public opinion in favor of women in combat. A *New York Times*–CBS News poll found that 72 percent of those surveyed thought women should be allowed to serve in combat units if they wanted to—the operative term being "wanted to." A *McCall's* magazine survey reported even stronger support for lifting restrictions—79 percent.[60]

Then, three years later, Bill Clinton became president, with the Democrats maintaining control of both houses of Congress. In December 1991, Congress had repealed Section 8549, the exclusion of women from Air Force combat missions.[61] During Clinton's first year in office, Congress repealed the statutory ban on women in naval combat, Section 6015.[62] Secretary of Defense Les Aspin then announced his intention to rescind the 1988 risk rule and replace it with a less restrictive ground combat rule. "Expanding the roles for women in the military is the right thing to do, and it's also the smart thing to do," he asserted. "It allows us to assign the most qualified individual to each military job. In all these actions, our overall aim remains the same, a high quality, ready-to-fight force."[63]

Aspin's instructions, issued in early 1994, included three new criteria for identifying direct ground combat units: (1) Will the unit engage an enemy on the ground with weapons? (2) Will the unit be exposed to hostile fire? (3) Does the unit have a high probability of direct physical contact with the personnel of a hostile force? He gave the services four months to provide "justification in detail why billets are being opened or kept closed."[64]

The secretary of the Army, Togo West, responded on June 1, 1994: "The issue at hand is not whether women will be in combat. Women are, today, in the fight. The issue is whether obstacles have been placed in their path, preventing them from reaching their full potential. Women should be assigned to any job they can perform."[65] West announced that women would be assigned to all positions except those involving the highest probability of direct combat with the enemy. "Direct ground combat," he specified,

> is engaging an enemy on the ground with individual or crew-served weapons, while being exposed to hostile fire and to a high probability of direct physical contact with the hostile force's personnel. Direct ground combat takes place well forward on the battlefield while locating and closing with the enemy to defeat them by fire, maneuver, or shock effect.[66]

West's decision to open more positions to women contradicted the findings of the Presidential Commission on the Assignment of Women in the Armed Forces, which Congress had established in the National Defense Authorization Act for Fiscal Year 1992–1993. Guided by the Army's statutory mission—the Army "shall be organized, trained and equipped primarily for prompt and sustained combat incident to operations on land"[67]—the fifteen-member presidentially appointed commission collected and studied evidence about the assignment of women to combat throughout 1992. The commission heard no evidence that putting women in combat would improve the Army's ability to accomplish its mission. The evidence, in fact, was to the contrary.

Lieutenant General J. H. Binford Peay III, the Army's deputy chief of staff for operations and plans, told the commission that "despite technological advances, ground combat is no more refined, no less barbaric and no less physically demanding than it has been through-out history."[68] Rear Admiral Raymond C. Smith Jr. testified, "Even if some women are strong enough to handle the physical demands of combat, the introduction of factors such as sexual entanglements and jealousies—even if the women don't invite such attention—would make the forward commander's job more difficult."[69]

A number of war veterans testified that women should not be assigned to ground combat because the physiological requirements over time are extreme, and any group is only as strong as its weakest member. In its December 1992 report, the commission found that women are shorter, have less muscle mass and upper-body strength, and weigh less than men, placing them at a distinct disadvantage when performing tasks—like ground combat—requiring a high level of muscular strength and aerobic capacity. No amount of training or education can change these physiological traits.

But the Clinton administration had an agenda, and it charged ahead. On July 29, 1994, the new secretary of defense, William Perry, opened eighty thousand more military jobs to women, bringing to more than a quarter million the number of positions opened to women by the Clinton administration.[70] The 1994 Defense Authori-zation Act required the Pentagon to justify changes to assignment policies that might cause women to be subject to a future draft.[71] Perry assured Sam Nunn, the Georgia Democrat who was chairman of the Senate Armed Services Committee, that the Pentagon's new ground combat rule still exempted women from "armor, infantry, and ground combat special operations forces (Army Special Forces,

Rangers, Navy Special Forces [SEALs] and Air Force Combat Controllers) units and career fields."[72]

The male-only Selective Service law—the draft—had been challenged in court in 1981 in the case of *Rostker v. Goldberg*.[73] The Supreme Court upheld the exemption of women from Selective Service registration because the law's purpose is to maintain a pool of potential combat troops. That argument was eroded by the Clinton administration's changes, which left more than 80 percent of all military positions open to women. Virtually all Air Force (99.7 percent) and Navy positions (94.0 percent) were now open, though the Army (67.2 percent) and Marine Corps (62.0 percent) were more restrictive. The Pentagon nevertheless insisted that women were still ineligible for ground combat assignments.[74]

Along with his announcement of eighty thousand new jobs, Perry promised, "Our over-arching goal is to maintain a high-quality, ready and effective force. By increasing the numbers of units and positions to which women can be assigned, the military services gain greater flexibility in the development and use of human resources."[75] Yet the Clinton administration never explained how liberalization of the female assignment policy would accomplish the goal of maintaining "a high-quality, ready and effective force." According to Perry, these changes were intended to expand "the opportunities for women in the military."[76]

Starting with the George W. Bush administration and accelerating in the Obama administration, even the relaxed 1994 rule was ignored except for direct-fire, close ground combat. Incremental changes, like the assignment of women to submarines, took place without the mandatory notice to Congress. Article 1, Section 8, of the U.S. Constitution gives Congress the power to "raise and support armies" and to "provide and maintain a navy." Congress makes the rules that govern the military, including those about women and their assignments. For many years, however, Congress has neglected its duty, allowing the executive—especially Presidents Clinton, Bush, and Obama—to flout its constitutional prerogatives.

This process has now culminated in the Obama administration's decision to open ground combat positions to women. In rescinding Aspin's 1994 rule exempting women from combat, Panetta directed the military services to report to Congress in May 2013 whether they intend to retain regulations regarding the assignment of women to combat units. These reports will not ask for Congress's approval but tell Congress the services' intentions. The burden will be on Congress to stop the administration's steamroller.

The Obama administration has every reason to employ this tactic to impose a monumental change on the American military. It worked like a charm to eliminate the ban on open homosexuals in the military. In his 2010 State of the Union address, President Obama called on Congress to repeal the policy known as "Don't Ask, Don't Tell." A week later, Secretary of Defense Robert Gates testified, "We have received our orders from the Commander in Chief, and we are moving out accordingly." Admiral Michael Mullen, the chairman of the Joint Chiefs, echoed his support with a personal endorsement that "allowing gays and lesbians to serve openly would be the right thing to do."[77] Gates then ordered a review of how to implement the repeal of "Don't Ask, Don't Tell," to be completed by the end of that year. Congress dutifully waited on the promised report, which arrived in November and was quickly followed by hearings featuring only the chiefs of the services. Then the lame-duck Congress repealed the law.

The administration is following the same script for putting women in combat, and the senior military leaders are capitulating on cue. Former Secretary of Defense Panetta has admitted that this change is about removing "as many barriers as possible." "Female service members have faced the reality of combat," he has said, and "proven their willingness to fight.... We are moving forward with a plan to eliminate all unnecessary gender-based barriers to service."[78]

Echoing Panetta at the January 2013 press conference announcing the change, General Dempsey insisted, "Ultimately, we're acting to strengthen the joint force." The only justification he offered, however, was enhanced "opportunity for everyone" followed by the obligatory bromide that readiness, morale, and unit cohesion will be as strong as ever. "We'll preserve our warfighting capability to defend the nation."

The Panetta-Dempsey power play set in motion a quick process to remove all remaining exemptions for women in combat. While the services started internal preparations to assign women to all combat positions, Congress was not officially notified until late spring and was thus denied the opportunity to conduct oversight hearings, much less halt or adjust the process.

The Ideology behind the Policy

In *The Art of War*, the ancient Chinese strategist Sun Tzu advised, "If you know your enemy and know yourself, you need not fear the result of a hundred battles." The U.S. military has ignored this counsel when confronting the radical feminists, who want to socially engineer it out of existence.

Feminists are using their considerable political clout to press politicians to undermine our armed forces, and the military's flag and general officers are astonishingly compliant. The feminist campaign that began decades ago is about to remove all combat exclusions for women regardless of the consequences for women themselves, the military, and the nation's security. This ill-advised policy sets aside common sense and millennia of human experience for the sake of appeasing a politically aggressive group of ideologues who despise all that the military represents. Even our most threatening international competitors have not succumbed to this nonsense despite their boasts of egalitarianism in the ranks.

"Feminism" understood as equality of rights and opportunities between men and women is not the enemy. But a movement that began in the nineteenth century with a reasonable and humane agenda developed a radical side in the twentieth. The original feminism focused on women's suffrage, working conditions, and education. Radical feminism—now enthroned in America's universities, the news and entertainment media, and much of the government— is at war with human nature itself. Among its chief targets for subversion are the family and the military, "patriarchal" institutions that must be destroyed or transformed. National security and the welfare of individual women are simply not the issue.

Maria Lepowsky, a professor of women's studies at the University of Wisconsin, testified before the Presidential Commission on the Assignment of Women in the Armed Forces in 1992 that putting women in combat will boost "female self-esteem," a staggeringly naïve assertion.[79] Failure in a brutally hard competition for which one is utterly unsuited—with potentially fatal consequences for oneself and one's comrades—is an unreliable path to self-esteem. Radical feminists treat combat as if it were a stage-managed reality show like *Survivor*, where men and women compete equally.

Radical feminists also dismiss the power of sexual attraction among young adults in conditions of intimate proximity. The experience of university students in mixed-sex dormitories is especially instructive. Undergraduates are approximately the same age as combat soldiers. Like soldiers on a military base, they are "captives" on their campus. Newly emancipated from parental oversight, these young people are prone to risky activity like the abuse of alcohol, drugs, and sex. The sociologist W. Bradford Wilcox, the director of the National Marriage Project at the University of Virginia, reports that 40 to 60 percent of college students participate in the campus "hookup" culture.[80] Coed living arrangements make this kind of sexual activity far more likely and are correlated with binge drinking.[81] The similarity of the isolated military community to dorm life is striking and may explain, in part, the military's problem with sexual assault and other physical and emotional traumas.

Feminists also reject the reality that men are hardwired to protect women from danger. The reflex to protect women could be especially dangerous on the battlefield, where a man might abandon his first responsibility to fight the enemy in order to rescue a woman in trouble.

While suspending the reality of human nature, radical feminists express prodigious confidence in the ability of a feminized military to avoid war altogether. In her testimony before the presidential commission, Professor Lepowsky mused, "What would be some possible consequences ... —if women were put in combat—on American cultural values and American society? ... I think there might be increased concern about committing troops to combat, also perhaps a good thing...."[82] Our experience in Afghanistan and Iraq, unfortunately, does not confirm her hopes. More than 154 women have been killed in combat and 964 wounded. Untold others have emerged from the conflicts with serious psychological scars.[83] Yet Americans didn't storm Capitol Hill demanding the war stop to save the women soldiers.

A related belief is that women are not as disposed to wage war as men are. Dr. Rob Sparrow, a bioethicist at Monash University in Australia, debunks that view. War, he writes, "is a political relationship between states and has nothing to do with the individual psychology of the individuals involved.… It's the political systems (capitalism/state/patriarchy) that drive the actions of those in power rather than the other way around.… In order to gain political power, women have to accommodate themselves to the needs of these systems as much as men do.…"[84] Maria Konovalenko, a biophysicist in Moscow, offers a dose of reality: "Women make a lot of emotional, spontaneous, and irresponsible decisions. In general, of course. I think if women were heads-of-state in all nations on earth, warfare wouldn't be reduced at all. In fact, it may be even worse."[85]

It is extremely unlikely that radical feminists' interest in the military is sympathetic. The greatest bastion of masculinity in American society, the playpen of patriarchy, the military, has been in feminists' crosshairs for decades. They want to build a "gender-neutral" culture, not a stronger military.

In spite of the incontrovertible physiological differences between the sexes,[86] the quest for an androgynous society continues with the aid of acceptable sex discrimination. If girls don't match boys' performance in math and science, the curriculum must be changed to encourage female participation. If young men show more interest in intercollegiate sports, then men's athletic programs must be cut back to achieve parity with women's. In the military, this tactic is known as "gender-norming." The 1992 presidential commission found that only one out of a hundred women could achieve the same physical fitness standards as sixty out of a hundred men. So, to level the playing ground, the military "gender-normed" the scores, giving a woman a top score for a performance that would have earned a man only a passing score. "Equivalence" is said to indicate "equality." But make no mistake: they are not the same.

The manipulation of the physical standards to ensure androgyny is all but certain if women are to be prepared for combat. The standards will be lowered until the desired quota of women is in the ranks of all combat units. Then our re-engineered, androgynous military will be as strong as the weakest link.

The most fantastic and tragic of the feminist assumptions behind the change in policy is that sending women into combat will be good for them.

General Dempsey tried to make this case in his remarks when the change was announced. He went so far as to make the illogical assertion that assigning women to combat units will *reduce* sexual harassment and assault. That might be true if infantry companies had a high percentage of women, but the reduction in the fighting ability of such companies would be catastrophic.

"Here we arrive at the bottom line of the sexual revolution," writes Stephen K. Baskerville, a professor of government at Patrick Henry College.

> For if courageous men, who do not hesitate to lay their lives down for their … country, are reduced to pathetic eunuchs when challenged by women, what hope do less determined and well trained men have. And indeed, if there is one word that explains the lightning speed with which the sexual revolution has spread throughout the Western world and beyond, with almost no opposition, it is male cowardice. But it is a new kind of cowardice, occasioned not by combat but by emasculation and driven not by competing men but by women.[87]

Radical feminists will do anything to eviscerate the military. Thanks to weak political leaders and cowardly generals, they have made giant strides toward that goal. Feminists have succeeded in framing the argument in the ideological terms of equality. Radical feminism, the Big Lie of our time, has been at war with human nature for fifty years. No enemy could have devised a more effective war against the national security of the United States.

Media's Enthusiasm for Women in Combat

The distinction between reporting and entertainment has nearly disappeared in America's media culture. Completely captive to feminist ideology, the media portray women as dominant, powerful, and ready for combat. The message of the interchangeableness of the sexes is ubiquitous on our flat-screen digital televisions, on streaming video, on iPads, in video games, and in the remaining daily newspapers. The effect on the American public, whose understanding of the military, to say nothing of combat, is extremely limited, is apparent in national polls that show overwhelming support for sending women into combat.

Former Congressman Allen West, an Army combat veteran, describes our society's credulity: "*G.I. Jane* was a movie and should not be the basis for a policy shift. I know Martha McSally [a former U.S. Air Force A-10 pilot now pushing the women-in-combat agenda in the media], have known women who are Apache and Cobra helicopter pilots, and served with women who were MPs, but being on the ground and having to go mano y mano in close combat is a completely different environment."[88] West is stating obvious truths that most civilians without military experience simply can't appreciate. Flying an aircraft is not comparable to sustained ground combat. Pilots return to a base, eat regular meals, and sleep in beds. Soldiers in sustained ground combat live in the dirt and grime, eat rations from packs, and conduct round-the-clock operations. West warns about the "third and fourth order effects" of the new policy: "This is the misconceived liberal progressive vision of fairness and equality, which could potentially lead to the demise of our military."

Hollywood routinely portrays young women in action films as heroines capable of great physical feats, more often than not intimidating men. The pictures released in 2012 included *Battleship*, depicting a female gunner's mate aboard the USS *John Paul Jones* who stops an alien invasion that threatens Earth. *The Hunger Games* features a tough young woman who is devastating with a bow and arrow. The fantasy film *Snow White and the Huntsman*, based on the German fairy tale "Snow White," portrays a butt-kicking 105-pound starlet whipping the bad guys in hand-to-hand combat and leading an army into battle.

Tough-talking women are the rule on the big screen. In the brutally violent *Dark Knight Rises* (2012), Catwoman is asked, "Hey, do those shoes make it hard to walk?" She kicks the questioner in the groin and responds, "I don't know. Do they?"

In 2013's *Zero Dark Thirty*, a female CIA operative interrogating captured terrorists, upon hearing about the death of friends to a terrorist strike, threatens, "I'm gonna smoke everybody involved in this op. And then I'm gonna kill Bin Laden."[89]

The portrayal of women in military roles goes back a number of years. In *Aliens* (1986), a male soldier asks a macho Sigourney Weaver, "Hey, Vasquez, have you ever been mistaken for a man?" She turns and asks him coolly, "No, have you?"[90]

Portrayals of heroines in combat grew in popularity in the 1990s. *Mulan* (1998) features a woman disguised as a man who becomes a great warrior and courageously saves her emperor and her country. And the 1996 film *G.I. Jane* epitomizes the genre of women in combat. Demi Moore plays the first woman (purely fictional) to go through Navy SEAL training, touted as the most rigorous combat training in the world. She battles for equal rights for women as she survives SEAL boot camp. During the final phase of that training, her class is called to active duty to fight the Libyans, and Moore becomes a heroine after assuming command of a rescue operation.

Television—both its news and entertainment programming—mirrors the movies with its depiction of women as ready for combat with little discussion of the risks. It wasn't always this way, however. Robert Altman's comedy *M*A*S*H*, which ran from 1972 to 1983, included the female nurse Major Margaret J. "Hot Lips" Houlihan, who earned the nickname by having sex with one of the doctors. Military women in earlier decades were generally comic characters, as in the short-lived series *Private Benjamin* (based on the Goldie Hawn movie) and the 1959 movie that became a television series, *Operation Petticoat*, about the misadventures of a fictional submarine with nurses aboard. But in the late 1980s, television's portrayal of women in the military went in a different direction.

The series *China Beach* (1988–1991), set at an American base during the Vietnam War, considered the lives of people sent to that country and how they dealt with the horrors and stresses of war. In *JAG* (1995–2005), Lieutenant Colonel Sarah "Mac" Mackenzie (Catherine Bell) is a military lawyer working with an elite legal team that prosecutes and defends those accused of military-related crimes.

The Public Broadcasting Service has aired documentaries promoting "a greater public awareness of the role women play in war and peace." *Lioness, Service: When Women Come Marching Home*, and *Women, War & Peace* explore the "emotional and psychological effect of war on women for the women's POV [point of view]."[91]

The entertainment media's enthusiasm for women in combat is matched by their counterparts in the news departments. The networks' January 2013 coverage of the Pentagon's announcement that it was lifting combat exclusions for women was a one-sided celebration of "equality in the services." The CBS News report quoted two supporters of the change but no opposing voice.[92] This was followed two days later by a puff piece featuring the Army's Colonel Christine Stark, who "absolutely" applauded the "landmark decision."[93]

NBC's Jim Miklaszewski delivered a story in perfect conformity with Pentagon PR. "Is the military prepared for women in combat?" he asked rhetorically. "There will be plenty of complaints about it. But I don't think it's going to have a negative effect on the actual strength of the force," replied one of many guests who was also prepared to defend the Pentagon's policy.[94] The story ended with comments from Congresswoman Tammy Duckworth, a Democrat from Illinois who lost both legs when her Black Hawk helicopter was shot down in Iraq. To Miklaszewski's question, "Are women ready for combat?" Duckworth answered with a non sequitur: "Well, I didn't lose my legs in a bar fight."

CNN featured two U.S. senators supporting the change and quoted the American Civil Liberties Union, which sued the Pentagon in November 2012 to have the combat ban lifted.[95] It was not until the following day's broadcast that CNN interviewed any dissenters from the decision. Even then, the story featured five supporters of the policy, who received five times the attention given to the two dissenters.[96] MSNBC and PBS's NewsHour likewise followed the party line, interviewing only supporters of the new policy.[97] Only Fox News gave approximately equal time to opponents.[98]

Reporting in the major newspapers was predictably supportive of sending women into combat. The *New York Times* and the *Washington Post* ran editorials celebrating the decision and roundly criticizing dissent. "The Pentagon's decision to end its ban on women in combat is a triumph for equality and common sense," wrote the *Times* editorial staff. Then it criticized "right-wing commentators" for rehashing "false stereotypes that women couldn't hack it."[99] The *Post* praised the "historic move—both sobering and exhilarating—that affirms the importance of women in defending this country and removes barriers that have impeded them in that work." Then it cited the primary feminist justification for the change: "One result will be a more level playing field for women … [and] they will no longer be hobbled by lack of official combat credentials." The glass ceiling has been shattered, and women can now rise to the heights of the armed forces.[100]

When Leon Panetta and his compliant generals rolled out their new policy on women in combat, they were confident that the media would report for duty. What does it say about the state of the American republic that the administration could impose, by bureaucratic fiat, a social change of unprecedented magnitude without the inconvenience of any meaningful debate among the molders of public opinion?

Popular Opinion Flips for Women in Combat

The American people overwhelmingly endorse lifting the ban on women in combat according to recent national surveys—a substantial cultural shift from two decades ago. National opinion polls published after the Pentagon's announcement of its new policy in January 2013 showed broad public support—as high as 75 percent—for the change. Opinions differed little between the sexes.[101] By comparison, a 1991 Gallup survey found only 38 percent of Americans favored putting women in combat.[102]

Political leaders of both parties seem convinced that public support for women in combat is broad. Their responses to the announcement ranged from enthusiasm to quiet acceptance; there were virtually no objections. President Obama himself assumed unanimous support for his decision: "Every American can be proud that our military will grow even stronger with our mothers, wives, sisters and daughters playing a greater role in protecting this country we love."[103] From a historical perspective, this was a momentous statement. The president of the United States was celebrating sending mothers, wives, sisters, and daughters into the most brutal violence known to man. "I can't conceive how anyone can say that," one Marine general told me. The military might be "better," he suggested, with "mothers, wives, sisters, and daughters" handling the VIPs at Andrews Air Force Base but certainly not with their serving as infantrymen.[104]

Republicans gave Obama no reason to doubt that "every American" supported the change. Speaker of the House John Boehner declined to comment on the issue, and Congressman Buck McKeon of California, the chairman of the House Armed Services Committee, released a one-sentence statement: "After a decade of critical military service in hostile environments, women have demonstrated a wide range of capabilities in combat operations and we welcome this review."[105]

Senator John McCain, a survivor of the Hanoi Hilton, accepted the change in principle. "We just have to make sure we maintain the same physical standards that we do for males, particularly in specialized units such as SEALS," he said.[106] Senator Kelly Ayotte of New Hampshire, a Republican who has been critical of Obama's defense policies, gave this one a strong endorsement: "I've seen firsthand servicemen and women working together in a range of dangerous operations to achieve our military objectives—and today's announcement reflects the increasing role that female service members play in securing our country."

The military leadership, of course, parroted the politicians. "Today we are acting to expand the opportunities for women to serve in the United States armed forces and to better align our policies with the experiences we have had over the past decade of war," General Dempsey said, assuring the American people, "Ultimately, we're acting to strengthen the joint force."[107] He had discussed the issue, he said, with the Army chief of staff, General Raymond Odierno, and with Marine Commandant General James Amos, adding, "I think we all believe that there will be women who can meet those standards."

The reaction of the political class (both inside and outside the military), which fears nothing as much as offending feminists, might not have been surprising. A more striking indication of how much public opinion has shifted is the extent to which cultural conservatives have given up the fight. The announcement of the new policy drew only limited opposition from the old culture warriors. Eleanor Smeal, the president of Feminist Majority and the former head of the National Organization for Women, remarked, "I think it's marvelous that there is no controversy around it."[108] She can be forgiven the modest exaggeration. Though some protests were heard, there was no groundswell of opposition like that which has greeted other Obama policies.

A few conservative Christian groups—the Family Research Council, the American Family Association, Concerned Women for America—denounced the new policy in press releases. Organizations like the Center for Military Readiness attracted some notice, usually at the bottom of an article. Ralph Reed, the former leader of the Christian Coalition, expressed a common sentiment: "While we generally defer to the Pentagon when it comes to military matters, putting women in combat situations is the latest in a series of moves where political correctness and liberal social policy are trumping sound military practice in the Obama administration."[109]

Perhaps the most remarkable silence was that of America's churches.

The breadth of public support for sending women into combat suggests that the citizenry has become desensitized to violence against women. The entertainment media certainly bear much of the responsibility. A study published in 2009 in *Psychological Science*, "Comfortably Numb: Desensitizing Effects of Violent Media on Helping Others," concludes, "People exposed to media violence become 'comfortably numb' to the pain and suffering of others and are consequently less helpful."[110] An earlier study, "The Effects of Mass Media Exposure on Acceptance of Violence against Women," found that exposure to films portraying violent sexuality increased male subjects' acceptance of interpersonal violence against women.[111]

Most of our social pathologies can be traced in one way or another to the deterioration of the family, and the increasing acceptance of violence against women is no exception. One in four American children is being raised by a single parent, the highest rate in the developed world, and that figure is as high as 72 percent for African American children.[112]

These single-mother households produce a lot of troubled men who become violent with women. Single-mother households themselves are marked by higher rates of domestic violence[113] and produce children who have a higher incidence of criminal activity.[114] A young man who commits violence against women is very likely to be fatherless.[115]

There is a correlation between the change of public opinion on women in combat and the decline in the portion of the population that has served in the military, suggesting that simple ignorance may be part of the explanation for Americans' changing views. Since the end of the draft in 1973, the number of people with military experience has dropped precipitously, with a predictable effect on the public's understanding of the military culture. Congress itself reflects this decline: less than a quarter of its members have any military service. Without personal experience or at least a reasonable familiarity with the military, people tend to make emotional decisions. To lifelong civilians, *G.I. Jane* is "fact."

Today, less than 1 percent of the population has ever been on active military duty, much less served in combat, compared with 9 percent in World War II. We now have two generations of men with no military experience on which to base their opinions. What they know about war and the military comes from movies and video games. Few have broken a sweat carrying a rucksack or running a combat obstacle course or have even fired a real weapon. Their lack of firsthand experience means that their opinions on women in combat will probably be shaped by whoever is shouting most loudly in the media—and that's usually the feminists.

Feminists have framed the question of women in combat as an equal rights issue. Further, they muddle our understanding of the combat environment by suggesting what we have seen in Iraq and Afghanistan is "high-intensity combat." With few exceptions, what women have experienced in those wars is an IED exploding as they ride from one safe area to another or small-arms ambushes along those same routes. Many young men and women have died in those situations, but they are not direct-fire, close ground combat.

Those hostile encounters were not the combat experienced in Ramadi, Hue, the Ia Drang, Chosin, or Guadalcanal. With some notable exceptions, counterinsurgency is best compared to high-intensity police work, not high-intensity conventional combat. Only 1.8 U.S. servicemen have been killed per day in Iraq, a rate that hardly compares to the 260 lost per day in World War II. The *intensity* is the major difference.

Perhaps, in the final analysis, it is no surprise that a culture that so degrades and devalues women is untroubled by sending them into combat. Americans once held women with high esteem, but, today, chivalry is practically dead. Respect for women went the way of marriage thanks to radical feminists who want to destroy that institution. Today nearly half (48 percent) of all firstborn children in America are born to a single mother.[116] This statistic suggests that men don't value women and their children enough to get married and provide for their families.

Whatever one might attribute public opinion to, sending women into combat is not good for women, and it's not good for our national security. Americans are falling for a historic deception.

CHAPTER 2

WHY PUT WOMEN IN COMBAT?

W hy do some women want to become ground combatants? The answers offered to this question range from equal opportunity and career advancement to patriotism and, inevitably, the elimination of sexism.

Female veterans and their male supporters make some compelling arguments for putting women in combat. Former Captain Laura Cannon, a 2001 graduate of West Point who served in Iraq (March to August 2003) with the Third Infantry Division, strongly endorses removing the combat exclusions for women. "No gender exclusions should exist," she insists, promising that "women are more than capable of filling infantry requirements." To prove her point, she says a female West Point classmate graduated from the Army Engineer Corps' Sapper School, "which might be tougher than Ranger School." (Cannon should know better. Sapper School is demanding, but according to a Ranger-qualified major who is familiar with the Sapper School, it requires nowhere near the sustained physical and mental demands placed on an aspiring Ranger.[1])

Retired Marine Colonel Steve McKinley served two tours in Iraq, where he commanded a 220-man civil affairs unit with ten women. He believes women are ready for combat, but he admits there won't be a "huge influx of women into infantry units." Still, he believes women will be "ready to the degree they have been trained."

Are Cannon and Colonel McKinley right? Is opening combat duty to women an idea whose time has come, or is it the triumph of ideology over common sense? Let's consider the most common arguments in favor of sending women into combat.

Argument No. 1: The Integration of Women into Combat Units Is Analogous to the Racial Integration of the Military and Lifting the Exclusion of Homosexuals[2]

This analogy is flawed as a matter of history.

First, sexual integration and racial integration are quite different questions, especially in a military context. In 1948, President Harry Truman signed Executive Order 9981, which declared, "There shall be equality of treatment and opportunity for all persons in the armed services without regard to race, color, religion or national origin."[3] That order led to the desegregation of the armed services, which improved the efficiency of the force. The policy that Truman changed was racial segregation, not exclusion. Racial segregation affected readiness, combat effectiveness, and military efficiency.

The success of moving soldiers from all-black units into racially integrated units does not justify lifting the sex-based exclusion from combat units. Unlike racial or ethnic differences, sexual differences extend to naturally occurring, unalterable anatomical, physiological, and psychological characteristics.

Before Truman's order, millions of blacks had fought for their country throughout its history. They distinguished themselves in every American war, including the Revolution, the War of 1812, the Civil War, the Spanish-American War, and both World Wars, all of which entailed sustained, conventional combat.

Second, lifting the combat exclusion policy for women is not comparable to removing the total service ban for open homosexuals. The American military had policies against homosexual conduct ever since George Washington commanded the Continental Army. It was not until the late 1970s, however, that the *Report of the Joint Service Administrative Discharge Study Group* recommended reaffirming the longstanding policy by adopting the principle that "homosexuality is incompatible with military service."[4] Congress put the ban on self-identified homosexuals into statutory form. That law was repealed in December 2010.[5]

Women have a long and honorable history of service in the American military. Their participation has been sanctioned, not prohibited, and today a quarter-million women serve in every military capacity except direct combat.

||||||||||||||||||||||||||||||||||||||||||||||||||||||||||

Argument No. 2: The Exclusion of Women from Combat Units Prevents Them from Obtaining the Training and Promotions Necessary to Compete with Men in the Military

Until January 2013, the combat exclusion policies prohibited women from serving in certain tactical career fields. And in some career fields that were open to women, the policies kept them out of important assignments that involved direct offensive ground combat. Those policies limited female service members to approximately 80 percent of all military jobs. Some combat branches such as aviation were opened, but for the most part only combat support branches were available.

Members of the service, especially officers, compete for promotion within a certain career field. Logisticians in general are not competing against infantrymen but against other logisticians. The argument that women must be in direct combat career fields to compete for promotion is false.

A 2012 RAND Corporation study for the Department of Defense of whether occupational restrictions on female officers account for any differences in their rates of retention and promotion found no statistically significant difference between the likelihood of a man's or a woman's reaching the rank of colonel (or Navy captain) after reaching the rank of major (or Navy lieutenant commander). RAND did find that female officers were less likely to be promoted to first lieutenant (or Navy lieutenant junior grade), captain (or Navy lieutenant), and major (or Navy lieutenant commander) than white males, though black women are about as likely to be promoted to captain (or Navy lieutenant) as white men. Further, retention rates for female officers at that level are also generally lower than those for males, though black women have a higher retention rate than white men. Today, according to RAND, women, who make up 14.6 percent of the total active force, account for 17.96 percent of all junior officers, 12.72 percent of officers from major to colonel, and 5.6 percent of general and flag officers.

This analysis suggests that young female officers are more likely than males of the same rank to leave the service. There are a number of possible explanations for the difference, such as the end of their service obligation (three to five years), marriage, children, and alternative careers. Women are less likely to join the military in the first place, and they are more likely than men to leave early.

Anecdotes are often helpful when examining a complex issue. An active-duty combat arms officer with two tours in Iraq who is married to a combat service support officer said, "There are a lot more joint domicile military couples now than before the war," and "usually the female soldier gets out … when they have kids." He explained, "I think a lot default subconsciously to the idea, 'I cannot be both a soldier and a mom and wife.'"[6]

This impression is confirmed by comments of dozens of former servicewomen, collected on a popular website for military women, about why they left the military.[7] Motherhood, of course, is a leading reason for leaving. "I got out when my son was 8 months old," writes one woman. "After I had my son, the Navy just didn't seem to fit in my life anymore. I was devastated about going back to work after my six weeks of maternity leave were up. The next few months were the most stressful of my life.… I would not recommend anybody being a mother in the Navy."

An eight-year Army veteran with two small children, including a special-needs four-year-old, warns other women to "think long and hard" before joining. A woman's life in the military "is a tough act," observes another woman, "but a military woman and mom is quite a different story." She found it overwhelming.

The "hardship and strain" of sea duty drove one woman from the Navy. And a brutally frank soldier explains why she couldn't wait to get out of the Army after her three-year enlistment: "There's the lovely field training with no showers or privacy, there are the 7-mile runs that the men have trouble staying in, but because you happen to be a woman it is always noticed when you fall out and you are yelled at." Then there are the clothes: "I don't care if I am a soldier or not, I still like to look like a girl and these baggy atrocities make it pretty damn near impossible. And let's not forget jumping out of airplanes—quite possibly the most testosterone-laden thing I've ever done.... I would just like to reiterate that the Army is not for most women. I think if you stay in too long, you begin to act and talk like a man, and who wants that anyways?"

A career in the military seems to hold little appeal for many women. "Of my [Officer Basic Course] class, I do not know of 5 female officers that intend to stay beyond their initial commitment," observes one weary woman soldier.

None of the nearly one hundred women quoted on the website cited the combat exclusion policy as the reason for her departure. Women leave for many reasons, but the combat exclusion policy—despite the protests of radical feminists—appears not be one of them. Much more research needs to be done before the Defense Department cites it as an obstacle to retention of female personnel.

||||||||||||||||||||||||||||||||||||||||||||||||||||||||||||

Argument No. 3: The Primary Role of the Armed Forces Is to Fight. Because Women Are Excluded from Fighting, They Serve a Secondary Mission and Are Therefore Second-Class Members of the Military.

No one disputes that the military's mission is to fight, but only one in five members of the military has a job that engages the enemy. Most military personnel—80 percent—support the fighters. There will always be divisions within military organizations based on function.

In the Air Force, for example, there are those who fly airplanes and those who don't. The flyers include fighter, bomber, and transport pilots, who pick at one another in jest. But each one knows that the others are critical to the overall mission. Likewise, women serving in support jobs in the combat zone share many risks with the male combatants. It is not necessary for women to prove themselves in man-to-man combat to be accepted, because most combatants know they are sharing with non-combatants considerable hardship and risk for the greater war effort.

The problem with pretending that women are equally capable combatants is that the enemy won't play that game. Colonel John Ripley, one of the most combat-experienced U.S. Marines ever to serve, warns, "If we see women as equals on the battlefield, you can be absolutely certain that the enemy do not see them as equals. They see them as victims. The minute a woman is captured, she is no longer a POW; she is a victim and an easy prey, and is someone upon whom they can satisfy themselves and their desires. That is the generally accepted view that our enemy has of the so-called woman warrior."[8]

Argument No. 4: Women Want to Be Equal Partners in Society, Which Means They Must Bear Equal Responsibility for National Defense

This notion of equality is based on the flawed assumption that we all have the ability to do the same things. American society has never been based on that kind of equality. A better term, perhaps, for what we seek is an equitable social order, which recognizes that we all have different abilities and strengths and that we should be judged by how well we do the things for which we are best suited.

Some people are gifted with special skills to repair cars, others are great cooks, and others perform brain surgery. Having demonstrated particular aptitudes and interests, the mechanic, the chef, and the surgeon undertook the appropriate training for their professions. Although these professions are remunerated unequally because of the varying rarity of the necessary skills, no one argues that one or another of them is not fully contributing to society or that they are not equal before the law.

The same applies to fighting wars. A logistician is no more important than the infantry grunt, and vice versa. Both are necessary to winning our wars, and both are at risk to death and injury, especially in today's counterinsurgency battlefield.

What distinguishes the military from other professions is its unique requirements and the nature of its operational environment. The judgment of the profession of arms backed by science has been that ground combat requires certain physiological and psychological attributes that men on average possess to substantially higher degrees than women do. That doesn't mean some women can't match a male in those attributes, but they are the notable exception.

Further, the military is a giant organization—2.1 million uniformed personnel—that sets standards by category for the good of the service and in the best interest of the taxpayer. For example, strict medical disqualifiers are detailed in regulations like the Army's 141-page *Standards of Medical Fitness*.[9] Many young Americans don't meet those standards, and few ask the Army to waive them, because they understand that the exclusions are intended to protect the armed forces' readiness and save the taxpayer unnecessary medical costs.

Women serve in critical military jobs, and no one should doubt that they are equal partners in society. They do not have to be ground combatants to prove their patriotism, especially if the military's long experience indicates that all-male ground units are uniquely well suited to combat.

ıı|ıılıılıılıılıılıılıılıılıılıılıılıılıılıılıılıılıılıılıılıılıılıı

Argument No. 5: Women Tend to Be Stabilizing Forces in Tense Periods

Some argue that men's natural belligerency can be counterproductive in war. A woman's touch, they say, would help calmer heads prevail.

A former Air Force security force commander with experience commanding women in Iraq told me how the female perspective defused some tense situations: "They are able to communicate at a more personal level than men, who tend to be more directive and harsh," this commander explained. "Women had a good ability to communicate more effectively."[10] But he was talking about police work, not direct combat.

Desiree Maxwell, a former Army sergeant, served a year as an intelligence specialist in Iraq and agrees that women bring something special to tense situations. "Their brains function differently.... It comes down to the way they handle and react to problems," she told me. When working with Iraqi soldiers, she said, the "male soldiers were straight forward, impulsive, while women would talk with the Iraqis differently, [and] think about the outcome."[11]

There is considerable merit to the argument women may be better at stabilizing tense situations than men engaged in police actions. That work, however, takes place before or after battle. Direct-fire, close ground combat generally takes place in an environment where talking has ceased and action becomes necessary.

||||||||||||||||||||||||||||||||||||||||||||||||||||||||||

Argument No. 6: We Are Evolving into an Androgynous Society, So the Military Should Embrace the Inevitability That Women Will Be in Every Job in the Armed Forces

Distinctions between the roles of the sexes are indeed being broken down at a dizzying pace. Women have moved into almost every traditionally male occupation, and men are now working in traditionally feminine occupations. Acceptance of homosexuality in the military is now mandatory, and even marriage itself is being redefined without regard to sex.

Ours is not the first culture to blur sexual distinctions, and the results of doing so have never been happy. This cultural "evolution," however, is not inevitable, and cultural norms cannot alter basic physiology. Men and women are genetically different with different capabilities that predispose one or the other to excel in certain tasks.

A truly sex-blind society is a fantasy. The sexes may be equal, or even equivalent, in most social areas, but they are not interchangeable, they are not equal in strength, and as long as the human race continues, sexual attraction will dramatically influence their relations with one another. Rather than accommodate itself to a supposedly "androgynous" society, the military, on which the very existence of our country depends, should organize itself on the basis of reality.

|||·|||||||||||||||||||||||||||||||||||||||||||||||||

Argument No. 7: Women Are a Readily Available Solution to the Shortage of Military Manpower

In World War II, Russian women volunteered to defend their motherland, and America would expect the same from her female citizens. But once there were sufficient men to fight at the end of the Second World War, the women were sent home to their families and to rebuild their communities. Even the "egalitarian" Soviets recognized the limitations of using female soldiers when suitable men were available.

America's armed forces will continue to recruit women into the ranks, and they will serve honorably in most positions. There is no evidence, either scientific or historical, that women can make up for an absence of men in combat.

III

Argument No. 8: Removing Sex-Based Barriers within the Military Will Improve the Fighting Force as a Whole[12]

That's what Leon Panetta asserted when he announced the new policy. But saying so doesn't make it so—even if you're the secretary of defense.

Lieutenant Colonel Charles "Chuck" Pudil, an active-duty infantry officer with multiple combat tours, draws an analogy with college football. Pudil, an ROTC instructor at the University of Arkansas, speculated what might happen if the university decided to feminize the Arkansas Razorback football team by insisting that three women be on the field for every play. "We couldn't tell the other football teams they must do the same, but the other teams aren't that foolish," observes Pudil. "What do you think might then happen? We won't win any games." He also suggested that the Razorbacks would become the laughingstock of the NCAA.

Combat units are like college football teams, Pudil explained. Only the best-qualified personnel get on the field to fight because "we are there to win." He admits that if women were considerably larger, stronger, and aggressive, then maybe they could play collegiate football. For that matter, they could fight in ground combat. But he doubts there is a population of women today willing and able to perform either on the gridiron or the direct combat battlefield.

CHAPTER 3

MYTHS ABOUT WOMEN IN COMBAT

I n the national debate about the wisdom of sending women into direct ground combat, it is important that we not fall into the trap of proof by assertion. We must test both sides' assumptions about women, about the military, and about combat. This is no time for politicians and generals to succumb to political intimidation from radical feminists.

In 2011, Major Jane Blair, a Marine reservist who served in Iraq, challenged what she called "five myths about women in combat" in an opinion piece for the *Washington Post*. The following objections to assigning women to combat units, she argued, were no more than empty stereotypes: (1) women are too emotionally fragile for combat; (2) women are too physically weak for the battlefield; (3) the presence of women causes sexual tension in training and battle; (4) male troops will become distracted from their missions in order to protect female comrades; and (5) women can't effectively lead men in combat.[1] Although Major Blair purports to meet each of those objections head-on, her attempt to debunk these so-called "myths" is a failure because she simply dismisses much of the contrary evidence, which is voluminous.

I have identified some myths about women in combat—six, to be precise. It is true that American women are performing well in combat zones and are exposed to combat incidental to their support missions, but they are not yet participating in direct-fire, close ground combat. Clearing away the prevalent myths and understanding the facts about such service is literally a matter of life and death.

Myth No. 1: The New Battlefield Is Woman-Friendly

The nature of war has changed, say those who want to open ground combat to women. In Iraq and Afghanistan, it has been impossible to protect women serving in support roles from the hazards of combat. Since future conflicts are likely to involve the same type of counterinsurgencies, women ought to be trained to share the direct combat burden with men.

This is a fallacious argument. Yes, the lines between combat supporters and actual combatants are blurred in counterinsurgencies such as those we have faced in Afghanistan and Iraq. But counterinsurgencies are operations of choice and not likely to be the way of the future.

Andrew Bacevich Jr., a professor of international relations at Boston University and a retired Army officer who lost his son in the Iraq war, asks, "If counterinsurgency is useful chiefly for digging ourselves out of holes we shouldn't be in, then why not simply avoid the holes?"[2] Wise leaders will take Bacevich's counsel and avoid the counterinsurgency "holes" in the future.

U.S. armed forces must prepare to conduct a broad range of operations, from security cooperation to major conventional wars, according to the Joint Staff's operations manual. The spectrum of operations includes thirteen "types" of military missions, tasks, and activities, such as conventional and stability operations, foreign humanitarian assistance, peace operations, and counterinsurgency.[3]

Iraq and Afghanistan began as conventional and counterterrorism operations, respectively, and then morphed into stability and counterinsurgency operations. That's a common transition along the conflict continuum.

Armies trained for conventional warfare can rapidly move to any of the other "types" of operations, as we saw in Iraq. The American-led coalition made a lightning advance up to Baghdad in the spring of 2003, employing massive conventional fire and maneuver operations. Focusing on conventional operations beforehand meant our forces were well prepared for that battle, saving lives and treasure. Had our forces entered Iraq after focusing on counterinsurgency operations, the march to Baghdad would have been very bloody, a lesson learned by Israel in 2006.

The Israeli Defense Forces fought the Iranian proxy Hezbollah in the summer of 2006 and, to their embarrassment, suffered substantial losses. According to the Israeli scholar Avi Kober, the IDF focused their training on counterinsurgency operations before the 2006 war rather than conventional operations. They were caught by surprise when Hezbollah employed conventional tactics and weapons, and they paid a heavy price.[4] Israeli forces were prepared neither physically nor operationally for the intensive, conventional, close combat (what is now being called "hybrid" warfare)[5] that was required in a number of cases.

America's Future Wars

What types of conflicts will the U.S. military face in the future if not counterinsurgencies? What effect will those operations have on women assigned to ground combat operations? The answer to the first question is that the United States will conduct the full spectrum of military operations in the future, as suggested in the operations manual. Many of those operations—civil support, foreign humanitarian assistance, noncombatant evacuation—will require few if any direct combatants. Female service members assigned to support jobs will participate in these operations, as will some direct ground combatants, albeit as helpers, not as fighters.

But as military operations develop into full conventional force-on-force warfare, ground combatants will move into the lead. The support units where women are assigned will be in the "rear," where they will not face dangers of the same magnitude or frequency as those that the direct conventional battle combatants face. That transition is happening today. Now that we are out of Iraq and moving out of Afghanistan, the services are rapidly refocusing training on full-spectrum conventional operations. The reason is that the penalties for failure are more severe in high-intensity conventional operations than in counterinsurgency operations, which necessarily take place over a longer period.

General Raymond Odierno, the Army chief of staff, described his service's refocus on "the higher end of the spectrum of military operations" in an article for *Foreign Policy*: "Our first priority remains being ready to deploy rapidly and defeat any adversary on land in any corner of the globe."[6] He gives a nod to past counterinsurgencies but explains that the future is about conventional combat. Specifically, "irregular warfare represents one subset of the range of missions that the Army must be ready to perform. [However,] we must reinvest in those fundamental warfighting skills that underpin the majority of our directed strategic missions," which are force-on-force conventional land wars. Those "directed strategic missions" are outlined in

President Obama's *National Security Strategy of the United States*,[7] the 2012 Defense strategic guidance, *Sustaining U.S. Global Leadership: Priorities for 21st Century Defense*,[8] *The National Military Strategy of the United States of America, 2011*,[9] the Guidance for the Employment of the Force (GEF), and the Joint Strategic Capabilities Plan (JSCP). These documents require our armed forces to be prepared to conduct the full range of military operations, including many contingency operations.

The nature of future military operations is hard to predict, as President George W. Bush learned on September 11, 2001, and in the difficult years of conflict that followed. In fact, since World War II, the U.S. military has failed to anticipate its future wars—the European Cold War against the Soviets, Korea, Vietnam, Afghanistan, and Iraq. As one surveys the current threat horizon, the list of potential military operations is as long and unpredictable as in the past: counterterrorism, stability operations, combating the proliferation of weapons of mass destruction, cyber operations, homeland defense, foreign humanitarian assistance, and a host of potential large-scale conventional operations against antagonists like Iran, Russia, and China.

The requirements of future military operations should govern decisions about the assignments of women. Many small-scale operations can be handled by special operations forces, which already exclude women, though crisis response, contingency, and outright conventional wars would include women in support jobs.

It is foolish to assume that most of America's future military engagements will be counterinsurgency operations, a type of war our nation should avoid in any case. We must be ready for the full spectrum of operations. Most of the time, those in support roles in full-spectrum operations, including most women, will not be exposed to the extremes of combat destructiveness.

Myth No. 2: Women Are Clamoring for Combat Duty

Both civilian and uniformed women, it is said, are clamoring for the "opportunity" to serve in ground combat units. In fact, there is little evidence that women, in or out of uniform, seek these brutally demanding positions. It would be a daunting challenge to raise and maintain a sizable corps of female combatants.

Consider what women have said about ground combat service, their motivations for joining the military, the demographics among those females who do serve, and the challenges associated with recruiting and retaining a female corps.

Polls of the American public find them an egalitarian lot, and a majority of them favor allowing women into combat units. There is no evidence, however, that civilian women want to enlist to serve in ground combat. Their views are mixed about whether that change might improve combat effectiveness and whether they support returning to a draft, should one become necessary to fill the military's ranks.

A Pew Research Center–*Washington Post* national survey conducted in January 2013 found that 66 percent of Americans favor allowing women to serve voluntarily in ground combat, with 26 percent opposed. The poll found further that 49 percent thought allowing women in combat units would neither improve nor hinder military effectiveness, 29 percent thought it would improve effectiveness, and 15 percent thought that effectiveness would suffer.[10]

A Quinnipiac University national poll conducted at the same time also found strong support (75 percent) for women "who want to serve in ground units that engage in close combat." A plurality of 41 percent thought that "women's presence in combat situations enhances military effectiveness," whereas 32 percent believe women would compromise effectiveness. The more interesting questions dealt with reinstating the military draft. Two-thirds (65 percent) oppose reinstating conscription, but if it were reinstated, 52 percent favor drafting women as well as men.[11]

By contrast, those closest to the issue, military men and women, have long expressed reservations about women serving in close combat units. Army surveys dating back to the 1990s indicate that the majority of female soldiers are strongly opposed to combat assignments, especially if they are forced into combat on an equal basis with men. A 2001 Army Research Institute survey found that few enlisted women favored placing women in combat on the same basis as men. Even officers opposed placing women in combat on the same basis as men—81 percent of female and 80 percent of male officers opposed assigning women to combat units. Only 10 percent of enlisted women supported the involuntary assignment of women to combat units.[12] Apparently the Army didn't like those results, because that line of questioning was dropped from the annual survey after 2001.

During the summer of 2012, the Marine Corps conducted an anonymous online survey asking fifty-three thousand service members about their views regarding women in ground combat. The results were sobering. Nearly one in four male Marines said he would leave the service if women were involuntarily posted in combat positions, and 17 percent of female Marines agreed with them. The survey did find growing enthusiasm among female Marines for the opportunity to serve voluntarily in combat.[13] Specifically, 1,558 female respondents (about 31 percent) said that they would be interested in a lateral move to a combat arms PMOS (primary military occupational specialty) if given the opportunity. And 2,083 female respondents (about 43 percent) said that they would have chosen a combat arms PMOS when they joined the Marine Corps had it been an option. If allowed, 1,636 female respondents (about 34 percent) would volunteer for a GCE (ground combat element) assignment.

Yet female enthusiasm for the combat arms quickly diminishes after the officer basic course, says one woman Marine officer. "You get worn out" during the mandatory course, she explained, and the women "change their tone" about volunteering for GCE.[14] Female Marines' chief concerns about classifying women into ground combat PMOSs included the obligation that male comrades would feel to protect the women, enemy targeting of women as prisoners of war, the risk of sexual harassment or assault, and the difficulty of maintaining modesty in billeting and hygiene facilities.

The interest of some female Marines in combat arms assignments was tempered by the Corps' recent single-standard tests. In September 2012, the Marines' infantry officer course managed to recruit only two eligible women volunteers to test their abilities against the grueling, three-month course at Quantico, Virginia. Both women quickly washed out along with twenty-six of the 107 men. One woman left the first day. The other—a top performer in her basic course who was given three months to prepare physically for the infantry course[15]—dropped out two weeks later for medical reasons.[16] A second test in March 2013 had the same outcome—both female Marines quickly dropped the course. The Marine Corps hopes to entice at least ninety more women for the challenging course as a proof of concept. But these failures suggest that more volunteers will be hard to find unless the standards change.

Female service members are understandably attracted to the increased opportunity that participation in combat units seems to promise. But there are plenty of fulfilling job opportunities already available to military women. "The job I want to do in the military does not include combat arms," said Sergeant Cherry Sweat, an Army communications specialist. "The choice to join combat arms should be a personal decision, not a required one."[17]

Pauline Jelinek, who writes for the Associated Press, indicates that Sweat's view may be typical among many servicewomen. Jelinek spoke with a female West Point graduate at the Pentagon and reported that "there's no groundswell of interest in combat jobs among female colleagues she knows." The West Pointer asked to remain anonymous because "in the military's warrior culture, it's a sensitive issue to be seen as not wanting to fight," according to Jelinek.[18]

Typically the opportunity to fight is not what motivates women to join the military. Most female veterans (eight in ten) say they joined to serve their country, to receive education benefits, or both. Others (70 percent) joined to see more of the world, and two-thirds (67 percent) joined to gain job skills, according to a Pew Research Survey. A major difference between men and women volunteers, according to Pew, was that 42 percent of women joined because jobs were hard to find, as opposed to only a quarter of men.[19]

Unemployment is especially high among blacks, and the allure of military jobs might explain why black women are attracted to the military.[20] Thirty-one percent of enlisted women are black, a figure twice that of the civilian population. By comparison, about 16 percent of the male enlisted population is black, about the same proportion as in the civilian population. Fifty-three percent of military women are white, as compared with a civilian figure of 78 percent. Despite the demographic overrepresentation of black women in the military, however, there is no evidence they are especially interested in combat service.

Jobs and good benefits are insufficient to attract enough qualified women to the military's ranks. In fact, recruiting a young woman costs the services twice as much as recruiting a man, according to the

1992 presidential commission.[21] Women are expensive to recruit because too few of them are interested in military service, much less combat. The Army, therefore, tailors its recruiting message to female audiences by glamorizing the lifestyle while downplaying the element of combat.

Melissa Brown, a professor at City University of New York, has studied decades' worth of recruiting materials. Those messages reassure young women that they won't lose their femininity in the Army, says Brown, "even though they are joining an institution known for conferring masculinity and making men out of boys."[22] Army advertisements depict young female soldiers in civilian clothing or non-combat garb like white lab coats or firefighters' gear, and they rarely show women carrying weapons. That's no accident, says recruiter Sergeant Marietta Sparacino, who recruited for the Army in 2008 across the Salt Lake City, Utah, area. "The males are much more into the range—shooting weapons and everything. The females not so much," Sparacino told the *Salt Lake Tribune*. Some women do express interest in military-specific activities like "jumping out of planes," she says, but she doesn't make that assumption when first speaking with a female candidate (she would with a male). Women's reservations about combat may explain why their numbers fell during the wars in Iraq and Afghanistan.

Once a woman does enlist, she is far less likely than a man to complete her initial training. A 2005 RAND Corporation study, "Success of First-Term Soldiers," found that of a hundred men recruited, seventy-six actually complete the first six months of active duty. Of a hundred women recruited, only sixty-three will be left after six months.[23] The economic costs of recruiting and training more women, then, are substantial, and they are not justified by a proportionate improvement in military readiness.

So despite public opinion in the civilian world, few women are motivated to serve in ground combat positions, especially in the face of tough standards like those of the Marine infantry basic course. And few women who are genuinely concerned about our national defense want standards watered down just to accommodate more women.

Myth No. 3: Women Are Already Effective at the Front

Women are already performing combat roles on the front lines, so we might as well make it official and give them the recognition and rewards they deserve. The problem with this seemingly reasonable position is that it's not true. Women continue to make great contributions to the war effort in Afghanistan, as they did in Iraq. Some have been killed and a few have performed heroically in their support missions, but they are not serving as frontline combatants.

Two young women earned the Silver Star for gallantry, which should make every American proud, but they were operating in support missions. The first of these women, Sergeant Leigh Ann Hester, was assigned to the 617th Military Police Company in Iraq, a National Guard unit out of Richmond, Kentucky.[24] On March 20, 2005, Sergeant Hester and two men from her military police unit were shadowing a supply convoy that was ambushed. Hester and her teammates quickly flanked the insurgents and cut off their escape. Dismounting, they then moved through the insurgents' "kill zone," launching M203 grenades at the insurgents who were firing from a concealed trench line. Hester is credited with killing three insurgents with her weapon. The ambush left twenty-seven insurgents dead and six wounded; one was captured. Later, Hester modestly observed, "It really doesn't have anything to do with being a female. It's about the duties I performed that day as a soldier."

Army Specialist Monica Brown earned her Silver Star in Afghanistan in April 2007 at the age of nineteen. A medic with the Eighty-Second Airborne Division's 782nd Brigade Support Battalion, Brown was accompanying a combat unit on a routine security patrol at dusk when insurgents attacked.[25] "We had just turned into a wadi (a streambed) when our gunner yelled at us that the vehicle behind us had hit an IED (improvised explosive device)," she explained. She jumped out of her Humvee and ran with the platoon sergeant a few hundred meters through a hail of insurgent small arms fire to aid the injured. While Brown hurriedly applied aid to the wounded, mortar rounds churned up the earth around her. Fortunately, another Humvee pulled up to shield her from the fire. With help, Brown moved the badly wounded into the vehicle while directing others to hold intravenous bags and assist as the vehicle sped out of the kill zone. "It was just a blur of noise and movement," Brown recalls. "Did I do everything right? It was a hard thing to think about."

These women acted with great valor in response to an all-too-typical counterinsurgency hit-and-run operation. Hester, an MP, was performing a routine convoy security mission. But Brown, a medic, should not have accompanied a company-level combat force on a security patrol that commanders knew was likely to encounter the enemy. The 1994 Pentagon rule, which was in effect at that time, excluded women "from assignment to units below the brigade level whose primary mission is to engage in direct combat on the ground." Brown's commanders seem to have circumvented this policy by "attaching" Brown's unit as opposed to "assigning" it to the combat unit below the brigade level—an important distinction in military practice. Evading the combat exclusion in this way had become fairly common for a number of reasons, including a lack of other support troops to perform a mission that had to be accomplished.[26]

Commanders routinely "attached" women to combat units not only as medics but also as truck drivers, as logisticians, and in the motor pool and personnel sections. One of the more innovative counterinsurgency-related roles devised for women was the female engagement team (FET). Captain Kelly Hasselman, a commander of FETs deployed with the infantry in Afghanistan, admits that "we're already here," in combat units, but "it's just not officially been in the books."[27] Her FET unit builds relationships with Afghan people, mostly women and children, whom cultural barriers otherwise render unreachable. FETs help building schools, bringing in medical care, and providing access to clean water. Women assigned to the FET do not engage in combat but are in a support role to infantry units. Their training includes combat and survival skills, enabling them to move, shoot, and communicate in hostile areas. They take culture and language classes, learn engagement and observation techniques, and participate in personnel searches and planning operations.

Male commanders tend to welcome women enthusiastically. "Gender, height, weight, religion, sexual preference, and race—I don't care," said Lieutenant Colonel Thomas Anderson, a battalion commander in Afghanistan. "It all comes down to your ability to do what the Army asks you to do," he told the *Los Angeles Times*.[28] But Anderson expects his female soldiers to be involved in firefights primarily because they are serving at his forward operating base. "They are no less capable than I am to react to and return fire," he insists. "Are my infantrymen better? Yes. That's not due to lack of ability. It is a lack of repetition." No doubt skills increase with drilling, but Anderson seems to be suggesting that females can perform to male standards on the Army physical readiness test if they just practice more. More push-ups will make the women the same as men.

The colonel's views are not shared by some of the women supporting his unit. Private First Class Rosie Darby, a medic at one of the battalion's combat outposts, calls the idea of women in combat a "terrible idea." She worries about the physical demands and how soldiers will react if a woman serving with them is injured. She explained the men in her platoon treat her like a little sister and would tend to neglect the fight to take care of her.

An active-duty Army officer and veteran of two Iraq tours, the second as a combat arms company commander in the fight, said the "hybrid threats of the contemporary battlefield blurred the distinctions between combat and non-combat. It is a mistake to conflate the idea that just because you or your unit get into direct fire contact with the enemy that all of a sudden you're capable of doing the same things as combat arms personnel. That is flawed logic."[29]

Some women in Iraq and Afghanistan demonstrated valor under fire in protecting their units and themselves. We should celebrate their courage but not abandon logic by pretending that they are case studies of women successfully joining in sustained, conventional combat.

Myth No. 4: Good Leadership Defeats Eros

Good leadership is the key to avoiding the damage that sexual relationships can inflict on military units. Wishing away human nature, however, is no way to build a strong fighting force. This myth collapses under the reality that the birds and the bees can't be totally contained even in the best-led units.

The sex drive is critical to the human species, and it has profound biological, psychological, and social consequences. The male sex drive reaches its peak in the teens and early twenties, the ages of most military personnel. Further, men are visually stimulated by the female figure, even when it is clad in unfeminine camouflage utility uniforms.

Years ago, I debated the pornographer Larry Flynt. We exchanged barbs on a national radio program about women in the military and the role of sexual attraction. What I remember after all these years is Flynt's assertions that every man looks at a woman and "undresses her in his mind" and that "men constantly think about sex." I doubt Flynt had any scientific evidence for his claims, but his success at selling smut to a mostly male audience did provide him with some insights.

The parents of male teenagers and the military squad leaders of young male troops will agree with Flynt that most young men are preoccupied with the opposite sex. Given the opportunity, they will "sow their wild oats" with young women. The pregnancy rates aboard Navy ships and in deployed Army units indicate that their amped-up hormones can overcome location, rules, and even the best military leadership.[30]

This is not just a male issue. Army Reservist Master Sergeant Sally Kennedy recalls a female subordinate deployed to Iraq. The young woman posted on Facebook a video of herself and a male soldier having sex in the back of a five-ton truck. Both soldiers were disciplined, but the female remained in the unit and kept many of her comrades happy for the balance of the tour.

A male aviation sergeant recalls the evenings in Kandahar, Afghanistan, where the soldiers he supervised—male and female—slept in tents crammed into a tight area. Coupling soldiers rocked the portable outhouses, and groans of pleasure filled the sultry nights. Nothing his chain of command did could stop these nightly liaisons. Indeed, they tacitly accepted the inevitable, especially in Iraq, where the forward operating bases generally afforded more privacy than those in Afghanistan. Military exchanges (commercial retail outlets at the FOBs) sold slinky lingerie, and medics handed out condoms and pregnancy kits—official acknowledgement that the war zone was also a sex zone.

"We don't really have any other choice than to go to each other" for sex, a male soldier stationed in Mosul, Iraq, explained matter-of-factly. "In past wars, they could go into town and there would be girls there or boys or whatever you want. Here, you can't really leave the base because you'll get killed." A woman in the 146th Transportation Company, also in Iraq at the time, estimated that anywhere from a quarter to three-quarters of female soldiers were engaging in sex while on deployment. "If you include all the girls who are having sex with girls, it's much closer to every one of us," she said. A female Marine officer stationed in Ramadi, Iraq, said something similar. "You have two choices: you can keep your pants on and be miserable and be harassed or you can take your pants off and you'll still get harassed, but you'll be a little less miserable."[31]

The suggestion that curbing all this sex is simply a matter of good "leadership" is unrealistic in part because the problem extends to the services' most senior officers. The Associated Press reports that at least 30 percent of military commanders fired between 2005 and 2013 lost their jobs because of sex-related offenses such as adultery and improper relationships.[32] The best-known recent example is the extramarital affair that ended General David Petraeus's brief tenure as director of Central Intelligence. Petraeus became intimate with his fellow West Point graduate Paula Broadwell while he was still on active duty in Afghanistan, though the relationship did not turn physical until after he had hung up his four-star uniform. Brigadier General Jeffrey Sinclair was at the center of another spectacular and demoralizing scandal. The former assistant commander of the

Eighty-Second Airborne Division was charged in September 2012 with forcible sodomy, multiple counts of adultery, and inappropriate relationships with female Army officers.

Sexual relationships like these destroy service members' confidence in one another and in their leaders. I saw this myself as an inspector general investigating general officer sex cases for the chief of staff of the Army in the early 1990s. My IG partner and I would start by speaking with the alleged victims and other unit members. We inevitably found that word of the improper relationship had reached every corner of the command, whether the unit was living in tents in the Saudi Arabian desert or at an Army post somewhere in the United States. Members of the command resented the breach of trust, the manipulation of authority, and the polarizing effects of the incident. These relationships *do* matter, and they are terribly damaging.

As if consensual affairs weren't bad enough, our armed forces also face an epidemic of sexual assault. The Pentagon's most recent annual report on such cases estimates that twenty-six thousand service members (12,100 females and and 13,900 males) suffered "unwanted sexual contact" in 2012, but only 3,374 reported the incidents.[33] Overall, 6.1% of women who participated in the military-wide survey indicated they experienced unwanted sexual contact in 2012, and most of this contact (67%) happened on military installations. Additionally, most of the offenders (57%) were military coworkers.[34]

There is a problem with the Pentagon's survey, however. The 2012 Workplace and Gender Relations Survey of Active Duty Military conducted for the Pentagon's Office of Sexual Assault Prevention and Response cites the twenty-six thousand figure as the number of service members who experienced some form of unwanted sexual contact in the year prior to the survey. The survey had an unscientific sample set

(108,478 service members received the survey; 22,792 responded), and the twenty-six thousand figure comes from extrapolating the survey's results across the entire military. It is therefore dangerous to draw any meaningful conclusions from the survey.[35] If one accepts the Pentagon's numbers, however, then the following are signifcant results that will not necessarily be heard from the mainstream media:

1. In the military, as in civilian life, women are more likely to be sexually assaulted than men
2. Overall, more military men are assaulted than military women. If we're tallying up the harm caused by sexual assault in the military, that number matters very much.
3. Estimated sexual assaults are up by 38 percent from 2010
4. Sexual assaults are down by 15 percent from 2006
5. When age and marital status are controlled for, the risk of contact sexual violence for military and civilian women is the same
6. Military women are less likely than civilian women to experience stalking or intimate partner violence
7. With few exceptions, the past year and lifetime prevalence (occurrence) of interpersonal violence and prevention, sexual violence, and stalking in the civilian and military populations are quite similar, with no statistically significant differences
8. Deployment history increases the risk of contact sexual violence

Perhaps the most publicized recent case occurred at Lackland Air Force Base in Texas, where male instructors were found guilty of adultery, rape, and inappropriate relationships with female trainees. This case mirrors in many respects the 1996 scandal at Aberdeen Proving Ground training command, in which twelve male noncommissioned officers were charged with sexual assault on female trainees. Why didn't the military learn enough from the Aberdeen scandal to prevent the scandal at Lackland? The failure was not due to a lack of involvement by senior leadership or of oversight by commissions or of monitoring. No, there's a more fundamental problem.

Desiree Maxwell, a former Army sergeant who earned a Combat Action Badge in Iraq when her convoy was ambushed, doesn't lay all the blame for the military's growing sexual assault problem on men. "Women bring sexual advances upon themselves by flirting and getting close to someone," she says. "Then, at the last minute they say no [to sex]. You have to be a strong woman to serve in the military and avoid peer pressure."

Master Sergeant Kennedy says "roofies," a date rape drug, are a problem in the Army today. They are "used to get a woman drunk and then sexually assault her," she explains. "I know as a first sergeant for three years we were briefed constantly about the problem ... [and] roofies are more prevalent now than before." When she was a new soldier at Fort Carson, Colorado, in the 1990s, female soldiers "were told to stay away from the 'Banana Belt,' the area where the infantry lived.... I knew how the infantrymen guys talked. They are foul-mouthed and vulgar. They make sexual gestures and women need to be careful if they bought her a drink," Kennedy recalls.

The sexual assault crisis has tainted even the legendary service academies, which are supposed to produce an elite corps of military leaders. The Defense Department's *Annual Report on Sexual Harassment and Violence at the Military Service Academies* for 2012 documents a serious and growing problem. Reported sexual assaults increased by 23 percent during the 2011–2012 academic year at the three academies, Army, Navy, and Air Force. But many more assaults were not reported. For example, some 135 female midshipmen said they were victims of unwanted but unreported sexual contact.[36]

The military's response to these sex-related crises has been clumsy. Specifically, for field units in places like Afghanistan, the military altered the rules to accommodate certain sexual liaisons. In 2008, the military command in Afghanistan changed General Order No. 1 that outlines allowable conduct for U.S. troops and civilians working for the military. Previously, "intimate behavior" between men and women not married to each other was forbidden and punishable by military law. Those rules were tossed out in 2008 to allow single men and women to visit each other's living quarters, as long as everyone else who lives there agrees and they are never "behind closed doors." Fortunately, not all commands in theater embraced that imprudent modification.

Changing General Order No. 1 wasn't enough to relieve some of the sexual tension among the troops, so General Dempsey now believes that assigning women to more combat positions will help mitigate the sexual assault problem. "We've had this ongoing issue with sexual harassment, sexual assault. I believe it's because we've had separate classes of military personnel—at some level," Dempsey said at a press conference when announcing his intention to lift the female combat ban.[37] "Now, it's far more complicated than that," he continued. "But when you have one part of the population that is designated as warriors and another part that is designated as something else, I think that disparity begins to establish a psychology that in some cases led to that environment. I have to believe that the more we can treat people equally, the more likely they are to treat each other equally."

That is a remarkably naïve view.

"You will inevitably have an explosion of sex in units," predicts Heather Mac Donald, a researcher at the Manhattan Institute. Eros in combat units "is an indomitable force," and "you are going to have a spike in sexual assault." Claims of sexual assault will be rampant, she warns. "The military will require sexual sensitivity training [and] the military will start looking like an Ivy League college with bureaucrats."[38] Mandatory sensitivity training programs already consume many service-member hours, and the military has more sexual assault response coordinators (twenty-five thousand) than it does recruiters (nineteen thousand), according to the Center for Military Readiness.[39]

Myth No. 5: Women Are Perfectly Capable of Handling the Rigors of Combat

As a matter of science, we are told, women are as physically capable of handling direct-fire, close ground combat as men.

The evidence, however, is all to the contrary. Numerous military studies have demonstrated that the average woman is physically incapable of performing at the same demanding level as the average frontline infantryman. This difference in ability, explains retired Rear Admiral Hugh Scott, a physician, "is due to the naturally occurring, unalterable anatomical and physiological differences in physical strength and endurance that exist between males and females, which is hormonal in nature, and cannot be ignored without jeopardizing the lives and safety of all members of a unit, and degrading its ability to carry out a successful mission." Those who would lift the Pentagon's ground combat exclusion of women—people like former Secretary of Defense Leon Panetta, General Martin Dempsey, and members of the Pentagon's 2011 Military Leadership Diversity Commission—simply dismiss the inconvenient evidence.[40]

Before considering the physiological evidence, it is essential to understand the physical requirements of ground combat. Infantrymen take the fight to the enemy in severe heat and cold and in deserts, mountains, and swamps. The experience of infantrymen in Afghanistan illustrates the stark demands. They carry a third of their body weight—half the body weight of the average Army woman—into combat, and they do so in the thin air of the Afghan mountains. Infantrymen must deal with debilitating fatigue and sleep deprivation. Combat losses—comrades wounded and killed—leave the survivors carrying more gear as the battle moves forward, further burdening every soldier.

The emergency-approach march gear of an infantryman in the Eighty-Second Airborne Division mortar section in Afghanistan in 2003 weighed 150 pounds.[41] The loads and combat tasks were shared equally among infantrymen, including their leaders. Even the company commander, the top on-the-spot leader, carried 110 pounds of gear.

A first sergeant who was with the 187th Regiment in Operation Anaconda in 2003 recalled how tough it was to carry all that gear: "We had extreme difficulty moving with all of our weight.... It took us 8 hours to move 5 clicks [almost three miles]. With just the vest [Interceptor hard body armor] and LBV [enhanced tactical load bearing vest] we were easily carrying 80 pounds. Throw on the ruck and you're sucking."[42]

Women are at a marked disadvantage in such conditions quite apart from how physically fit they may be. "The hormonal nature of the physical and physiological differences between males and females is due to the secretion, metabolism, and chemistry of the male sex hormone, testosterone," says Admiral Scott. Referring to the authoritative *Textbook of Medical Physiology*,[43] he summarizes how testosterone gives men an enormous physiological advantage over women:

Testosterone is a naturally occurring steroid hormone from the androgen (male) group that is primarily secreted in the testes of males and to a much lesser degree in the ovaries of females, with small amounts also being secreted, in both sexes, by the adrenal glands. On average an adult male produces about ten times (300 to 1,200 ng/dl) more testosterone than does an adult female (30 ng/dl to 95 ng/dl).

In the male, testosterone has a profound effect on protein formation and increased muscular development that begins after the start of puberty, during which there is a doubling of the muscle mass of all muscle groups. While men and women have an equal number of muscles and muscle fibers, the strength difference relates exclusively to muscle size that is determined by testosterone levels. Because women have less testosterone than men, they have smaller muscle fibers that result in the development of small-size muscles; in effect, women have less muscle to activate. That also is the reason why women develop less muscle when training with weights and exercising.

The anabolic effects of testosterone make men at least 30 percent stronger than women, especially in the upper body musculature, which provides a greater capability for doing the kind of heavy manual work associated with combat arms, such as carrying full packs on forced marches, along with lugging weapons and ammunition, carrying radios and batteries, and, when necessary, lifting and carrying a wounded or dead comrade. There is little overlap between the distributions of male and female upper-body strength.[44]

Testosterone also increases the total quantity of bone matrix and calcium retention, all of which result in a heavier and stronger male skeleton. More specifically, testosterone affects the anatomy of the male pelvis, narrowing and lengthening the pelvic outlet. The resulting funnel-shaped pelvis adds greater strength for load-bearing tasks and more efficient locomotion. In females, the lack of testosterone coupled with the effect of the female hormone estrogen results in the development of a broad ovoid pelvis that is better suited for child-bearing and delivery than for carrying heavy loads.

Finally, testosterone increases the basal metabolic rate by as much as 15 percent, an indirect result of its effect on protein anabolism, increasing the activities of all cells. Males therefore have larger hearts and lungs and produce greater amounts of red blood cells. The average male has about seven hundred thousand more red blood cells per cubic millimeter than the average female, giving him 40 percent more aerobic capacity than women and greater endurance in performing hard physical work. The smaller female heart must pump more blood than a man's at a given level of exertion because there is less hemoglobin in the blood to carry oxygen. These differences would put women at a distinct disadvantage in ground combat, which requires strength and physical endurance, because they must operate at a higher percentage of their maximum capability, leaving them with a smaller reserve capacity.

The 1992 Presidential Commission on the Assignment of Women in the Armed Forces concluded: "The average female Army recruit is 4.8 inches shorter, 31.7 pounds lighter, has 37.4 fewer pounds of muscle, and 5.7 more pounds of fat than the average male recruit. She has only 55 percent of the upper-body strength and 72 percent of the lower-body strength."[45] These discrepancies inevitably affect

performance. The commission found that only "the upper five percent of women are at the level of the male median," and "the average
20-to-30-year-old woman has the same aerobic capacity as a 50-year-
old man."[46]

These dramatic differences in physical capacity are amplified in
ground combat. A Walter Reed Army Medical Center report, *Load
Carriage in Military Operations*, outlined the differences between the
sexes' ability to carry loads:

> Compared with men, women walk with shorter stride
> length and greater stride frequency. As loads increase,
> women's stride length decreases, whereas men's stride
> length does not show significant change. With increasing
> load, women also show a more pronounced linear increase
> in the time that both feet are on the ground (double sup-
> port time) than do men. To bring the center of the load
> mass over the feet (base of support), women tend to
> hyperextend their necks and bring their shoulders farther
> forward than do men, possibly to compensate for less
> upper body strength. Many of these differences between
> men and women persist even when differences in body
> size and composition are taken into account.[47]

The pronounced physiological differences between the sexes put the
female body at much higher risk of injury in physically taxing conditions. The shape of the female pelvis, for example, puts women at a
disadvantage when marching, running, or carrying weight at the
extremes of endurance.[48] When a mixed platoon of recruits marches
at the male stride (forty-five centimeters) rather than the shorter

female stride (thirty-eight centimeters), which happens when most of the recruits are male, there is an increased incidence of stress fractures of the pubic ramus among the women.[49]

As you would expect, then, military women experience more than twice the number of lower-extremity injuries and over four times the number of stress fractures as men. A 2006 study of first-term female Marines found that 44 percent suffer lower-extremity injuries, and they were less likely to complete their first-term enlistment.[50] A 2010 study found the non-battle injury rate for women in one U.S. unit serving in Operation Iraqi Freedom was 167 percent higher than that for men, and the skeletal-muscular injury rate was almost equal to that of men from all causes.[51]

In the civilian world, rational minds recognize the fundamental differences between the physical capacities of men and women. Dr. Mary Lloyd Ireland, a Kentucky orthopedic surgeon, studied why female basketball players suffer twice as many serious knee injuries as males and six times more anterior cruciate ligament tears. She attributes the problem to women's bodies' being less suited than men's to absorb the driving and pounding of the sport.[52] Anne Loucks, who teaches physiology at Ohio University, found that hard physical work coupled with a caloric deficit—common conditions in combat—may over the long run damage a woman's reproductive system and deplete bone minerals, making her prone to osteoporosis.[53]

This same rationality used to be found in the military as well, but the last thirty years have seen a persistent effort to extirpate it. When a 1982 review of the Army's policies for women found that only 8 percent of female soldiers were capable of lifting one hundred pounds (the definition of "very heavy" work), the Army devised the Military Enlistment Physical Strength Capacity Test (MEPSCAT) to help match recruits with jobs. But because such a test might interfere with the political goal of expanding the female presence in the Army, MEPSCAT was never implemented.[54]

In 1996 Congressman Robert Dornan, a Republican from California, asked the General Accounting Office to review the sex-neutral occupational performance standards in the military. In its response, the GAO pointed out that in 1976 it had recommended that the services develop standards for measuring recruits' strength and stamina because some service members were unable to accomplish the physically demanding tasks of the jobs to which they had been assigned.[55] The Army had responded to that recommendation by classifying occupational specialties according to their physical demands and giving recruits a weight-lifting test. There had been an improvement in matching recruits with suitable jobs, but the standards had tended to keep women out of certain positions. The Army discontinued the weight-lifting test in 1990 without explanation.

Instead of testing soldiers' fitness for particular jobs, the Army began using surveys to ascertain how soldiers were performing in the jobs to which they had already been assigned. Surveys in 1989, 1994, and 1995 revealed that substantial minorities of soldiers had difficulty with the lifting that their jobs required, though there was no explanation of what happened to those soldiers. They ought to have been reassigned, but it is likely that they remained in their positions and other soldiers had to carry their loads.

In its 1996 investigation, the GAO found that the Army's surveys were not working. Supervisors reported that they worked around individuals' physical inabilities or "redistributed" tasks (that is, made others pick up the slack, hurting morale) and that problems were rarely channeled to higher levels of authority. (The other services, according to the GAO, did not even attempt a systematic assessment of their members' physical fitness for their jobs.)

Before the GAO's report was published in July 1996, the Army announced the results of its own preemptive study. The Army Research Institute of Environmental Medicine selected forty civilian women between the ages of eighteen and thirty-two to engage in physical training for twenty-four weeks. Funding for the $140,000 study came from a women's health research project pushed by Congressman Patricia Schroeder, a Democrat from Colorado and a leading proponent of women in combat.[56] The subjects were supervised five days per week, ninety minutes per day, by experts in strength training and conditioning. They lifted weights, hiked with backpacks, and ran.

At the conclusion of the training, 78 percent of the women could lift over one hundred pounds, qualifying for the most demanding military occupational specialties and apparently casting doubt on female exclusions.[57] The subjects increased their repetitive lifting ability, substantially improved their ability to run with a seventy-five-pound backpack, augmented their aerobic capacity by 14 percent, and dramatically increased their hip and thigh muscle strength and endurance.

These results were no surprise to Lori Gilstrap, a strength and conditioning coordinator with the U.S. Olympic Committee. She warned, however, that women shouldn't be expected to match men in strength because they have much lower levels of testosterone.[58] "You don't need testosterone to get strong," countered Everett Harman, the Army scientist who headed the study. Consistent training and conditioning "can be very effective in improving the ability of women to perform physically demanding military jobs."[59]

But another study by the same Army institute found that women, because of their smaller stature and higher body fat percentage, will seldom meet the physical requirements of the military's heaviest jobs. Aerobic capacity, according to the authors of that study, is a function of body fat percentage, and strength is a function of lean muscle mass. Only people with lean muscle mass of 110 pounds can perform heavy work jobs, yet the average woman has a muscle mass of 36-percent muscle mass[60] or fifty-eight pounds.[61]

The 1996 training study is suspect on its face because it didn't include a male control group for a comparison of changes in strength. It also did not address the impracticability of keeping women at such a high standard of training, especially when they are away from the "artificial" lab environment with its barbells and Olympic trainers. An important question is whether women can achieve *and maintain* the physical standards for combat. Studies of soldiers in World War II showed a marked decrease in muscle and fitness under prolonged combat conditions. Those were men, of course. For women, a corresponding loss of fitness might prove catastrophic.

Nature gives women far less strength and aerobic capacity than men. The 1992 presidential commission found that only 3.4 percent of women achieved a score equal to the male *mean* score on the Army Physical Fitness Test (APFT).[62] William Gregor, of the School of Advanced Military Studies at Fort Leavenworth, Kansas, compiled the APFT results of 74,838 cadets attending the Army Reserve Officers' Training Corps Advanced Camp, now known as the Leader Development Assessment Course, from 1992 to 2008. Because of their training, ROTC cadets generally display a much higher degree of fitness than do enlisted recruits, but the same disparities between the sexes that we have seen elsewhere were apparent among these highly motivated cadets.[63]

The three components of the APFT—push-ups, sit-ups, and a two-mile run—test physical fitness only; they don't correspond with actual military tasks, much less combat requirements. The APFT, nevertheless, is a useful indicator of general physical wellness, and women ROTC cadets dramatically trail their male counterparts. Specifically, only 2.9 percent of the women were able to attain the male mean score for the two-mile run, and only 1.5 percent of the women achieved the male mean for strength. This is why the Army has "separate but equal" female APFT test tables, which are less strenuous than the male test requirements. The standards may be "equivalent," but they're not "equal."

These Army figures complement the results of a Navy "damage-control" test that revealed enormous differences in performance between male and female sailors. The Navy's damage-control procedures were designed around the ability of the average man. Ninety-six percent of the men tested met standards for two damage-control evolutions (carrying a P-250 water pump), and 100 percent met standards for a stretcher carry. The percentage of women meeting standards for the same tasks was 1 percent and 12 percent, respectively. The Navy attributed the difference to women's having only about 60 percent of the upper-torso strength of men.[64]

The British Army toyed with the idea of putting women in infantry units. But a 2002 study revealed that only 0.1 percent of female applicants and 1 percent of trained female soldiers "would reach the required standards to meet the demands of these roles." The report concluded, "To admit women would … involve a risk with no gains in terms of combat effectiveness to offset it." So, in 2010, the British government reviewed its policies and opted to retain its ban on women in combat.

The physical differences between men and women are stark and impossible to overcome, even with Olympic trainers and plenty of time.

The experience of Kristen Scharnberg, a *Chicago Tribune* reporter who was embedded with the 101st Airborne Division during the invasion of Iraq in 2003, is a fitting cautionary tale with which to conclude.[65]

Scharnberg is clearly no shrinking violet, but she acknowledges her discomfort with the impossibility of personal modesty and the lack of hygiene on the front lines. She was "sick to death of having to pee in front of men," but what persuaded her that ground combat was not a place for a woman was the physical demands.

Early on she promised herself that "no matter how tired I was or how physically strenuous a mission became, I would never let one of the soldiers lug my rucksack or equipment for me." She broke that promise halfway through a four-mile hike carrying a seventy-pound rucksack to which, in the hope of charging her computer and phone, she had added a car battery. When she was about to give out, a soldier asked, "Ma'am, can I carry that battery for you?"

> All my resolve failed. I handed the battery to the young man—who already was lugging a much heavier load than I was, including a fully loaded M-4 assault weapon that he would be expected to use in case of an attack.
>
> The decision nagged at me for days. Not only had I not been able to pull my own weight, I also had potentially put that young soldier at risk.

Months later, back home in Chicago, a female colleague asked Scharnberg if her experience in Iraq had given her an opinion about sending women into combat. She told the woman the story about the battery and how she had seen "big, tough, burly male soldiers nearly collapse during 10-kilometer hikes with rucksacks, ammunition, TOW missiles, radios and machine guns."

I'm not qualified to say that no woman could do that job, but I suspect that it would be a rare one who could. I had run a marathon not long before the war and worked out almost every day. I grew up on an Iowa farm where manual labor was part of the bargain. But I had been bested by a car battery, and when I handed my load to that soldier, I admitted that I never could have cut it in the infantry.

Myth No. 6: Other Countries Put Women in Combat

It is true some countries allow women to serve in combat jobs, and those women are making important contributions. The experiences of other countries, however, can be of limited applicability to the U.S. military. There is also a great deal of politically motivated overstatement in reports about women in foreign combat forces.

Seven countries are often cited for their progressive employment of female combatants, but under closer scrutiny, those examples yield more questions than answers. The enormous size of the American military—an active force of 1.46 million not counting National Guard and Reserve forces—makes comparisons difficult.

Australia

Australia, one of America's closest Asia-Pacific allies, is just starting its grand experiment with female combatants.

In 2012, Australia's active military included 47,135 personnel backed up by 29,396 reservists. Women make up 14 percent of the active Australian forces (7,861), and they account for 10 percent of the country's deployed forces.[66]

In 2011, the Australian government announced its intention to remove all sex-based restrictions from Australian Defense Force combat roles. That decision, which was driven by a string of sex scandals, is being implemented over five years.[67] The Australian military is going to offer women "try before you buy" deals to encourage them to take on full combat roles. But the move has so far generated little response. No serving army or air force women have sought combat posts. A defense spokesman said the navy had three responses to its call, though formal applications in the navy started only in January 2013.[68]

The first phase of the plan began in January 2013, when currently serving women could apply for combat roles provided they met all the requirements. New female recruits can begin entering directly into combat roles in January 2016.

New Zealand

New Zealand, an island nation in the South Pacific, has no restrictions on women serving in combat and no known enemies. Its miniscule armed force (4,290 active, 1,824 reservists) permits women who qualify to serve in the Special Air Service and infantry, armored, and artillery units. The New Zealand Defense Force is 16-percent female.

Norway

Norway, a Scandinavian nation that enjoys protection from the North Atlantic Treaty Organization, has a tiny armed force of eleven thousand uniformed professionals plus roughly eight thousand conscript soldiers. The professionals may serve on expeditionary missions as well as duties at home, but conscripts may fulfill only the latter role.[69]

Norwegian military women may serve in all combat jobs. They make up 9.1 percent of the professional force and 10 percent of the conscripts. The Norwegian Ministry of Defense has set targets for female conscripts of 25 percent by 2015 and 20 percent for military professionals by 2020.[70]

"The few women that are attracted by the infantry and cavalry do a great job in the Norwegian Army," said Colonel Ingrid Gjerde, an infantry officer in the Norwegian military for twenty-five years, as reported by *National Geographic*.[71]

"I have to be clear: You have to meet the physical standards, because the job is still the same. It works very well as long as women hold the standards," explained Colonel Gjerde, the former commander of Norwegian forces in Afghanistan in 2012. "It's not a big deal because women who go into these fields know the standards, and it's not that hard for women to train up to the standards if they really want."[72]

Germany

Germany is Europe's economic powerhouse, but its military is now a shadow of its former Cold War self. Today, German women serve in most military occupational specialties, but that was not always the case. Women were excluded from the German armed forces—the Bundeswehr—from its establishment in 1955 until 1975, when they were permitted to serve in the medical and music corps.

That changed in 2000 when the European Court of Justice ordered Germany to allow women to serve in more military positions than previously permitted. Subsequently the German government amended its constitution, replacing the prohibition against women's carrying weapons with the provision that women cannot be forced to carry weapons. That change led to a substantial influx of young women into the Bundeswehr.

Conscription was abandoned in 2011, and today the German armed forces are a professional, all-volunteer force. Currently 10 percent of all military personnel are women, according to the

Bundeswehr's chief of staff, General Volker Wieker. "Our goal," he says, "is a combined ratio of 15 percent [women] in all units and 50 percent in medical units."[73]

The all-volunteer Bundeswehr includes approximately eighteen thousand women, out of a total of 185,000 active soldiers. They are found throughout most military specialties, including combat arms, where an estimated eight hundred female soldiers serve. A few combat specialties such as special operating forces, however, do not include women.

It hardly matters where women are assigned in the Bundeswehr, because that army doesn't fight much and is unlikely to in the near future. A series of secret internal reports on the German army leaked to the tabloid *Bild* exposed German soldiers' poor state of training and antiquated equipment on the Afghan battlefield. "German soldiers mostly don't know how to use their weapons.... [They] have no or little experience driving armored vehicles," according to *Bild*.[74] Furthermore, before Germany joined the Afghan war coalition in 2009, it had no officers with combat experience.

Russia

Russia is often celebrated as a powerhouse of feminine combat power. In World War I the provisional government formed a few women's battalions that numbered five thousand and were overseen by male officers. The women "had their heads shaved and were otherwise defeminized in appearance and segregated from males." At least two of those units fought in active combat, but their casualty rate was high. The experiment was declared a failure—but so was the Russian army—in 1917.[75]

It is true that an estimated eight hundred thousand women served in the Soviet armed forces during the Great Patriotic War (World War

II), some in support and others as combatants. There was a Women's Reserve Rifle Regiment and a Central Sniper Training Center for Women. The 122nd Air Group graduated six hundred women pilots. By 1943, Soviet women served in the infantry, anti-aircraft defense, armor, artillery, transportation, communications, nursing, and the partisan resistance.[76]

"The relative effectiveness of Soviet women in World War II is hard to measure," an Army Research Institute report concludes. Female units developed their own cohesiveness, but most women served in mixed units. "Soviet sources reported women having trouble with tasks involving upper-body strength," like throwing grenades, and there were cases of "self-inflicted grenade deaths among women." There was a German account of tearful Soviet women pressed into artillery service and of men who were contemptuous of them.[77]

A quarter of Soviet women who served were decorated, including eighty-nine who received their nation's highest award, the Hero of the Soviet Union. But that rich tradition died with the demise of the former Communist state.[78] When the war ended, so did the exigencies requiring women as stopgap combatants. They were removed from combat units because of the inefficiencies and their lack of capability.

Today, Russian women are far less evident in the armed forces. "Compared to 2007, the number of servicewomen (officers and warrant officers) has shrunk from over 30,000 to a little over 11,000 today," said Yelena Stepanova, a lieutenant colonel with a Russian armed forces sociological research center. The reduction is part of a broader process of personnel cuts across the armed forces, Stepanova said. Russia's armed forces have more than two million service members.[79]

There is also a debate within Russia about the role of women. Yelena Knyazeva, Russia's sole female army general, said women should not replace the thousands of men dodging military service, but they should bring up children instead. Last year, according to the general staff, some 250,000 Russian men dodged the draft.[80]

The Duma is considering legislation that would introduce voluntary military service for women with similar terms to the conscript system for men. If passed, the legislation would allow female recruits to fill the current deficit of male conscripts.[81]

Israel

Israel is usually the first example cited in arguments for women in combat, but it is a mistake to think of the Israeli Defense Forces as the home of the female warrior. "We have misconceptions. We have been brainwashed about what women can do and what women cannot do. This is a big, big mistake," said General Yitzhak Gershon, a thirty-two-year veteran of the IDF and now national director and CEO of the nonprofit Friends of the IDF.[82]

Israel's Military Service Law was amended in 2000 to grant women the right "to serve in any role in the IDF." Today most (90 percent) IDF roles are open to women, although women are found in only 69 percent of all positions.

Modern Israel is the size of New Jersey with a population of only seven million. It is surrounded by enemies and has a long history of wars. By necessity, Israel conscripts young citizens of both sexes. With few exemptions, women serve one year and nine months, while men serve three years.

It is a myth, however, that women have always been fully integrated into Israel's fighting forces. They served during Israel's 1948 War of Independence, making up about 20 percent of the total force and filling support roles: nursing, signal, and convoy escorts. The few women who served in combat units were withdrawn because Arab enemy units became more fanatical and less likely to surrender because they were fighting women. Contributing to that decision was the possibility of women combatants' falling into enemy hands as prisoners of war and being abused.

Dr. David Gutmann, professor emeritus of psychology and behavioral sciences at Northwestern University medical school in Chicago, spoke at a 2009 symposium on "Islamic Terror and Sexual Mutilation," warning about the abuse female POWs might face. "During the Israeli War of Independence Jewish fighters, including female soldiers captured by Arab irregulars, were routinely tortured and mutilated in the most obscene ways (by contrast, water-boarding would have furnished a pleasant interlude), and IDF officers warned their troops against being taken alive," Gutmann said.[83]

After the War of Independence, a women's corps was formed, known by its Hebrew acronym, CHEN (which means "charm"). Women were subsequently trained in armed self-defense, and in 1949 women became subject to conscription, but not on the same basis as men.[84]

Since those days, and because of politics and national security, Israel has reversed its decision by returning women closer to the front lines. Today, women provide significant combat support by serving as military police, border guards, and flight instructors and by training tank crews. Women hold 1.6 percent of all IDF combat jobs, and the army wants to increase that number so as to employ women in new Iron Dome anti-missile units that proved so effective against Hamas rockets and mortars in November 2012.

Women do not serve as combatants with the IDF's elite direct-fire, close ground combat units. Some perform support functions, but according to a now-retired U.S. Army officer who attended the Israeli Armored Corps Commander's Course, the Israelis are adamant that women will not be allowed to fight. Every unit was assigned vehicles to remove the women to the rear at the outset of hostilities. Much of this was due to Jewish cultural views as much as the inability of women to perform tasks in direct combat.[85]

Most of the women in combat-related jobs serve with the anti-aircraft division, search and rescue units, border police, and the one-of-a-kind Caracal Battalion, a 70-percent-female, light infantry battalion. The Caracal Battalion is part of the 512th Brigade in Israel's Southern Command, which serves along the Jordanian and Egyptian borders, mostly in a border patrol–like capacity. The unit trains with specialized weapons—machine guns, sniper rifles, and mortars—and has a reputation as a no-nonsense and reliable battalion.[86]

Some combat-hardened senior commanders are concerned that Israel is going too far pushing for women closer to direct ground combat. Retired Major General Yaakov Amidror told the Associated Press that women will never be a match physically in frontline units. "If anyone thinks women are going to fill the fighting ranks, they're wrong," he said.[87]

Retired Major General Yiftach Ron-Tal, who led the process of integration of women into combat units a decade ago, now expresses strong reservations about further integration of women into combat units. "It turns out that the amount of stress fractures suffered by soldiers is dozens of percentage points higher among women than among men. As a result, the female soldiers are not required to carry as much weight," Ron-Tal explained.[88] He adds, "I think that women's service in combat roles in the IDF should not be widened. I cannot even imagine a female soldier serving inside a tank or in elite infantry units, mostly because of operational considerations. The army must not allow this thing to interfere with its operational ability." General Ron-Tal said the inclusion of women in combat units placed "the military in a nearly impossible situation," and it "will be a grave mistake that will damage the prowess of the army. Women's service in roles that are not suited to them might harm state security."

Canada

Canada's alleged success with women in combat always comes up in debates about the issue. Canada has a "no exclusion policy," which means women can compete for all positions, including direct ground combat. As of 2011, women made up 12 percent of Canada's regular and reserve forces (which number 68,250 and 47,081, respectively),[89] and in the same year, 310 Canadian women were deployed to Afghanistan in combat positions such as infantry, field artillery, combat engineers, armor, and pilots.[90]

There are many glowing testimonials in the press about the performance of Canadian military women in Afghanistan but no objective data. One media report indicated some Canadian female combatants felt excluded from the real fighting. When asked about that report, Canadian forces refused to provide statistics on how often the women were used in combat. A military spokesman did say that "participation on operations is based on the physical and mental abilities of soldiers.... This process does not include gender considerations."[91]

Some women deployed as combatants to Afghanistan were sidelined in administrative jobs. Corporal Kimberly Ashton, a combat engineer, said she never left her forward operating base the entire tour. Infantry corporal Katie Moman had a similar complaint. She spent her six-month tour inside a Kandahar FOB, never getting the chance to fight, a common complaint reported in the *Wall Street Journal*.

A former senior Canadian commander in Afghanistan said some male colleagues had a desire to "protect" the women and looked out for them by carrying their gear or protecting them in the battlefield. This may explain as well why female combatants were used so sparingly in combat. Apparently there was need to protect the women in combatant ranks, but not only from the enemy. In a letter to her husband, Captain Nichola Goddard, the first Canadian woman killed in action, wrote, "There were six rapes in the camp last week, so we have to work out an escort at night." She didn't indicate whether the perpetrators were Canadian or Afghan army or police.[92] It's a problem U.S. women face throughout the war zone, so men have to escort them around camp after dark.

Canada is finding it difficult to recruit enough women for its grand feminist experiment. They occupy 2.4 percent of the combat jobs, according to the Canadian government.[93]

The experience of these countries confirms that women can competently fill a number of combat support roles. The United States should learn from other countries' experiences and avoid their mistakes, but the world's sole superpower cannot blindly follow their military personnel policies. Less consequential powers may get away with allowing fashionable opinion to shape their military policy. The United States, on which the stability of the world order depends, does not have that luxury.

CHAPTER 4

THE RISKS OF PUTTING WOMEN IN GROUND COMBAT

T he feminist vision for America's military is portrayed in *Battlestar Galactica*, a 1978 television science fiction series that spawned movies, books, comics, and video games. The androgynous crew of the *Galactica* share wardrooms, bunkrooms, and bathrooms. In this world without patriarchy, men and women fight without regard to their opponents' sex.[1]

The truth is that the radical feminists who are pushing women into combat see America as a patriarchal society in which men are the oppressors of women. To rectify that situation, feminists oppose standard sex roles and seek the radical reordering of society.[2] The greatest bastion of patriarchy, in their view, is the U.S. military. They are determined to remake it in the image of *Battlestar Galactica*—a sex-blind society in which men and women are interchangeable.

The armed forces have been a key battleground in the culture war since the mid-1970s, and the sexual egalitarians have made great strides in winning the American people's sympathy. Targeting the military was audacious—it was possibly the most conservative institution in the country, as well as one of the most powerful—but strategically brilliant. They astutely worked from inside the Pentagon through political appointments to change military policies one by one. With astonishing swiftness, they have reached the threshold of a victory that was unthinkable a generation ago—transforming the world-conquering United States armed forces into an androgynous job corps that happens to fight, but not as well as it once did.

Now it is up to the American people to decide which military they want: the one that vanquished every totalitarian threat it encountered during the twentieth century and made the United States the greatest global power in history, or a gender-normed jobs corps, in which multiculturalism and radical feminism have replaced readiness as a strategic imperative.

The Feminist Agenda

Breaking the combat glass ceiling for women entails substantial risks for the female combatants and their children. Even before the insertion of women into ground combat units, the casualty lists from Afghanistan and Iraq provide a progress report on feminism in the military. Mothers sent into the combat zone are coming home to their children in body bags. Among them are Lori Ann Piestewa, twenty-three, mother of two preschoolers; Melissa J. Hobart, twenty-two, mother of a three-year-old; Jessica L. Cawvey, twenty-one, single mother of a six-year-old; Pamela Osbourne, thirty-eight, mother of three children, ages nine through nineteen; Katrina L. Bell-Johnson, thirty-two, mother of a one-year-old.[3] But for feminists, it's worth the risks. The agenda that feminists pursue at any cost, writes the military historian Martin van Creveld, is to compel the forces to pretend, against all the evidence that soldiers and doctors can muster, that women are as fit for war as men: increase the proportion of women from near zero to as many as 10–13 percent of the troops; turn training into a mockery and humiliation for those men who are involved in it alongside women; absorb the extra costs involved in paying for everything from separate toilets to pregnancy cases and from special uniforms to post-natal leave of absence; deny or cover up any damage done and loss suffered; and ignore or silence or discharge anybody who objects.[4]

Risky Business

There are eight major risks to the armed forces and American security in placing women in direct ground combat roles.

1. **Compromised standards:** If feminists and their political allies in the Pentagon, the White House, and Congress are to succeed, they must first compromise military training and operational standards. That will inevitably drain combat effectiveness, and the nation will be less secure.

2. **Failure to match capabilities with job assignments:** The armed forces have already tried sex-neutral standards based on job requirements, but they had to be abandoned because they eliminated too many candidates. Feminists will not be content with performance standards that women can't meet.

3. **Physical suffering:** Young women who serve as ground combatants by choice or compulsion will suffer disproportionate physical and psychological harm. The

government will bear the expense of those injuries, many of which will last a lifetime.

4. **Destruction of the warrior spirit:** Feminizing our ground combat forces threatens to destroy the warrior spirit, that masculine mindset that glues fighters together and fuels their aggression to kill our enemies. Damage that spirit and you condemn our military to defeat.

5. **Increase in sexual assaults:** Our military already faces a serious problem of sexual assault within the ranks. Pushing women into ground combat units will make it worse.

6. **Forcing women into combat:** By and large, enlisted women are not eager to join combat units. But such assignments will become necessary because there won't be enough female volunteers to make the feminization of combat units work.

7. **Reduction of retention rates and decline of quality:** Lifting the ban on women in combat will hurt both retention and recruitment. The effect of feminization will become noticeable as the economy improves and as the military completes its postwar downsizing.

8. **Subjecting women to the draft:** If combat is open to women, there is no longer any reason to exempt them from Selective Service registration and from a future draft.

These are the likely consequences of opening ground combat duty to women. Let's look at them in more detail.

Risk No. 1: Compromised Standards

There is good reason to believe that once women are forced into ground combat, readiness standards will be degraded. The consequences for the women, our ground forces, and the nation will be serious.

The Obama administration and the Pentagon brass deny that this will happen. Former Secretary of Defense Panetta insisted that it is critical to maintain the same high standards we have always had for combat units, but he also said that "the department's goal in rescinding the rule [against women in combat] is to ensure that the mission is met with the best-qualified and most capable people, regardless of gender."[5]

The "department's goal," however, is driven by the "diversity metrics" outlined in the 2011 report of the Military Leadership Diversity Commission (MLDC), which called for eliminating women's ground combat exemptions so that more women could advance to the stars over qualified men and at the expense of readiness.[6] "The Commission's lodestar," writes Kinglsey R. Browne in a careful and devastating study of the report, "was diversity, not military effectiveness, and it failed to take into consideration a wealth of information bearing on its recommendation."[7] The MLDC's recommendations are not based on authoritative sources, says Browne, and its "analysis of the sources that it did consult was superficial and in conflict with some of the facts, as opposed to the 'spin,' contained in these very sources." For example, the commission downplayed sex differences in strength and physical capacities, ignored pregnancy's substantial effects on readiness, and claimed that there was "little evidence" that the integration of women harmed cohesion.[8]

Following that report, General Dempsey revealed that the readiness of the force was no longer the Pentagon's highest priority. In the press conference announcing the rescission of the 1994 rule excluding women from ground combat units, the chairman of the Joint Chiefs stated, "If we do decide that a particular standard is so high that a woman couldn't make it, the burden is now on the service to come back and explain to the secretary, why is it that high? Does it really have to be that high?"[9] In a dangerous world, General Dempsey had just set his foot on a very slippery slope.

The question Dempsey ought to have asked is, "Do we have the personnel we need to meet the current high standards for combat units?" The answer right now is yes. There is no shortage of able-bodied male volunteers who meet the existing, battle-tested standards for ground combat positions. So why ask the services to consider changing the standards? Because this is about politics. If women are to serve in ground combat units, the standards must change because very few women will meet them.

Further, in order for sexual integration of combat units to work, says Dempsey, there must be a "critical mass" or "significant cadre" of women in each unit, by which he means 10 to 15 percent of a force. In a hundred-man infantry company, that's two squads of women.[10]

What happens if only 5 percent of women can meet the standard? The diversity umpires will likely force the services to adjust their "faulty" standards in order to achieve that "critical mass" of women. The objective determines the standard, and the objective is bringing women into combat units, not building combat units that are ready to fight. The standards will drop by necessity.

General Robert Cone, the head of the Army's Training and Doctrine Command (TRADOC), acknowledges that "soldiers—both men and women—want fair and meaningful standards to be developed for accepting women into previously restricted specialties. I think that fairness is very important in a values-based organization like our Army."[11] General Cone knows that the battlefield is not "fair" and that lowering standards is dangerous. His true objective is evident when he says, "Army officials will look at 'traditional impediments'—the attitudes regarding the acceptance of women into previously male-only jobs." He continues, "The Army will take proactive measures to mitigate resistance to women going into specialties." After all, "We want the right environment for women."[12]

In the new military, units will inevitably become subject to commissars of political correctness. This has already happened at West Point, where each company now has a "cadet respect officer," who, armed with the necessary coercive powers, insures that everyone displays the proper attitudes.

The "barriers" that everyone now wants to dismantle are standards of readiness that have stood the tests of time and combat. To feminists, however, they are a "glass ceiling" impeding the rise of women to the highest ranks of the military that the feminists themselves despise. The Army chief of staff, General Raymond Odierno, promptly pledged his conformity to the new order of women first, readiness second, promising to examine the Army "in order to develop strategies to overcome these barriers."

The military's track record of maintaining high standards while achieving sexual integration is not impressive. It is a warning of what lies ahead as the final obstacle to a fully feminized military falls.

Politically Inspired Sexual Integration Scuttles Navy Flight Standards

In 1991, one hundred Navy and Marine Corps aviators were alleged to have sexually assaulted at least eighty-three women and seven men at the annual Tailhook Association Symposium in Las Vegas. Investigations followed, leading to punishments for some alleged officer offenders. The Tailhook scandal caught the attention of the national media, embarrassed the Navy, and became a weapon in the hands of liberals like Senator Barbara Boxer of California, who forced the Navy to accept women into naval combat aviation. The

Navy accordingly lowered its standards, and soon Lieutenant Kara Hultgreen became the first woman to "qualify" as an F-14 Tomcat pilot. A report by the Center for Military Readiness later concluded that fighter training was compromised because of her sex. She received one-on-one tutoring after repeated failures to qualify. Males normally would not receive such intense tutoring. Hultgreen's records indicate that she was pushed through training and certified for combat although her superiors knew she wasn't ready.[13]

The Navy lowered its aviation standards in order to "win a race" with the Air Force to produce the first female combat pilot, according to an inspector general's report. When then F-14 naval flight officer Lieutenant Patrick Burns voiced concerns about the standards issue, Commander Tom Sobieck told him, "You don't understand. These women are going to graduate regardless of how they perform."[14] Burns told the men in his chain of command that he "expected a catastrophic mishap to take place concerning one of these individuals sometime during their fleet tour."[15] He was tragically prophetic. Hultgreen was killed when she lost control of her aircraft while attempting to land on the carrier *Abraham Lincoln* in 1994. Fortunately, the Navy realized what it had done and raised the standards again.

Mixed-Sex Basic Training

We compromise combat standards at our peril, and General Dempsey promises he won't let that happen. But when pressed in the past to accommodate women, the Pentagon has cut corners to pull off the sexual integration of basic training. That experience provides valuable insights for combat commanders faced with further sexual integration in the future.

The Army reported to the Presidential Commission on the Assignment of Women in the Armed Forces that in October 1977 it

began integrated basic combat training at Fort Jackson, South Carolina, with three-one and two-two male-female platoons per company
(a basic training company consists of four platoons). Mixed-sex basic
combat training companies followed suit at Forts Leonard Wood,
Dix, McClellan, Bliss, and Sill.[16]

Although TRADOC and the Army declared the mixed-sex basic
training program a success, the Army stopped the program for reasons that became public in 1982. To wit, the male recruits were not
being physically challenged enough to reach their full potential. A
male trainee in an early mixed-sex basic program put a positive spin
on his experience: "A lot of us think the women slow us down—but
still, it helps a lot just having them around. You can talk to them in a
way you can't talk to men."[17] Not everyone shared this sunny perspective, however. The Army's director of initial entry training warned
about the psychological effects of mixed-sex training on new male
soldiers. For example, he said all-male companies improved esprit de
corps, encouraged competition, and pushed trainees beyond minimum standards.[18] This is hardly an endorsement of mixed-sex units.

Years later, under heavy political pressure, the Army resumed
mixed-sex basic training, and today the Marines are the only service
not following the practice. The problems, however, continue, and they
have been the subject of numerous studies. In 1997, Secretary of
Defense William Cohen and Senator Nancy Landon Kassebaum of
Kansas declared that mixed-sex basic training was "resulting in less
discipline, less unit cohesion, and more distraction from training
programs."[19] In 1999, the Congressional Commission on Military
Training and Gender-Related Issues, chaired by Anita Blair of the
Independent Women's Forum, came to a similar conclusion: "Whether
[mixed-sex basic training] improves the readiness or the performance
of the operational force is subjective."[20] Elaine Donnelly, president of

the Center for Military Readiness, has unearthed a briefing presented to the secretary of the Army in 2002 finding that mixed-sex basic training was "not efficient" and was "effective" only in sociological terms. While endorsing the practice anyway, the briefing concluded that including women in basic training introduced a host of problems:

- Less discipline, less unit cohesion, and more distraction from training programs;
- Voluntary and involuntary misconduct due to an emotionally volatile environment for which immature recruits are not prepared;
- Higher physical injury and sick-call rates that detract from primary training objectives;
- Diversion from essential training time because of interpersonal distractions and the need for an extra week of costly "sensitivity training" (mandated after Aberdeen);
- A perceived decline in the overall quality and discipline of sexually integrated basic training, a lack of confidence in the abilities of fellow soldiers, and the need to provide remedial instruction to compensate for military skills not learned in basic training;
- Redefined or lowered standards, gender-normed scores, and elimination of physically demanding exercises so that women will succeed;
- Additional stress on instructors who must deal with different physical abilities and psychological needs of male and female recruits;
- Contrivances to reduce the risk of scandal, such as extra changing rooms, security equipment, and personnel hours to monitor barracks activities, and "no talk, no

touch" rules, which interfere with informal contacts between recruits and instructors;

- No evidence of objective, military-oriented benefits from sexually integrated basic training (social effects primarily benefited women in subjective ways); and
- Little or no evidence that restoration of single-sex training would be detrimental to women or men.[21]

These "inefficiencies" are instructive for combat leaders facing forced sexual integration. Although they address basic training situations, most of the "inefficiencies" apply to regular units now facing sexual integration.

Before the Army first ended sexually integrated basic training, officials knew they had a serious problem. In February 1981, the acting assistant secretary of the Army for manpower and reserve affairs, William Clark, told the Senate Armed Services Committee that the service intended to study the effect of female soldiers on the Army's combat readiness, and he requested a "pause" in female recruitment and enlistments.[22] Field commanders questioned the effect of women soldiers on the readiness of their units, he explained. Acknowledging that women were doing their jobs and that the issue wasn't their exposure to combat, he expressed concern about "the combat effectiveness of the organizations as you have large numbers of women in them."[23]

Today, after a multitude of studies over the last few decades, the Army still can't answer Clark's question. Politics, not readiness, continues to drive decisions about women in the armed forces.

President Clinton Keeps Up the Effort to Compromise Standards

As soon as President Clinton took office, he started conducting social experiments with the military, beginning with his attempt to lift the military's long-standing exclusion of homosexuals. Then, in April 1993, Secretary of Defense Les Aspin announced the administration's intention to open more combat positions to women. That order followed Congress's repeal of the Section 6015 combat exclusion law. The following January, Aspin announced, "We've made historic progress in opening up opportunities for women in all the Services. Expanding roles for women in the military is right, and it's smart."[24]

Aspin's announcement prompted each of the services to review its job categories and present recommendations for opening more positions to women. Secretary of the Army Togo West Jr. announced the assignment of women to many new positions, stressing that the Army "recognized the importance of training male and female soldiers to work together as a cohesive team. In an attempt to enhance gender cohesion, the Army will integrate basic training at all basic training installations." He promised that "these recommendations will open non-traditional positions for women to serve as role models, thereby encouraging other women throughout the Army to seek out additional challenges. All of these outcomes will enhance readiness."[25]

West offered no evidence to contradict the lessons learned from the Army's previous attempts at sexually integrated training. Incredibly enough, when the GAO conducted its study of mixed-sex basic training in 1997, the records supporting the 1982 decision to abandon the practice were not available for its review. "The Army has no records of those programs or their results to compare with those on its current program and results," the report reads.[26]

Service Academies Compromise Standards

The integration of women into the service academies resulted in different standards reflecting the differences between men and women. The differences begin with the six test events in the U.S. Military Academy's candidate fitness assessment; women must complete seven pull-ups, compared with eighteen for men.[27]

Females first joined the academy's long grey line in 1976, and according to Brigadier General Anne Macdonald, a member of that class, "The expectation for the women to perform was the same as [for] the men."[28] It quickly became clear, however, that physiological differences made those standards too tough on the young women. "Many women suffered injuries from the road marches with full gear and running in combat boots or our suede Converse sneakers up and down hills for miles at a time at a pace often under 8 minutes per mile," recalls retired Colonel Debra Lewis, another member of the first coed class.[29] "Frequently turning purple by the end of the runs, I decided early on that I would pass out before I let myself drop out of a run."[30]

That class started with 119 women. Sixty-two were graduated four years later—6.8 percent of the class.[31] A 1994 GAO study found that two-thirds of female cadets thought women were treated the same as male cadets, while about half of the male cadets agreed. The men did better academically and against military performance indexes than the women. Women's average physical education grades were much better than male cadets', but the physical standards were quite different. "Gender-norming" insured that females scored higher even when they did not meet the same standard as males. That same GAO study found that women had a higher rate of attrition.

Prior to the arrival of women in 1976, every West Point graduate, unless he was medically disqualified, was appointed to a combat position, such as infantry, armor, or artillery. After women arrived, graduates were given the opportunity to go into all Army branches for which they qualified and were permitted by policy and quota, seriously degrading West Point's warrior ethos.

Standards Compromised in the Marine Corps

More recently, in September 2011, the Defense Advisory Committee on Women in the Services heard a presentation on the Marine Corps' plans to evaluate male and female volunteers on six "common ground combat element standard dismounted tasks"[32] to determine their physical strength and stamina. But once the testing began, the six tasks were reduced to three.[33] The toughest tasks were taken out to accommodate women's lower capabilities.

The Marines also tested two female officer volunteers to see if they could survive the tough thirteen-week Infantry Officer Course (IOC) at Quantico, Virginia. Part of the Corps' research to determine what additional jobs could be opened to women, the test began in September 2012. Both women and a quarter of the men washed out, but the Corps maintained its standards.

Two more female Marines attempted the IOC in March 2013, but both failed the obstacle course and were dropped. Colonel Todd Desgrosseilliers, commander of the Basic School, which includes the IOC, says the standards "are gender-neutral now." "They aren't hard to be hard. These are the things they need to be able to do to be infantry officers." He says he is confident that women will eventually pass, but that does not mean they will automatically join the infantry. That is up to the Corps to decide. "Almost all of the killing in the Marine Corps will be done by your men," he told the Marines who survived the Combat Endurance Test.[34]

Allies Set the Example by Compromising Standards

Our allies had to reduce standards to bring women into their ground combat forces. Canada lifted all combat exclusions to accommodate women, according to the 1992 U.S. Presidential Commission on the Assignment of Women in the Armed Forces, which studied

Canada's experience. "The Canadians invited women from both inside and outside the military to join the infantry. Although 103 women were interested in joining the infantry, none of them were pre-screened or required to meet any minimum standard. Consequently, attrition was severe due primarily to physical and endurance factors, with only one woman graduating. Shortly after graduating, she was reassigned to another unit."[35] That translates to a less than 1-percent success rate at great cost to the taxpayers and military.

The Canadians quickly "modified" their infantry physical fitness requirements to "reflect actual requirements." For example, the physical test was modified so soldiers only had to carry another soldier of the same weight, and backpacks were limited to fifty pounds. It is perhaps more accurate to say that the modifications to "reflect actual requirements" were made to "reflect political concerns."

The Danish military likewise lowered its physical training standards to accommodate women. When the U.S. presidential commission asked a Danish military briefer why his country lifted the combat exclusion, he responded, "Combat readiness is not an overarching concern of the Danish military. They believe they will have ample time to prepare their forces as conflicts present themselves."[36] Such an approach might work for the Danes, but it is obviously not an option for the United States.

Setting Sex-Blind Standards

One former Army commander understands how to apply standards in a sex-blind manner. Retired Major General Patrick Brady explains how his system worked in a mixed-sex medical battalion unit.[37] He praises women's performance and conduct while recognizing that most couldn't perform heavy-lifting tasks such as loading litters in helicopters, carrying the wounded to safety, and even lifting tool chests. In those jobs, more often than not, men had to cover for the women, and so two people were required when only one should have sufficed. Brady came to the common-sense conclusion that most men will not treat women as they do other men; they almost always help the women with the physical tasks. The military, he reasons, should acknowledge sexual differences, just as the rest of society does. In the Olympic Games, there are separate events for men and women. Most direct combat jobs require a high level of cardiovascular fitness. Combat standards have developed over hundreds of years, and they shouldn't be changed to "satisfy the crazes of the president's feminist supporters."[38]

Such common sense is becoming rare in the upper levels of leadership. General Dempsey wonders why standards "have to be that high." Some women in the military who have had a taste of combat have an answer for him.

"I am here to tell you that we are not all created equal," writes Marine Corps Captain Katie Petronio, a combat engineer officer with five years of service and two combat tours, "and attempting to place females in the infantry will not improve the Marine Corps as the nation's force-in-readiness or improve our national security."[39] She doubts that even the fittest women can "endure the physical and physiological rigors of sustained combat operations." She warns, "We haven't even begun to analyze and comprehend the gender-specific medical issues and overall physical toll continuous combat operations will have on females."

Captain Petronio is critical of lowering standards in order for more women to serve: "The bottom line is that the enemy doesn't discriminate, rounds will not slow down, and combat loads don't get any lighter, regardless of gender or capability." The Diversity Commission frets about women moving into the senior ranks, but women thrust into combat positions won't be physically fit enough to serve at those levels. "Even if a female can meet the short-term physical, mental, and moral leadership requirements of an infantry officer, by the time that she is eligible to serve in a strategic leadership position [general or flag officer], at the 20-year mark or beyond, there is a miniscule probability that she'll be physically capable of serving at all. Again, it becomes a question of longevity," explains Petronio.

The Marine Corps' standards "are designed to ensure safety, quality, and the opportunity to be placed in a field in which one can sustain and succeed," Petronio maintains. "What are we trying to accomplish by attempting to fully integrate women into the infantry?" This battle-tested combat engineer disagrees with assigning women into the infantry because it "will rock the foundation of our Corps for the worse and will weaken what has been since 1775 the world's most lethal fighting force."

Ryan Zinke, a Montana state senator and a former Navy SEAL, understands the physical demands of combat. Putting women in direct combat roles, he warns, is "nearly certain" to cost lives because standards will be compromised.[40] He admits that "there are some women who can do the physical training." "When I was a SEAL instructor … I watched some Olympic-caliber women athletes run through the [SEAL] obstacle course better than certainly many of the SEAL candidates could do," Zinke says. "I think there are some women who can do it. But, what are the unintended consequences? This is not a Demi Moore movie."

Zinke believes that pushing women into all combat jobs will provoke a blizzard of gender-sensitivity training that will seek to "eradicate endemic male sexism" and reduce the aggregate strength of combat units where physical strength can make the difference between winning and losing.

Marine Sergeant James Webb, the son of Jim Webb, the former Virginia senator and former secretary of the Navy, said, "If you admit women into the infantry, you must ask them to be men. This is completely unfair, as women are not physically just smaller men—they are completely different."[41] Those differences are obvious and consequential. That's why in the Olympics "there are separate events for both men and women."[42]

"The infantry itself is a lot like your university's football team," Webb writes. Young men join the infantry "to push themselves to the limits of human endurance," where few women can go. Infantry training breaks even the strongest men, he explains. Serving as a Marine grunt "was the most physically taxing and damaging thing I have done to myself." Even at his peak physical conditioning—twenty-six pull-ups, running three miles in under eighteen minutes—"the sheer magnitude of the equipment I had to carry [in combat] took its toll. An easy day was carrying around half my body weight. At times, it was significantly more."[43]

Webb agrees with Zinke that dropping standards to allow more diversity would result in "nothing short of a marked drop in effectiveness on the battlefield, which in turn results in needless deaths of our people." Our future enemies are not going to check our "diversity" cards before the fight. They "could care less about whether or not we have women on the battlefield. Their only concern is how easy it is to kill our people."[44] Assigning young women to ground combat units will inevitably compromise long-held, necessarily high standards. That compromise will cause resentment, hurt morale, and, Zinke says, cost lives.

Commanders will gender-norm the standards to avoid soaring injury rates among female soldiers who, as Webb sensibly points out, are not men. But men will have to assume more of the physical burden, jeopardizing themselves and the mission.

The Army Physical Fitness Test is a good example of gender-normed standards. It accounts for men's superior upper-body strength and cardiovascular system. A perfect push-up score for women between the ages of seventeen and twenty-one is 40 percent lower than for men—forty-two verses seventy-one push-ups in two minutes. Those same women get a perfect score for running two miles at a rate 17 percent slower than men—fifteen minutes and thirty-eight seconds verses thirteen minutes flat. The sit-up standard for seventeen- to twenty-one-year-olds is the same for both men and women, seventy-eight in two minutes. Women's hips and hip muscles make this event easier for them.[45]

Changing the standards becomes necessary to the primary diversity goal of "setting women up for success" rather than fielding the readiest combat units. This is not only a feminist and politically correct assault; it is plain stupidity that will degrade the armed forces' ability to defend the country.

Risk No. 2: Failure to Match Capabilities with Job Assignments

Most experienced combatants (a group that does not include General Dempsey or the Army chief of staff, General Odierno) don't expect women to meet the current high standards required to join their ranks. Many take comfort in General Dempsey's promise "to assess, develop, and validate gender-neutral standards" before bringing women into combat jobs.[46] But the general's promise might mean something quite different from what these people think, and our tough combat standards are by no means secure.

The hidden meaning of General Dempsey's assurance that we will "assess, develop, and validate gender-neutral standards" most likely is that standards will be adjusted downward. And experience suggests that the vetting of ground combat candidates, as a consequence, will be inadequate. The leaders saddled with the task of guiding ground combat units through this process should beware.

The so-called "gender-neutral" standards that General Dempsey announced might be based on effort rather than results. David Burrelli of the Congressional Research Service has warned that the law already permits the services to judge candidates based on how much energy is exerted on a task, "regardless of the work that is actually accomplished."[47] The same lowering of standards, John Leo points out, afflicts many American schools, where As are given just for showing up. The outcome is not as important as the effort.[48] Unfortunately, the battlefield is a dangerous place to test this egalitarian principle.

No one who has followed the feminization of the military over the past four decades should be surprised by Dempsey's political word game. The Pentagon has used gender-norming for years to reward equivalent effort rather than equal results. That technique has given the military its current physical fitness double standards, which award a female soldier the same physical fitness score as a male of the same age who runs two miles two minutes faster.

Given the physiological differences between men and women, no one objects to gender-norming as a measure of personal fitness, but it makes no sense when setting standards for performance in combat, where the result, not energy expended, is what matters. But that is what General Dempsey appears to be advocating.

Remember what he said at that January 2013 press conference: "If we do decide that a particular standard is so high that a woman couldn't make it, the burden is now on the service to come back and explain to the secretary, why is it that high? Does it really have to be that high?"[49] A leader in command of the facts would place the burden of proof on those who want to change the standards. But Dempsey made it clear at the same time that his intent is to "expand the opportunities for women." The service chiefs all reportedly agree with the chairman's intent, and they understand that expanding opportunities for women will require changes to current standards.[50] Objecting to such changes, they know, would end their careers.

That puts the combat ground force services in a difficult position. What should be the standards for physically demanding combat jobs, and how should candidates be vetted to determine whether they are up to the challenge? Currently, Army and Marine Corps basic recruits must satisfy relatively low physical fitness standards. For example, the Marines' initial strength test (IST) requires a nineteen-year-old man to perform two pull-ups, do forty-four crunches in two minutes, and run a mile and a half in thirteen and a half minutes. The IST standards for women are much lower than the men's.[51]

Many of those male Marines will go on to ground combat training at the School of Infantry after boot camp. The assumption is that these male recruits have the potential, with time and a lot of hard training, to become capable of performing the most physically demanding combat tasks. No such assumption can be made about female recruits. Their potential is limited by physiology. If the services don't define the physical standards for each combat specialty and then design tests to determine which recruits, male or female, are up to the challenge, a lot of time and expense will be wasted on unqualified personnel.

Part of the problem is that the military has a poor record on job placement, especially for women. The General Accounting Office reported in May 1976 that military women were being assigned to specialties "without regard to their ability to satisfy the specialties' strength, stamina, and operational requirements."[52] That report prompted the services, the Army in particular, to try to determine the physical requirements of each military occupational specialty (MOS) in order to develop sex-neutral physical standards. In 1978, the Armed Forces Examining and Entrance Stations started using what it called the "X-Factor" test, which related a candidate's weight-lifting ability to the physical requirements of particular jobs. Unfortunately, the X-Factor test was only used to advise enlistees on job suitability and was soon dropped.[53]

In the early 1980s, the Army developed the Military Enlistment Physical Strength Capacity Test (MEPSCAT), which matched the physical abilities of recruits, regardless of sex, with the physical job requirements using four physical tasks: lift, carry, push, and pull. General Maxwell Thurman, the TRADOC commander who oversaw the program, promoted MEPSCAT as a "gender-free" physical strength test that would benefit Army women. "What we are trying to do is match the person with the job, both mentally and physically, so they will have a more even-handed chance to stay with [the Army] and get promoted," Thurman said.[54]

The Army chief of staff, General Edward C. Meyer, liked MEPSCAT, and he defended it before the Senate Appropriations Committee:

> Previously, the Army had a personnel system which virtu-
> ally ensured women soldiers would fail. We were ordered
> to take in a whole bunch of women, and we put them in
> jobs where they really had no opportunity to succeed.
> There was never a [female] platoon in basic training that
> won "Best Platoon." So they felt ill of themselves. The males

felt they were not pulling their fair share of the load when we put them all together. From a physical point of view, we put women into jobs which they weren't able to carry out. The men thought the women were not doing their job, so we had harassment occurring.[55]

MEPSCAT nevertheless fell out of favor because it tended to eliminate most women from key jobs, and soon it went from being mandatory to being used on an advisory basis.

Anecdotal evidence suggests that the Army's vetting system isn't much better today than it was decades ago. We still assign both men and women to jobs that require more strength than they can deliver. This is especially true for women.

Miranda (last name withheld) graduated from the Army's transportation advanced individual training at Fort Leonard Wood, Missouri, in March 2013. In her mixed-sex training unit, she said, "there were things the women couldn't carry." The women were graduated and sent to their units even though they lacked the strength to perform critical physical tasks.[56]

Sergeant Michael Shaffstall is an aviation mechanic at Fort Bragg, North Carolina. On a recent tour in Afghanistan, he found that most of the women in his unit "couldn't carry their own gear off the C-17 [a transport aircraft]. They would ask other soldiers [males] to carry their stuff." Female mechanics "constantly asked the male soldiers to carry their toolboxes for them."[57] An aviation mechanic's toolbox weighs approximately fifty pounds.

First Sergeant Charles Buzzatto, who retired in February 2013 after twenty-two years of active duty as a military policeman with combat tours in the Balkans and Iraq, supervised both men and women. "Few women," he says, "can pick-up a battering ram with which to knock down a door in a raid." So the male soldiers in his MP unit did the heavy lifting.

In these situations, the units were able to work around the women's limitations with a little good will from the men. But those same limitations could be fatal in a combat unit, arguably the most demanding MOS. Knowing whether a combat soldier will be able to perform the tasks that his or her position requires is a matter of life or death. The British army understood this. When it considered putting women in combat, it put all its combat candidates to a realistically rigorous test. Very few women passed, so the defense ministry scuttled the idea of assigning women to combat units. The U.S. military should do the same thing.

Here is how we might test candidates for three combat arms positions—a tank crewmember, an infantryman, and a Navy sea-air-land (SEAL) sailor.

One common task for all armor crewmembers is loading the M1A2 Abrams tank for combat with its basic load of ammunition. Each of the basic loads of forty rounds, which are carried in the ammunition racks inside the tank, weighs between forty-one and fifty-six pounds. The three-man crew also loads another thousand pounds of machine gun ammunition. Candidates should be able to load the tank in no more than 1.5 times what an experienced crew requires. If a soldier drops a 120mm tank round, he or she automatically fails.

The resilience demanded of an infantry private requires a rigorous vetting process. A good test for a would-be infantryman would be to put a hundred pounds of gear on his back plus an individual weapon (seven pounds), then have him conduct a quick-paced twelve-mile foot patrol over uneven terrain. At the objective, the candidate must dig a fortified position with overhead cover that can safely absorb artillery fragmentation. The test continues with a night of patrolling, guard duty, and at best a couple hours of sleep. This daily routine is to be repeated for up to four days, interrupted at least twice a day by two simulated firefights that require quick movements with full gear and negotiating a variety of difficult climbs, crawls, and water obstacles without compromising the mission. This test is best conducted on half rations and when the weather is hot (ninety degrees or more) or cold (twenty degrees or less). The standard for the infantry test should be no more than 1.5 times what it takes the experienced infantryman to conduct the same tasks under similar conditions. Of course, quitting or being injured at any point is an automatic failure.

The Navy's SEALs are an especially tough group that must maintain high standards. A Naval Health Research Center report describes three actual SEAL missions that could be modified and used to vet candidates:

- Walk (i.e., "hump") 15 km (9 miles) over uneven terrain at night, carrying a 125-pound pack (with radios, etc.) in 70°F temperature to objective; then, retrace steps to extraction point.
- Serve as point (trail breaker) for an element, walking a distance of 42 km (26 miles) through dense jungle (up and down), in tropical heat and humidity, during a 3-day period, carrying a 60-pound pack and weapons.
- Perform a "duck drop," followed by an 29 km (21 nm [nautical miles]) transit (3 hours) in 48°F air temperature, then swim a distance of 2,000 meters in 56°F water carrying a limpet mine and using a Dräger; return to Zodiac without limpet, then travel 6 km (4 miles) to extraction point (10 hours total).[58]

The gateway for each combat specialty must be a realistic test that determines who is physically and mentally prepared for the job. An active-duty officer with combat command experience provides some much-needed perspective on the question of putting women in combat: "Is it about increased capability in these units, or is it about social experimentation? The number of females who would want to join combat arms is small and the numbers who could hack it are smaller." He believes recruiting to fill female combat jobs will be a nightmare; failure will "mean females involuntarily serving in combat arms."[59]

Risk No. 3: Physical Suffering

Women will suffer physically and mentally, their units will experience a drop in readiness, and the financial costs for the nation will rise if women are pushed into combat.

Women's bodies are different from men's. As punishing as combat is for men, it takes a far higher physical toll on women. The serious risks for women in combat are well documented:

1. A U.S. Navy study found the risk of anterior cruciate ligament injury associated with military training is almost ten times higher for women than men.
2. A sex-blind study by the British military found that women were injured 7.5 times more often than men while training to the same standards.
3. A U.S. Army study found that the most frequent causes of medical evacuations for females in Iraq were mental and musculoskeletal disorders. The men were most often evacuated for battle injuries and musculoskeletal disorders.

4. According to a U.S. Army study, "12 percent of female soldiers are pregnant at any time," which means they are non-deployable and assigned to light duty for at least six months per pregnancy.

5. Women suffer twice as many lower-extremity injuries as men, an Army study found, and they fatigue much more quickly because of the difference in "size of muscle," which makes them more vulnerable to non-battle injury.

6. A *Psychiatric Services* study found that female veterans are three times more likely to commit suicide than female non-veterans. In 2012, the armed forces suffered more suicides than ever before.

Women Will Suffer as a Result of the Policy Change

Women assigned to ground combat units are placed in exceptionally dangerous circumstances. Captain Katie Petronio of the Marines puts the matter in perspective.[60] Her concern is not whether women can conduct combat operations, because "they can." It's that few women can endure the physical and physiological rigors of *sustained* combat operations. The Pentagon, she warns, has not studied the medical implications of continuous combat operations for women. Low-intensity combat and sustained conventional combat are very different, and the United States has participated almost exclusively in the low-intensity variety since 1973.

Captain Petronio, a college hockey player who graduated near the top of her Marine classes, spent an "excessive amount of time ... in full combat load" during her two combat tours. The rigors of her engineering job in a combat environment contributed to a severe case of restless leg syndrome and compressed nerves in her lower back, which caused neuropathy. In the fifth month of her second combat deployment, she recounts, "I had muscle atrophy in my thighs that was causing me to constantly trip and my legs to buckle." She lost agility and mobility and then received a diagnosis of polycystic ovarian syndrome, which resulted in infertility.

The constant stress, lack of rest, and inadequate nutrition that attend combat duty, coupled with the drive to complete the mission, increase the risk in women of weight loss, altered menstrual patterns, and bone thinning, says Petronio.

Psychological stress or insufficient nutrition can suppress the secretion of hormones by the hypothalamus, pituitary, and ovaries, causing menstrual dysfunction. The long-term effects can include infertility and bone damage.[61]

The punishment that ground combat inflicts on the female body should be a matter of enormous concern. A number of studies demonstrate the marked differences between men's and women's susceptibility to injury while engaged in ordinary military training, which is far less demanding than the ground combat seen in Iraq and Afghanistan.

The department of orthopedics at the U.S. Naval Academy evaluated the risk of anterior cruciate ligament (ACL) injury for female midshipmen from 1991 to 1997. The risk of an ACL injury while participating in sports was three times higher for women than men. But women's risk of an ACL injury in military training was *nine times* that of men.[62]

When the British military experimented with "gender-free" physical standards in the 1990s, imposing precisely the same requirements on women and men,[63] there was a tremendous increase in the injury rate for military women. Fractures of the tibia (shin bone) rose from 12.6 to 231.2 per ten thousand personnel, and stress fractures of the feet increased substantially as well.[64] These experiences were reported in the *Journal of the Royal Society of Medicine* in 2002: "This study confirms and quantifies the excess risk for women when they undertake the same arduous training as male recruits, and highlights the conflict between health and safety legislation and equal opportunities legislation."[65]

A second British test[66] yielded the conclusion that women should not fight on the front lines. The combat-effectiveness gender study found that fewer than 2 percent of female soldiers are as physically capable as the average male soldier and that women are up to eight times more likely to be injured in sex-blind training. The results of that test showed the following:

1. Most (70 percent) of the women failed to carry ninety pounds of artillery shells over measured distances, while 20 percent of the men failed.
2. Almost half (48 percent) of the women failed to complete a 12.5-mile road march carrying a sixty-pound combat load followed by range firing under simulated combat conditions; 17 percent of the men failed.
3. Women were slower than men in combat exercises involving "fire and move" situations in which the soldiers sprint from one position to another while in their combat gear.
4. In close-quarter combat tests that involved hand-to-hand fighting, the women suffered higher injury rates than the men.

In an admirably clear-eyed report of November 2010, the British secretary of state for defense concluded that he "was satisfied that the continued exclusion of women from ground close-combat roles was a proportionate means of maintaining the combat effectiveness of the Armed Forces and was not based on a stereotypical view of women's abilities but on the potential risks associated with maintaining cohesion in small mixed-gender tactical teams engaged in highly-dangerous close-combat operations."[67]

The Assignment of Women to Ground Combat Units Will Impair Readiness

The assignment of women to ground combat units will produce lower rates of deployable service members, making it more difficult for commanders to maintain the readiness of their forces.

Combat units maintain a state of readiness that allows them to deploy at a moment's notice with as many of their trained personnel as possible. The rate at which members of these units are unavailable to deploy is a matter of obvious importance, and for women, that rate tends to increase as their training and operations become more demanding. A 2007 Army Medical Department study of disease and non-battle injuries (DNBI) in a brigade combat team (BCT) deployed to Iraq found that women "had a significantly increased incident-rate ratio for becoming a DNBI casualty" as compared to men.[68] Of the forty-seven female soldiers evacuated from the BCT, thirty-five (74 percent) left because they were pregnant. These women most likely became pregnant while serving in a combat zone, a clear violation of the military's rules on sexual relations.[69] Once a pregnancy is diagnosed, the woman leaves and seldom returns to her forward-deployed unit.

Military pregnancy policy specifies a postpartum deferment period—six months for the Army, the Air Force, and the Marine Corps. During that period women are not required to deploy or redeploy. In fact, once a service member is confirmed to be pregnant, she is removed within fourteen days from the forward-deployed unit.

Because her position is seldom if ever backfilled, another soldier must pick up the slack, which understandably hurts morale.

Dealing with pregnancies is even more difficult in the Navy. If a sailor on sea duty becomes pregnant, she is transferred after her twentieth week of gestation to a shore-based command that meets certain criteria, such as being close to a Navy medical center. The length of that assignment was extended in June 2007 from four months after the child's birth to twelve months. Combined with a nine-month pregnancy, that puts expectant mothers on limited duty for up to twenty-one months. According to an inspector general's report based on site visits to Hampton Roads, Virginia, in March and April 2013, shore industrial and aviation commands are receiving more pregnant sailors—from 15 to 34 percent of authorized billets, in some cases—who are unable to fulfill essential duties. "If pregnancy trends remain constant," says the report, "the new pregnancy distribution policy could have over 2,500 sailors counting against shore duty commands in ratings where they are not able to conduct mission-essential work within industrial or hazardous material-type conditions."[70] That situation doesn't bode well for female members' careers or, most importantly, the readiness of their operational units.

Pregnancy is common among the servicewomen who are near the peak of their fertility (twenty-three to thirty-one). A 1996 Army study of forty thousand female soldiers deployed during Operation Desert Shield and Desert Storm (1990–1991) determined that 12 percent of Army women were pregnant at any time. If the rate is the same today among the 76,694 active-duty women, then there are 9,203 non-deployable pregnant women in the Army—the equivalent of fourteen battalions. That non-deployable number jumps to 48,680 if we apply the same 12-percent pregnancy rate to all 405,669 active, reserve, and National Guard Army women.

The 1992 presidential commission found that soldiers' pregnancies often occur just before or during deployments. The commission cited a Roper poll of the military that found 56 percent of those who were deployed in Desert Shield and Desert Storm with mixed-sex units reported that women in their unit became pregnant just prior to deployment or while deployed in the Gulf. Forty-six percent of that group reported that pregnancies harmed unit readiness, and 59 percent reported harm to morale.[71] Across all services, females were three times less deployable for Desert Shield and Desert Storm than males for a variety of reasons, including pregnancy.[72] Army Master Sergeant Sally Kennedy, who was attending advanced individual training at the beginning of Desert Shield in 1990, recalls most of the young women in her unit saying they would get pregnant to avoid being sent to the war.[73]

Despite all efforts, including family planning seminars, the Navy continues to experience increasing rates of unplanned pregnancies and of operational deferments for those pregnancies that occur while on sea duty. A recent survey found a 74-percent unplanned pregnancy rate among female sailors; only 31 percent of those women were using birth control at the time they conceived. By comparison, according to the Centers for Disease Control and Prevention, half of all pregnancies in the United States are classified as unplanned.[74]

Pregnancy is not the only reason women are often non-deployable or evacuated. A 2013 Government Accountability Office study of the Navy found that women, who make up 16 percent of that service, accounted for nearly a third of all reported patient encounters aboard naval vessels during fiscal year 2012. Their most frequent diagnosis was lumbago, or lower back pain, which often made them unavailable for physical tasks.[75]

Evaluating medical evacuations from Iraq and Afghanistan from January 2003 through December 2011, the GAO found that women's evacuations were most commonly attributed to mental disorders, musculoskeletal disorders, "signs, symptoms, and ill-defined conditions," and non-battle injuries. The same report found men left primarily for battle injuries, musculoskeletal disorders, non-battle injuries, and mental disorders, in that order.[76] Female evacuations for mental disorders are a serious issue that is only recently beginning to receive the attention it warrants.

Contending with a substantial portion of its personnel that is prone to injury and illness is a daunting challenge for the armed forces. The previously mentioned 1996 Army Medical Research and Material Command study resulted in the publication of a revealing booklet about women's health, *Sustaining Female Soldiers' Health and Performance During Deployment.*[77] Based on lessons learned from the deployment of forty thousand women in Operation Desert Shield and Desert Storm, the booklet recommends preparatory and preventive measures to ensure the good health and performance of female soldiers. Commanders who ignore these precautions do so at their own peril and put their female personnel's health at risk.

The booklet acknowledges that women suffer twice as many lower-extremity injuries as men and that they fatigue more quickly, putting them at greater risk of non-battle injury. Stress fractures occur because fatigued muscles cannot neutralize the "tensile stress" in the surrounding bones, as healthy muscles can.[78] A combat unit with women must therefore adjust its rate of march to avoid musculoskeletal injuries among the women.

Pregnancy, illness, and injury among deployed female service members are serious enough, but the deployment of substantial numbers of women to hostile environments for combat or humanitarian reasons requires the military to support feminine personal hygiene in the most challenging circumstances. The proponents of expanding the presence of women in combat zones often dismiss the issue as trivial, but it affects women's health, attitudes, practice, work, morale, coping, and general performance. In other words, it is hardly trivial.

In remote areas like the sides of mountains in Afghanistan, combatants will go weeks at a time without bathing, but women are susceptible to a variety of problems if they go even short periods without bathing. "Bathing on a regular basis for men may be a luxury, but is an absolute necessity for women; without it we invite a host of gynecological problems that directly affect our readiness capability," wrote Marine Gunnery Sergeant Beth English. But more than water is required, she adds. "There has to be a delivery system of some sort and then an area for segregating the women for privacy."[79]

Feminine hygiene encompasses not only regular bathing but also the need to wash various parts of the body, managing urination, defecation, and menses, as well as selecting and caring for clothing and planning and maintaining appropriate facilities.[80]

The Army's *Sustaining Female Soldiers' Health and Performance During Deployment* encourages women to bathe daily and to use a host of personal hygiene items to avoid increased urinary infections, which "affect readiness." That precaution should be taken seriously. The researchers at Fitzsimmons Army Medical Center found that one-third of 450 female soldiers surveyed experienced problematic urinary incontinence during exercise and field training activities.[81]

While serving in the field, without ready access to bathing and toilets, women are more prone to develop infections of their urinary tract and vagina. The incidence of infections will vary with the environment; hot, moist environments encourage the growth of fungal organisms and yeast infections, while the incidence of urinary tract infections increases when adequate fluid is not consumed or as a result of "holding" the urine because of privacy concerns or lack of toilets and other facilities.[82]

To prevent infections women need to maintain regular hygiene by keeping clean and dry, avoiding tight clothing, wearing cotton underwear to absorb moisture, and allowing air to circulate. But that is easier said than done, a military woman complained when interviewed in an American Academy of Nurse Practitioners study: "It is real hard to change your underwear because you are afraid that if you put your boots down in the middle of the night, something is going to crawl in your boots…. If you tried to go in the port-a-potty and change your underwear you weren't able to do that because you were falling over and there wasn't enough room."[83]

Another military woman stated, "I had a lot of trouble, I would be standing there trying to get everything off, and your pants are fairly tight, and then get them down, and instead of sit, I would put one hand back like this and hold onto the door to try and squat standing up to pee rather than sitting down on it. The seat area was covered with urine and feces and I had no desire to sit down there, so, trying to stay clean as possible was my goal."[84]

The Army's women's health booklet recommends women modify their uniforms for quick disrobing and carry special comfort items for rest stops. Of course, disrobing while in full combat gear takes more time for a woman, and some women tend to dehydrate in the field because of lack of privacy and time constraints. The booklet encourages commanders "to give women special levels of privacy and longer rest breaks," treatment that is often dangerous and could slow the mission.

No experienced leader wants his troops to become dehydrated. He knows how quickly dehydration hurts physical and mental performance and can turn a soldier into a heat casualty. Well-disciplined units force water on troops conducting strenuous activities, but such measures can increase the frequency of urination and slow the units down.

Defense Costs Will Increase if Women Are Assigned to Ground Combat

Women could produce a much greater long-term medical bill for the Pentagon than men. Captain Petronio's warnings about the devastating repercussions of combat on women's health deserve serious study before the Defense Department pushes women into combat positions.

Besides the physical risks we have considered, women in combat zones are subject to serious psychological problems, as the 2013 GAO study of medical evacuations reveals. But the most sobering measure of the problem is the suicide rate—it increases threefold when women go to war. The National Institute of Mental Health is working with the Army to identify categories of soldiers most at risk for suicide. Researchers speculate that the problem stems from women's feelings of isolation in a male-dominated war zone or their heightened anxieties about leaving behind children and other loved ones.[85]

The problem doesn't go away when women warriors come home. A study published in *Psychiatric Services* among female veterans eighteen to thirty-four years old found they are three times more likely to kill themselves than non-veterans.[86] Male veterans, according to another study, are twice as likely to commit suicide as non-veterans. "When we broke out the statistics on females with military service, it was shocking," said Mark Kaplan, the coauthor of the study. "Why were women killing themselves at such a disproportionate rate?"[87]

The stress on military women who leave children behind can be especially acute. Mona Ternus, a professor at George Mason University and an Air Force Reserve lieutenant colonel, studied seventy-seven women returning home from deployment to children aged ten to eighteen.[88] She reports a "strong correlation" between the amount of time deployed and the appearance of diverse health problems in the women. But her findings about the children left behind are perhaps more troubling: "A longer deployment leads to increased risk behaviors among adolescent children such as non-accidental physical injury, physical fights, incidents involving weapons, cigarette smoking/chewing tobacco, alcohol, illegal drug use, self-mutilation, drop in school grades and attempted suicide." These behavioral problems are not magically solved by mom's return home: "While 75 percent of the adolescents exhibited no risk factors prior to deployment according to parental responses, just as many of the children engaged in risk behaviors during and after deployment." "Adolescence," concludes this researcher—who herself was deployed several times away from her teenage daughter—"is a turbulent period with an increased number of risk behaviors. It follows that separation from the military mother during these potentially dangerous deployments has an impact on the adolescent." In sum, the suffering described in this new literature is the product of a head-on collision: The military's needs—for personal endangerment, for longer and more distant deployment—are inimical to the need of a child for mommy, and vice versa.

More evidence of the suffering of children left behind by deployment was reported in 2009 in the journal of the American Academy of Pediatrics. Analyzing information from interviews with over four thousand families, the study found "a positive association between the number of deployment months and child difficulties, suggesting that with greater total months a parent is deployed (or absent from the home), the stressors of maintaining a healthy home life increase."[89]

Before separating mothers from their children, the Army issues them a collection of literature on "children and deployment" (one of the accompanying pictures is of a woman cradling an infant). These materials recommend books on "family-change situations," such as *All Kinds of Families* and *The Good-Bye Painting*. "The child may become confused and fearful that Mommy or Daddy will abandon them," the Army counsels. "The 'I want my daddy/mommy syndrome' can be helped by supplying the child with a laminated photo." It is not uncommon for mothers still nursing their children to be deployed. Since many of the mothers in the military are single—women in the military are twice as likely as men to be single parents—many luckless children are left with no parents.

The Defense Department is wrestling with other mental health issues, such as post-traumatic stress disorder, to which women are twice as susceptible as men.[90] Women at war are subject to the same battlefield trauma as men are, of course, but they are also exposed to sexual harassment and sexual assault.

None of this research directly addresses the question whether the benefits of sending mothers of young children to war outweigh the increasingly obvious costs. Nor does it consider whether at least some of the women whose sufferings are so compellingly described are victims of an egregious failed experiment in social engineering. Indeed, the Army's policy of separating mothers from their toddlers is a point of pride, cast as a principled refusal to surrender the feminist ideal that men and women must carry the same responsibilities if they wish to enjoy the same benefits.

One thing is clear, though. Sending women into a combat zone is expensive. The fiscal year 2012 National Defense Authorization Act directed the GAO to conduct "a review of the female-specific health care services provided by DOD to female service members." The GAO reported:

> DOD has put in place policies and guidance that include female-specific aspects to help address the health care needs of servicewomen during deployment. Also, as part of pre-deployment preparations, servicewomen are

screened for potentially deployment-limiting conditions, such as pregnancy, and DOD officials and health care providers with whom GAO met noted that such screening helps ensure that many female-specific health care needs are addressed prior to deployment.[91]

The integration of women into combat units will require more female-specific medical equipment and expertise, examination rooms, and more. Military health-care costs will inevitably increase.

The higher costs associated with the policy change—women suffering, readiness dropping, and medical costs increasing—come at a time of dramatic cuts in defense spending. That alone should prompt close scrutiny by Congress.

Risk No. 4: Destruction of the Warrior Spirit

"Whichever army goes into battle stronger in soul, their enemies generally cannot withhold them," said the Greek mercenary Xenophon.[92] That soul is a mindset, a commitment to excellence in battle. It is the intangible but decisive factor in the fight. It is the warrior spirit, and inserting women into America's combat units will destroy it.

The men who embody that spirit can be an otherwise unsavory lot. Throughout history they have earned the titles "the Great," "the Terrible," and "the Conqueror." These warriors seek violence and love a good gunfight. They look for an edge over the enemy and exploit his weakness. These rough-hewn men with their often alarming characters win the hard-fought victories.

History is filled with the stories of warriors whose spirit contagiously spreads within cohesive units. You will search in vain for stories of women's superiority in war or even their equivalence to men in combat. In fact, in three thousand years of recorded history, no country has thought sending women into battle is a good idea; those who have tried it in sustained conventional combat, such as the Soviets, have abandoned the notion.

That is why the military recruits or conscripts young men for fighting. Men are naturally better equipped for combat than women, both physically and psychologically. I have discussed the physical differences between the sexes at some length, but the psychological differences are no less important. They include risk-taking, physical aggression, and coping with fear.

Men's inclination to take risks in every aspect of life makes them better combat candidates. Even in civilian society, men are overrepresented in risky occupations and suffer 90 percent of all workplace deaths. Summarizing the social science research, Kingsley Browne concludes that males take risks even when doing so is a bad idea, while females are "disinclined to take risks even in fairly innocuous situations or when it was a good idea to take a risk."[93] Women, Browne writes, "are more likely than men to perceive risk, and even when they perceive the same level of risks as men, they have higher levels of fear about the risk." A practical measure of this difference in risk-taking is the Carnegie Hero Fund Commission's awards for heroism, 90 percent of which have been given to men. That commission finds that men are more likely than women to accept risk to foil robberies, chase down purse snatchers, and thwart carjackers. Men are also far more likely than women to help a stranger in distress.[94]

Risk-taking and fear are related as well. Girls tend to experience higher levels of fear than do boys from childhood through adulthood, according to a 2009 study in the *Clinical Psychology Review*. Browne cites a number of military-related studies that found women experience significantly more psychological stress than men both when faced with actual or perceived threats.[95]

Physical aggression is critical for combatants, and men have a much higher propensity to demonstrate aggression from an early age than girls. Aggression studies found young men between eighteen and twenty-one years of age were by far the most aggressive of all groups. That is no surprise to those who follow criminal behavior.

The Bureau of Justice Statistics indicates that men account for 77 percent of homicide victims and nearly 90 percent of the offenders. A man is nine times more likely than a woman to murder someone. Further, young men eighteen to twenty-four years old—the same people the military recruits—have the highest offender rate of all age groups.[96]

This otherwise troublesome segment of the population, fueled by testosterone (nature's risk-taking, fear-suppressing, aggression-enhancing wonder drug), is just the group the military is looking for, seeking to channel their dangerous proclivities in a productive way—killing our enemies.

There might also be a genetic explanation for a young male's readiness for combat—more risk-taking, less fear, and more aggression. An Australian study from 2012 indicates that the SRY gene, which directs male development, may promote aggression and shape the male reaction to stress. "The aggressive fight-or-flight reaction is more dominant in men, while women predominantly adopt a less aggressive tend-and-befriend response," according to the researcher Dr. Joohyung Lee.[97] The SRY protein is present in a number of vital organs in the male body, including the heart, lungs, and brain. "This suggests SRY exerts male-specific effects in tissues outside the testis, such as regulating cardiovascular function and neural activity, both of which play a vital role in our response to stress," writes Lee.

Apart from hormones, there is evidence men are more motivated to engage in combat than women are. Browne's analysis indicates the male's motivation on the battlefield is not fear of death and injury as much as fear of being labeled a coward. Why is fear of cowardice such a motivator? Above all, men have a need to "appear a man amongst men," and battle is the "acid test."[98] A World War II study of American soldiers showed that they saw combat as a "dare," and "one never knew for sure that he could take it until he had demonstrated that he could."[99]

The benefits of male psychology and combat motivation are especially effective when they permeate entire, cohesive units, especially all-male units. Masculine virtues are critical to military success, and men want to keep it that way, according to the 1998–1999 Triangle Institute for Security Studies Project on the Gap between Military and Civilian Society.[100] That survey found men in all groups place a high value on masculine culture.

Gender theorists have come up with the label "hypermasculinity" for extreme forms of masculine culture. That culture prevails in the military and is reinforced through socialization with peers. One definition of "hypermasculinity" sounds like a description of a combat infantry unit: "In essence, normative standards of masculinity that emphasize aggressiveness, dominance, and independence, and that minimize sensitivity, gentleness, and other stereotypically feminine characteristics have been found to be associated with heightened propensity to commit rape."[101]

One study that tested the relationship between culture, sexual integration, and unit cohesion found that the more "masculine" the culture of a unit is, the lower the chances are of successfully integrating women into the unit. A second study found, logically enough, that units with a higher percentage of women were less likely to have a highly masculine culture. Therefore, according to some researchers, the solution to sex-based problems is to assign more women to units. And so General Dempsey has indicated that some as-yet-unstipulated minimum number of women will have to be assigned to ground combat units. That approach might work in a nonprofit that cares for sick children, for example. But it is a deadly prescription for a unit that is supposed to kill the enemy.

Other studies, however, find an inverse relationship between cohesion and the percentage of women in a group. Studies of five military deployments to the Persian Gulf, Somalia, and Haiti found that in four of them, the more women in the unit, the lower the cohesion. Other studies have found that the longer a unit is deployed, the more "hypermasculine" it becomes.[102]

It certainly isn't women's fault that men are hardwired to protect them and won't readily follow them into combat, and it isn't their fault that masculinity fuels cohesion. But whether you think it's a matter of evolution or nature or divine design, that is, in fact, how men are.

The pastor John Piper offers an illustration. Two young people, Jason and Sarah, are walking after dark and are suddenly threatened by a man with a knife. And suppose Jason knows that Sarah has a black belt in karate and could probably disarm the assailant better than he could. Should he step back and tell her to do it? No. He should step in front of her and be ready to lay down his life to protect her, irrespective of competency. It is written on his soul. That is what manhood does.[103]

Men feel the need to protect women in dangerous situations, particularly if there is an emotional attachment between them. The combat environment can complicate that relationship, especially in conditions like those that Ryan Smith, a Marine infantryman, described in a now-famous column in the *Wall Street Journal*.[104] Smith was a squad leader during the 2003 invasion of Iraq, and he rode with twenty-four other Jarheads in the back of an amphibious assault vehicle designed for only fifteen. They sat on each other with full gear and were unable to get out of the vehicle for over forty-eight hours.

They urinated and defecated in empty water bottles and food bags inches from the faces of their comrades. "It is humiliating enough to relieve yourself in front of your male comrades; one can only imagine the humiliation of being forced to relieve yourself in front of the opposite sex," he writes. There was no hygiene for a month. All the while they were suited in chemical protective suits that kept the heat in as the outside temperature soared in the Iraqi desert. After a month in those suits, their bodies covered with sores and the skin peeling off in layers, Ryan's unit was lined up naked and hosed off with pressure washers.

Would introducing a couple of women into that vehicle have made Smith's unit more cohesive, more effective in battle? Cohesion is built through the consistent and close association over time that produces mutual trust and confidence. It holds the group together under the stresses of combat, and it is reinforced by shared values, strong leadership, and good order and discipline.

Sexual differences can undermine unit cohesion. Women's lack of stamina and their lower load-carrying ability make them in many cases a weak link in a ground combat unit. Add to that the lack of privacy and inevitable sexual relationships, and you weaken rather than strengthen cohesion.

Lieutenant Colonel Stephen Smith, a 1991 Gulf War infantry commander, told the 1992 presidential commission:

By introducing women, even women who have the physical capability to lift the rucksacks, walk the distances, raise the hatches, load the TOW missiles, break the track on those vehicles and put it back together again, you are still introducing into that equation other factors that weren't there before: sexual jealousies, intentions, our own social or moral values come into play, and they make more difficult that job of that commander who is forward.

I believe that women in those squads would reduce the combat effectiveness of those squads, and I think we would pay for that in casualties.[105]

Lieutenant Tom Downing, a Navy aviator, agreed:

Men in general will act differently amongst men. They will act differently when women are involved. And I think the penalty that you pay when you put a woman into that particular unit is going to decrease the overall effectiveness of that unit to go out there and actively engage the enemy and kill people.[106]

There is no evidence that integrating women into small, highly cohesive warrior units like Ryan's Marine platoon will enhance effectiveness. There is every reason to expect that it will damage unit confidence. The United States has the world's finest fighting forces. The world is too dangerous to put them at unnecessary risk.

The American military is highly successful at recruiting young males with the raw material to become outstanding warriors. Those fighters are then assigned to combat units where their skills and cohesion allow them to operate in some of the most challenging environments known to man. We put this treasure at risk when we force women into those units.

Risk No. 5: Increased Sexual Assaults

The U.S. armed forces have a problem with sexual harassment and assault, and the reason, according to the chairman of the Joint Chiefs of Staff, is that "we've had separate classes of military personnel, at some level." Mixing the sexes even more intimately, General Dempsey seems to suggest, will relieve the problem. Unfortunately, he offers no evidence from history or social science to justify his view.

When the military has created mixed-sex units, the assault problem has increased. A recent example is the scandal in the 737th Training Group at Lackland Air Force Base in San Antonio, Texas, where at least seventeen basic training instructors sexually preyed on dozens of female trainees. Sexual predation is indefensible, and perpetrators should be punished to deter further abuse. But pushing more young women into combat units will likely make the problem even worse and will certainly be enormously expensive.

"The most striking aspect of the [congressional hearing on the Lackland scandal]," observed Heather Mac Donald, "was the glimpse it provided into the military's existing gender infrastructure—complete with 'sexual-assault response coordinators,' etc. This massive bureaucratic apparatus will only grow in the wake of the decision to introduce females into combat roles."[107] Indeed, the Defense Department's Sexual Assault and Response Office's budget increased from $5 million in 2005 to $23 million in 2010. Overall, sexual harassment and assault cost the Pentagon more than $113 million a year.[108]

The rate of violent sexual crime in the military increased 64 percent from 2006 to 2012, according to a Pentagon study released in January 2012. "Rape, sexual assault, and forcible sodomy were the most frequent violent sex crimes committed in 2011," the study found. And the situation is worse than it appears. "We assume this is a very underreported crime," said Secretary of Defense Panetta, and he indicated that the incidence of sexual assault is roughly six times higher than actual reports.[109] In 2012, there were 3,374 reports of sexual assault throughout the U.S. military, but, as discussed in chapter three, the Defense Department says the real number is around twenty-six thousand.

General Dempsey admits sexual assault is "far more complicated" than simple sex-based discrimination. That problem is much like the daunting problem the military faces with suicides, now at the highest rate ever. The 349 military suicides in 2012 exceed the 295 American combat deaths in Afghanistan during the same year and the 301 suicides in 2011.[110]

Dempsey's response, however, is to blame the exclusion of women from combat: "When you have one part of the population that is designated as warriors and another part that's designated as something else, I think that disparity begins to establish a psychology that in some cases led to that environment." Anu Bhagwati, the executive director and cofounder of the Service Women's Action Network and a former Marine Corps company commander, echoes this view. "When you have legalized discrimination against women, there's no doubt in my mind that there's a link there [with sexual harassment and assault]," she told the *Christian Science Monitor*.[111] The idea that throwing men and women into uninterrupted intimacy under the highest imaginable stress is a prescription for reducing sexual harassment and assault is an affront to common sense. But ideology has a way of overcoming common sense—this time at grave cost to America's military defenses.

There is a contrary view of what Dempsey admits is a "complicated" issue. Putting young, virile men in close quarters for extended periods with young women results in lots of sex, and some of it turns violent. As one active-duty sergeant at Fort Bragg, North Carolina, says, "In the end, Joe will do what he wants to do." In those circumstances, all the threats against breaking General Order No. 1, no sex while deployed, won't overcome nature's most powerful drive. Are men incapable of self-control? Some are, and sexual assaults take place even in the most disciplined units. Forcing more young women into the toughest and most primal military setting will only contribute to the problem.

Let's be frank: there is a lot of sex in the war zone. Laura Cannon, a 2001 graduate of the U.S. Military Academy, wrote in the *Washington Post*,

> I had no idea that a combat zone would be such a sexually charged environment. Blame it on amped-up testosterone pouring out of aggressive, athletic men. Or blame it on combat stripping even the strongest of men and women down to their core, raw emotions. Combine that with forming special bonds with comrades who promise to do whatever it takes to ensure your safe return home, including sacrificing their life for yours. What do you think happens? Let me tell you, covert combat sex (or in my case, hard-core making out, because I was too scared to go "All-In") ranks high on the list of life's thrills.[112]

Chief Warrant Officer Bradley Greer, an OH-58 helicopter pilot at Fort Bragg with tours in Iraq and Afghanistan, warns that when you assign a young woman to an infantry squad and put them at a remote outpost, you will "get trouble. You will get allegations of rape. You will get claims of sexual harassment."[113]

The risk of such accusations causes male leaders to take extra precautions, like insisting on having a witness present during counseling or other encounters with female subordinates, a disruption that diverts personnel from other duties.

However serious the threat of sexual violence that women in the combat zone face from their fellow American servicemen, it pales in comparison with the threat posed by the enemy. War histories demonstrate conclusively that all women, and especially female prisoners of war, are at high risk of sexual assault or worse.

Women at Risk of Becoming POWs, and Implications

Assigning women to combat zones makes them vulnerable to capture, which for women can be especially tragic. The military knows the risk. The Air Force's "survival, evasion, resistance, and escape" (SERE) training tries to prepare aviators for captivity and torture.[114] Years ago, the training included a "rape scenario" in which the mock captives had to endure the sounds of sexual torture, the purpose being to condition men to overcome the inclination to help women in distress. After interviewing SERE trainers, the presidential commission reported:

> If a policy change is made, and women are allowed into combat positions, there must be a concerted effort to educate the American public on the increased likelihood that women will be raped, will come home in body bags, and will be exploited. The consequences of not undertaking such a program would be large scale disillusionment with the military should the United States get in a protracted military engagement.[115]

That fear has become a reality in recent wars. Two well-known cases of American non-combatant female soldiers taken captive in war illustrate the dangers. Major Rhonda Cornum was captured in the 1991 Gulf War, but it was years before she admitted that she was sexually assaulted. The five-foot-six, 110-pound flight surgeon suffered broken arms when her Black Hawk helicopter was shot down over southern Iraq. Her Iraqi captor sexually assaulted her in the back of a truck, she acknowledges, though she dismissed the assault, saying, "It didn't make a big impression on me … getting molested was not the biggest deal of my life."[116]

In 2003, Private Jessica Lynch's support convoy was ambushed in Nasiriya, Iraq. The nineteen-year-old army supply clerk now acknowledges that she was raped and sodomized by her captors.[117]

Both Cornum and Lynch kept their assaults secret at the time, perhaps to quell criticism of the policies that led to them. Cornum's capture and abuse occurred around the time Congress repealed the statute prohibiting women on combat aircraft and shortly after the Pentagon eliminated the 1988 risk rule, which had kept women out of positions that carried "significant risk of capture." The authors of that rule had been rightly concerned about the danger of women's being taken prisoner. The effects of sexual assault are more than physical. Despite Cornum's dismissive attitude, victims can suffer psychological consequences for years.

In the last hundred years, from World War I through Afghanistan, 142,246 Americans have been captured and interned by the enemy. Fewer than one hundred of those POWs were women, and eighty-three of them were nurses held by the Japanese after their conquest of the Philippines in World War II. If women, who constitute approximately 15 percent of the armed forces, are placed in all combat jobs, we can presume that they will account for 15 percent of all casualties and 15 percent of all POWs. Since 2001, 154 women have been killed and 964 wounded in the Iraq and Afghanistan wars. If those female casualty numbers were equivalent to the male numbers, 978 would have been killed in action and 7,553 wounded.[118]

Because the Iraq and Afghan wars have been counterinsurgency operations, the number of POWs has been extremely small. But if women had been present in past wars as they are today, then many thousands would have become POWs. Those numbers will only increase as we push women to the front, and that is when sexual assault becomes a substantial risk for women. The International Red Cross describes the danger: "Although both men and women are subject to sexual assault, a distinction needs to be drawn between them. Sexual torture as such, particularly during interrogation, with its full spectrum of humiliation and violence can, and often does, culminate in the rape of the victim, and is more common with women prisoners."[119] Women who have been raped, of course, face the risk of pregnancy, which incarceration would turn into a horrific experience.

Feminists talk about women soldiers' sharing the burden of war on an equal footing with men. But the burden of women in combat will not be equal to men's. Once they are taken captive, based on the history of warfare, especially since World War II, women will face the additional trauma of sexual assault at the hands of their captors. Even so, women will not be only victims of such abuse. The 1992 presidential commission heard from Vietnam POWs, who said hearing the screams of women would have made their captivity all the more difficult. Colonel Fred Cherry of the Air Force, who spent seven and a half years in a North Vietnamese prison camp, testified:

> I am certain had the cries and screams and being next door
> to my fellow prisoners being tortured and given the rope

treatment and the bamboo beatings and the rubber straps—I'm sure I would—it would have affected [me] more severely had that been a woman, rather than a man.[120]

Air Force Colonel Norman McDaniel, also a POW in North Vietnam, said, "There is no doubt in my mind it would make a difference ... there is no question in my mind, I would certainly lean toward giving the enemy something if I knew they were raising hell with a fellow female prisoner."[121]

Colonel John W. Ripley, a Marine infantry commander in Vietnam, was never a POW, but he experienced a lot of direct-fire, close ground combat. The experience of Private Jessica Lynch was on his mind as he testified about the consequences of sending women into combat:[122]

> Those that permitted this to happen, who sent [Lynch] on that mission, should be themselves admonished, if not court-martialed, because that is the way the enemy sees women in combat; all of our enemies. And that is why they will treat—that is the way they will treat female captives or the female wounded left on the battlefield. That is precisely what will happen to them. We know that. We have seen the enemy.

Colonel Ripley did not mince words. "I have seen the enemy, and I know what they do to Marines. They skin them alive—one of my compatriots at Con-Tien—nail them to trees. I've seen that, with bridging spikes." He saw other atrocities—"a man's privates cut off and stuffed in his mouth, or his fingers cut off so they can pull his rings off." The ideological arguments for sending women into combat are unpersuasive to a man with Colonel Ripley's experience. Should women fight? he asks. "Hell, no! Never."[123]

A 2013 report produced by the U.S. Institute of Peace (USIP) on wartime sexual violence graphically addresses the frequency of sexual violence during war. Rape by combatants is widespread in many conflicts, such as the civil wars in El Salvador and Sierra Leone, in which the sexual violence was state-sponsored, and the Balkan war, which was marked by gang rape, sexual slavery, and sexual torture.[124] USIP cites a study of forty-eight conflicts in Africa between 1989 and 2009 that found that 36 percent of the armed groups in the conflicts engaged in some form of sexual violence. Another study, of wartime rape in eighty-six major civil wars, found that 62 percent of those conflicts included either massive or numerous reported rapes over at least a one-year period.

There were also incidents of rape as a substitute for consensual sex, such as the "comfort women" system established by the Japanese commanders in World War II. In the Democratic Republic of Congo, officials claim that widespread rape occurred because the fighters couldn't afford to pay sex workers.

Perhaps the worst and most widespread sexual violence took place in Europe during World War II. A horrific wave of sexual violence accompanied the collapse of the Third Reich. Soviet soldiers are estimated to have committed two million rapes. One Soviet veteran excused his youthful behavior in gang raping a twelve- or thirteen-year-old girl. "If she cried, we put something in her mouth," he said, explaining that he and his companions were just farm boys and hadn't been with a woman in four years.[125] Sexual atrocities abounded on the Nazi side as well, of course.[126]

The rape of captured American servicewomen would be an inevitable consequence of assigning women to combat. "War is hell" for men, but it reserves special torments for women, not all of whom would dismiss their rape with Major Cornum's easy bravado.

Risk No. 6: Forcing Women into Combat

Far more women than ever will die or be wounded in future wars if the Pentagon moves forward with its plan to push females into direct-fire, close ground combat units. There are a number of reasons for this conclusion, but first let's examine the blood cost of past American wars.

Wars take a tragic toll on American youth. The Second World War claimed 405,399 American lives (2.5 percent of the 16,112,566 participants), and 670,846 (4 percent) suffered non-mortal wounds. More recent wars have been decidedly less deadly, in a large part because of advances in emergency medicine. But even with the best emergency care, the human costs of the Vietnam War were considerable: 58,220 dead (0.6 percent of all military personnel who served) and 303,644 (3.5 percent) wounded.[127]

Female battle casualties became noticeable to the public for the first time after the September 11, 2001, terrorist attacks, which launched 2,333,972 U.S. military personnel, 10 percent of whom were women, into war in Afghanistan and Iraq. Together, those wars claimed 6,656 American service-member lives (0.2 percent of those who served), with another 50,608 wounded (2 percent). Men shed the most blood in Iraq, with 4,299 killed (97.5 percent of the total deaths) compared with 110 women (2.5 percent). So far 2,182 men have died in Afghanistan (98 percent of the total deaths) compared with forty-four women (2 percent).[128] The numbers of wounded men and women in those wars are proportional to the killed-in-action figures.

The number of women killed and wounded is as small as it is because women have been shielded by the Pentagon's long-standing combat exclusion policy. Barred from assignment to any unit below brigade level whose primary mission is direct combat, women serve in support positions. Nevertheless, in Afghanistan and Iraq, those combat restrictions do not entirely "preclude women from being involved in ground combat," said Eileen Lainez, a spokesman for the Defense Department.[129]

Most of those so-called "ground combat" engagements involving women were chance encounters connected with support missions. In those cases, women were killed or wounded by improvised explosive devices that detonated near their vehicles while they were hauling supplies or by other hostile acts. Other women served in units like military police temporarily attached to combat formations supporting convoy operations and may have encountered hostile fire during movements. Those circumstances put women in grave danger. Of course, all female service members in theater are trained to react to such attacks by dismounting and setting up perimeter security. In some instances these women have distinguished themselves under fire, but with the exception of Sergeant Leigh Ann Hester,[130] they did not mount direct ground combat attacks against a determined enemy. That is the job of combatants.

It is the nature of a counterinsurgency that the enemy blends in with the population, leaving no place totally safe. The absence of clear front lines puts servicewomen in harm's way, blurring the boundary between combat and support jobs, and prompting feminists to claim that they are "already in combat." Counterinsurgency, however, is not the same as sustained conventional combat.

Advocates for lifting the combat exclusion policy for women rely on the expectation that future wars will be counterinsurgency operations like Iraq and Afghanistan. This betrays not only a misunderstanding of women's roles in Iraq and Afghanistan but of our future military threats as well.

Future Warfare a Cornucopia of Operations

General Raymond Odierno, the Army chief of staff, outlined his view of America's future combat challenges in February 2013 in the journal *Foreign Policy*.[131] "We were right to focus on building counterinsurgency expertise given our mission over the past 12 years," he wrote. "However, irregular warfare represents one subset of the range of missions that the army must be ready to perform." The nation's ground forces are quickly returning to a conventional, traditional focus, though Odierno promised "not to walk away from the [counterinsurgency] experience."

"We must reinvest in those fundamental warfighting skills that underpin the majority of our directed strategic missions, from deterring and defeating aggression to power projection," Odierno cautioned. To be ready for these conventional operations, "we must refocus on our core warfighting skills while improving our ability to distribute and reassemble our forces rapidly, building the mass necessary for our central mission: to fight and win the nation's wars."

The Army chief of staff's message is clear. We are returning our forces to conventional operations because that is the foreseeable threat. The chairman of the Joint Chiefs, however, is not singing from the same page. General Dempsey's decision to open ground combat units to women is based on the assumption that future wars will be like Afghanistan and Iraq.

In his memorandum to the secretary of defense about eliminating "all unnecessary gender-based barriers to service," Dempsey states that "to successfully integrate women into the remaining restricted occupation fields," it is necessary "that a sufficient cadre of midgrade/senior women enlisted and officers are assigned to commands at the point of introduction to ensure success in the long run."[132] In other words, sexual integration of the combat units won't work if only a few women are introduced here and there. There has to be what Dempsey calls a "critical mass" of women—what the rest of us call a "quota." The only way to achieve this quota is to impose it on combat units through the work of feminist enforcers (Dempsey's "cadre of midgrade/senior women"), who will keep the men in line, allowing the "assimilation of women" to be successful. The forced integration of women into combat units will somehow take place, Dempsey assures us, without any diminution of "unit readiness, cohesion, and morale."

The phrases "sufficient cadre" and "critical mass" come from the Defense Advisory Committee on Women in the Services and theorists in other countries, such as Canada. They remain vague, and Dempsey has never defined what percentage of combat troops must be female to make integration work. The terms, nevertheless, are often interpreted to mean a cohort of 10 to 15 percent of a unit since anything less would be tokenism. So a hundred-man infantry company would need at least ten to fifteen women. If so, then a substantial portion of the casualties in future wars will be female.

Even in the counterinsurgency operations of Afghanistan and Iraq, the vast majority of casualties have been combatants. Had those combat units been 15-percent female, then the number of American servicewomen killed in Iraq would be 663 instead of 110. Wounded servicewomen would number 4,789. In Afghanistan, the count would be 334 women dead and 2,802 wounded.

This calculation assumes that women in infantry units would suffer casualties in proportion to their numbers. The grim reality, however, may be that women, who are physically less suited than men to the work of the infantry, will suffer disproportionate casualty rates in combat.

Feminist political power is so intimidating, however, that many military leaders talk glibly about policies that will guarantee a dramatic rise in the number of American women maimed or killed in war. Lester L. Lyles, the now-retired Air Force general who chaired the Military Leadership Diversity Commission that recommended abolishing the combat exclusion policy, justified his position by saying, "Women serving in combat environments are being shot at, killed, and maimed. But they're not getting the credit for being in combat arms."[133] Surely General Lyles understands the difference between "combat arms" and the support positions in which women are now serving. The question that Lyles leaves conspicuously unanswered is if women are being killed in support arms, how many more would be killed in combat arms? We might also ask, what is this "credit" to which Lyles refers and to whom is it important? Is it really worth thousands more female casualties?

Risk No. 7: Reduction of Retention Rates and Decline of Quality

The military's recruitment and retention of service members has been robust in spite of twelve years of war. The effort has been aided by several years of high unemployment and the decision to reduce the size of the force. The Army alone plans to cut at least one hundred thousand troops. As the economy improves and downsizing is completed, though, the military will have to compete in a difficult marketplace. Lifting the ban on women in combat will make that task considerably tougher.

Worried Marines

The Marine Corps is concerned that putting a "critical mass" of women into combat units will harm performance because of pregnancy (12 percent Army servicewomen are pregnant at any given time), health problems, and morale-busting preferential treatment for women.

In 2012, the Corps distributed an anonymous questionnaire to its 200,225 members and received fifty-three thousand responses. The results of that survey cast a shadow on the Pentagon's plans to insert thousands of women into combat positions.[134] A significant number of both male and female Marines indicated that pushing women into ground combat units will influence their decisions to remain in the Corps. Specifically, 17 percent of male Marines and 4 percent of females who otherwise planned to stay in the service or were undecided said they would be likely to leave if women were able to volunteer for combat positions, while 22 percent of males and 17 percent of females would be likely to leave the Corps if women were forced into combat positions.

Women worried about being targeted by enemies as POWs (and history shows that they're right to worry), about sexual harassment and assault by their male comrades, and about hygiene and privacy in the austere, rough-and-tumble world of the Marine combatant. They were also concerned about whether male Marines would accept them in combat roles and whether they would be physically able to keep up with the men.

In spite of these reservations, however, 31 percent of the women—1,558 female Marines—expressed interest in becoming ground combatants, and 34 percent—1,636—said they would volunteer for ground combat assignments. The relatively high number of would-be warriors suggests that these women don't understand how tough Marine ground combat jobs can be. Answering a survey is different from actually trying to meet the standards in a real trial. Captain Katie Petronio certainly thinks so.

The need to achieve a "critical mass" of women in combat units raises questions about how voluntary such assignments will be. Only 3 percent of the women responding to the survey said they would not have joined the Corps if ground combat had been open to women. (The figure was 13 percent for men.) But 23 percent of the female respondents said they would not have joined if women could be involuntarily assigned to combat units.

Military Times 2013 Poll Finds Mixed Response to Women in Combat

The 2013 edition of an annual survey conducted by the *Military Times*, an independent publication, reveals widespread skepticism about the Pentagon's new policy on women in combat and raises concerns about retention and recruitment.[135] Thirty-nine percent of those surveyed believe the change will have a "significant/major negative impact" on military readiness. A plurality (46 percent) of "combat troops" (a term that was not defined) "think it's a bad idea," and another 17 percent "will wait and see." The military's best recruiters are current service members and veterans who encourage their sons and daughters to join. A particularly interesting question in the *Times* survey, therefore, is, "If you had a son [or daughter] who was planning to join the military, would you support that decision?" A sizable majority, 67 percent, would support a son's decision to join, but most, 52 percent, would not want a daughter to enlist. Those answers raise doubts about General Dempsey's assurance that putting women in combat would make the military more attractive to young women and their parents.

Risk No. 8: Subjecting Women to the Draft

The Obama administration's decision to lift all combat exclusions for women virtually guarantees that the Supreme Court will declare male-only conscription unconstitutional.

Four times the United States resorted to conscription to field an armed force: during the Civil War (1863–1865), World War I (1917–1918), World War II (1940–1947), and the Cold War, including

Vietnam (1948–1973). In each case, the draft met with resistance, especially in the late 1960s and early 1970s, when college campuses exploded over the issue. Richard Nixon was elected president in 1968 promising to end the draft, which the government finally abandoned in 1973. We have now produced two generations of young men who have no military experience, and civilian society is consequently ignorant about most military issues.

The Selective Service System operates today as a standby agency in the event of a national emergency. Its best-known function is registering all eighteen-year-old men, a practice resumed in 1980 by President Jimmy Carter in response to the Soviet invasion of Afghanistan and continued as a hedge against underestimating the number of servicemen needed in a future crisis.[136] The agency's work is governed by the Military Selective Service Act (MSSA) of 1971, amended as recently as 2012, which provides for the maintenance of an armed force adequate to "insure the security of this Nation." Congress declared, "In a free society the obligations and privileges of serving in the Armed Forces and the Reserve components" should "be shared generally.… To this end, it is the intent of the Congress that whenever Congress shall determine that units and organizations are needed for the national security in excess of those of the Regular components of the Ground Forces and the Air Forces," it will order citizens to active federal service "so long as such necessity exists."[137]

Section 453 of the MSSA provides for draft registration: "Except as otherwise provided in this title it shall be the duty of every male citizen of the United States, and every other male person residing in the United States, who, on the day or days fixed for the first or any subsequent registration, is between the ages of eighteen and twenty-six, to present himself for and submit to registration."[138] There is no mention of female citizen registration.

Expect any future draft to be very different from the Vietnam-era version. The famous college deferment for full-time students no longer lasts up to four years. The new system postpones induction only until the end of the current semester, though a senior may postpone service entry until the end of the academic year. Local draft boards must be representative of the race and ethnicity of the registrants in the area, and selections are based on a lottery calling men classified 1-A, eighteen and a half through twenty-five years old, oldest first.[139]

When President Carter reinstated registration in 1980, he requested that women be included. Congress decided that since women were excluded from combat service by statute and military policy, women would not be required to register. The congressional debate gave life to a lawsuit first filed in 1971 claiming that male registrants were being discriminated against on the basis of sex.[140] The Supreme Court decided the case, *Rostker v. Goldberg*, in 1981, holding, "Since women are excluded from combat service by statute or military policy, men and women are simply not similarly situated for purposes of a draft or registration for a draft, and Congress' decision to authorize the registration of only men, therefore, does not violate the due process clause."[141]

Since the *Rostker* decision, however, military policies have radically changed, and the basis for the Court's decision has been dismantled. In April 2013, the National Coalition of Men (NCM) filed a lawsuit in California challenging the male-only Selective Service registration. Citing the Pentagon's announcement that women will be "allowed" to enter all combat positions, the NCM's complaint argues that "the sole legal basis for requiring only males to register with the [Selective Service System] for the military draft no longer applies, and Defendants should now treat men and women equally." The plaintiffs seek "injunctive relief ordering the Defendants to end the sex-based discrimination in its military draft registration program and to treat men and women equally."[142]

This NCM case may be dismissed because the issue is not ripe for litigation, since the issue of women in combat is under study by the executive branch and congressional debate. Unless Congress writes the combat exclusion into law and the Obama administration agrees to restore those barriers, however, the Supreme Court, in a matter of a couple years, will require female registration for the draft.

Though the change in combat policy lays the constitutional groundwork for including women in the draft should it be restored, the question of drafting women into the military seems purely theoretical to most Americans. Given the violent unpopularity of the draft the last time we had it, we assume that the possibility of its restoration is remote. That, unfortunately, is a mistake. The enormous cost of the all-volunteer force (AVF) and the expected requirements of future military operations make the return of the draft far more likely than most people realize.

The Impending Personnel Crisis

When the AVF was established in 1973, no one imagined how expensive retirement and benefits would become. Retirement costs climbed from $4.4 billion in 1973 to over $50 billion in 2011. In only a decade, from 2001 to 2011, health care costs climbed from $19 billion to about $55 billion. Both costs are still rapidly rising.[143]

Of course, the fastest way to cut the defense budget is to reduce the size of the force, which in 2013 stands at 1.46 million active-duty personnel and about 1.1 million reserves and National Guard members. The Pentagon also employs 790,000 full-time civilian employees, not counting the sixty thousand who are assigned to the military health-care system. Cuts are in the works.

The 2013 budget request for military personnel was about $150 billion to fund the pay and benefits of current and retired members of the armed services, according to the Congressional Budget Office. That figure does not include the $130 billion provided to the Department of Veterans Affairs to cover health care and service-connected disabilities for eligible veterans. The CBO forecasts that military personnel costs—even with major personnel cuts over the next few years—will approach $200 billion by 2022.

There is a hidden personnel cost that is seldom mentioned but nevertheless substantial. The AVF has become accustomed to battlefield support from contractors who fill roles formerly held by military personnel and units. The more than two hundred thousand contractors in Iraq and Afghanistan in 2008 actually outnumbered our troops. Most of that cost—which was handsome—was borne by annual "overseas contingency operations" appropriations, which are not commingled with Defense Department appropriations.

The AVF has become dependent on private contractors and will remain so. These contractors replace soldiers in the war zone, substantially increasing operational costs and giving the administration political protection when speaking of the size of the forces deployed for operations.

We could afford the current force with contractors if the U.S. government became disciplined enough to control non-defense spending. After all, defense spending as a percentage of overall discretionary spending is dramatically lower than it used to be. At the height of the Vietnam War, in 1968, the Pentagon consumed 45.1 percent of federal discretionary spending. At the peak of the wars in Afghanistan and Iraq, that figure was 19.9 percent.[144] Thanks to sequestration and other spending-cut deals between Obama and Congress, defense spending is falling further.

So how large of a force do we really need? The standard answer is that we need to maintain a force large enough to respond to future requirements.

Presidents in the AVF era have called upon the military far more than their predecessors did. There were nineteen overseas military deployments during the twenty-seven years of the last draft (1946–1973). During the thirty-nine AVF years of 1973–2012, there were 144 deployments—five times more. Why the escalation in the use of our forces?

Retired Lieutenant General Karl Eikenberry, a former commander and ambassador in Afghanistan, thinks that decision-makers feel freer to deploy a professional force than a draft force. "If we had a conscripted military good enough to accomplish the same missions assigned our current volunteer forces (admittedly a bold assumption), would the U.S. have invaded Iraq in 2003 and had almost 100,000 troops stationed in Afghanistan one decade after 9/11?" Eikenberry asks.[145] He suggests the country would be less sanguine about deploying a conscripted force.

Apart from costs, a decision to reinstate the draft could be driven by the military's inability to recruit enough volunteers of the requisite quality. At least once in the 1990s, the services hit a dry recruiting spell. Recruitment has been steady in the Obama years in part because unemployment has been high.

If the United States continues to demand a large standing military force, and if the AVF proves to be unsustainable because of the expense or poor recruitment or both, then Congress will have the unpleasant job of deciding how to fill the ranks. The Supreme Court will insure that male-only conscription is a thing of the past, and young women will then be forced into the military. Some of them will be placed in combat jobs. Americans must decide now if they are ready for Uncle Sam to take their daughters, put them in army boots, and send them into the trenches with men, because that is the inevitable consequence of the policies that the Obama administration is putting into place.

CHAPTER 5

WHAT SHOULD WE DO?

The Obama administration did an end run around Congress, as it has done in numerous other policy areas, when it rescinded the 1994 rule exempting women from ground combat units. Nevertheless, the Pentagon is required to report the change to Congress and to address how it affects the constitutionality of male-only draft registration.

Congress has an opportunity to act. The question is whether it will fulfill its constitutional duty or whether it will play dead, as so many leaders in the military have done.

Radical feminists have pushed hard to open combat positions to women, not to improve military readiness or because more than a tiny fraction of the women in the military want those positions. Their motive is being able to compete directly against men for a shot at senior combat command positions. But to do that, they will have to game the system by "gender-norming," that is to say, by lowering the physical standards for combat duty to make women and men "equals" on the battlefield.

General Dempsey and the service chiefs make the case for women in combat on the basis of "diversity," while carefully avoiding any discussion of whether the presence of women will improve or diminish combat effectiveness. This is the toxic effect of political correctness. Combined with the go-along-to-get-along operational philosophy that pervades the higher ranks (can anyone image a place for George Patton in today's Army?), it has allowed ideologues who despise America's traditional military culture—the culture of "duty, honor, and country"—to cripple the institution that performs the government's most basic task—protecting the nation from its enemies, both foreign and domestic.

Congress's record of overseeing the U.S. armed forces in recent years is not encouraging. It declined to get involved in 2006 when Admiral Michael Mullen, then the chief of Naval Operations, directed the Navy to make "diversity" a "strategic imperative" and its number one priority. Then in 2007, as chairman of the Joint Chiefs of Staff, Mullen made diversity a strategic imperative for the entire armed forces, and again Congress did nothing. In 2009, Congress established the Military Leadership Diversity Commission, which eventually proposed an aggressive agenda to promote women at every level. Going far beyond "equal opportunity," this feminist wish list called for deliberate discrimination in favor of women (under the rubric of "diversity metrics") and, to enforce it, "accountability reviews." Congress then directed the Pentagon to implement these proposals. A Congressional Research Service report reviewing that history notes that the language of this legislative mandate "makes no mention of the effects on military readiness such changes may produce."[1]

So we have reached the point where, with the blessing of the Joint Chiefs of Staff, multiculturalism in the form of "racial and gender diversity" has become the highest personnel priority of the United States military. There is not much time to restore common sense to national security policy, and if we are to do so, Congress must summon the courage to lead the way.

Nothing restores common sense as quickly as a bracing encounter with reality. Only a tiny fraction of the population has any acquaintance with military combat, but the gripping firsthand accounts of ground combat that follow offer a realistic picture of the hellish environment into which the political and military leadership of this country, along with its slumbering citizenry, is preparing to send American women.

To stop this policy, Congress must take certain steps. First, it must hold hearings on the administration's announced changes, thoroughly considering all of the challenging issues. Second, Congress must address what can best be described as the evident lack of moral courage among our top uniformed leaders. The Founders tried to insulate the military from politics by dividing the authority over the armed forces between the executive and legislative branches. But today, our military is infected by political correctness. The imposition of uniformity in thought, speech, and behavior regarding the strategic imperative of diversity, including the assignment of women to combat, prevents any reasonable discussion of the risks of degrading the military's capacity to perform its mission.

Finally, Congress must write into law commonsense restrictions on combat service that recognize the contributions of female service members without jeopardizing the effectiveness of the force.

What Is Ground Combat?

None of the current service chiefs has had personal experience in direct-fire, close ground combat, but they all endorse sending women into it. Does it matter that none of these leaders has served in the infantry and gone "eyeball-to-eyeball" with an enemy determined to kill him by any means possible? "Yes, it matters a lot," says General Carl Mundy, the former commandant of the Marine Corps. "I did see that kind of battle in Vietnam." Direct ground combat is "smashing heads, shooting the enemy at a range of six feet, and wrestling the enemy to the ground in a death struggle," he explains. That sort of experience influences your thinking.

To judge from current programs of combat instruction, the ground services still believe that future combat will include "eyeball-to-eyeball" fighting that is different in many important respects from the counterinsurgency and counterterrorism operations the services have conducted in Afghanistan and Iraq. That's why our senior leaders must closely study past conventional ground combat operations to ensure that our units are properly manned, equipped, and trained. Fortunately, we have experienced veterans still in the ranks and older warriors still alive to share their lessons learned.

Some of the most valuable insights into brutal ground combat come from Operation Iraqi Freedom's battles in Najaf and Fallujah. These were horrific and exhausting fights to the death.[2]

A hundred miles south of Baghdad, Najaf is the home of Islam's third-holiest shrine, the Imam Ali Mosque, and the adjoining Wadi-us-Salaam cemetery, the largest in the world. In the summer of 2004, the mosque and cemetery became the site of some of the toughest ground combat of the Iraq war.

In July 2004, the Multi-National Force—Iraq commander, General George W. Casey Jr., ordered the Eleventh Marine Expeditionary Unit (MEU) to quell an uprising in Najaf spawned by the renegade cleric Muqtada al-Sadr's Mahdi "messiah" militia.[3]

Battalion Landing Team, First Battalion, Fourth Marines (BLT 1/4) faced tougher fighting than any other Eleventh MEU ground

combat element. An active-duty Marine infantry officer who served
with BLT 1/4 described the fight in Najaf in an interview with me. He
was also part of the Marine force that fought its way to Baghdad during the "March Up" in 2003. He said the enemy encountered during
the earlier fight was rarely as determined as those the Marines faced
in Najaf in 2004.

Here is that officer's account:

> The Najaf fight started in earnest when a Marine helicopter
> was downed by hostile fire near the Imam Ali Mosque, the
> most sacred of all Shi'a shrines, and by prior political
> arrangement the shrine was a no-fire area. Of course, the
> Mahdi forces used the mosque complex as a sanctuary for
> staging operations, for employing medium and heavy mor-
> tars, and to provide treatment for their fighters wounded
> in battle without fear of reprisal and with good effect.
>
> The Marines' rescue operation to secure the downed
> Huey helicopter lit the fuse that started the worst of the
> fight, but it was the Mahdi's attack on the nearby An-Najaf
> police station that launched the Marines into the toughest,
> close-in direct ground fighting of the war to that point.
> The Mahdi used the massive cemetery, which was adjacent
> to the mosque, as a staging ground for the attack on the
> police station.
>
> From the outset the Marines were under constant and
> very accurate mortar fires guided by Mahdi observers on
> rooftops. Evidently the Mahdi pre-registered targets
> throughout the area, which were marked for ease of iden-
> tification. Then when calls for fires came by radio, Mahdi
> mortar crews, which were sequestered safely inside the

mosque grounds, quickly fired as the Marines maneuvered near the pre-registered targets.

It soon became obvious that the only way to stop the militia, given the strict rules of engagement, was to pursue them into the cemetery. The Marines scaled the cemetery walls from multiple points to methodically move from headstone to crypt to mausoleum, clearing each through-out the three-by-four-mile area.

The Mahdi had good command and control, pre-coordinated indirect fires throughout the cemetery, hundreds of command-detonated pre-positioned improvised explosive devices, grenades, machine guns, and small arms. They used their arsenal to good effect throughout the three-day battle. Further, the Mahdi fighters were a determined enemy and died by the hundreds as the Marines cleared every inch of each sector in the cemetery.

Throughout the battle the Marines constantly overcame immense physical and mental challenges while battling the enemy. Examples of such challenges included climbing over tombstones and mausoleums [up to fifteen feet high], on top of and inside grave sites, and in and out of mausoleums while killing Mahdi fighters in close combat, hand grenade fights. Some of these fights resulted in Marine casualties, which subsequently had to be carried out [on other Marines' shoulders] of the cemetery maze, over hundreds of meters, by foot [because litters could not negotiate the sharp turns and obstacles presented by the densely packed headstones and mausoleums]. Additionally, due to the enemy's intense, near continuous, and extremely accurate small arms and medium and heavy mortar fire, stationary support-by-fire positions mounted on top of Marine vehicles became increasingly vulnerable. After suffering multiple casualties and numerous extremely close calls while in support of one of the BLT's rifle companies, one of the BLT's heavy machine gun and anti-armor platoons identified a multi-story Iraqi government building that would provide cover and concealment from enemy fire while also enabling continued support for the rifle company.

The heavy weapons platoon proceeded to clear the multi-story structure and then returned to their vehicles to dismount their heavy weapons.

Then the Marines rapidly moved these heavy weapons one hundred meters, while under near continuous [mortar and small arms] fire, from their vehicles into the upper levels of the building.

The Marines, who were already weighed down with personal gear and rifles, dismounted the heavy weapons— the .50 caliber machine guns (127 pounds each) and Mark 19 grenade launchers (137.5 pounds each)—and many hundreds of pounds of ammunition, and then raced across a fire-saturated hundred-meter open area to the cleared buildings. They climbed with the gear to a middle floor overlooking the cemetery, where they set up the heavy weapons after creating firing positions by knocking large holes in the walls and filled sand bags to stabilize the weapon tripods. This quick action was done as the 130-degree Fahrenheit temperature cooked the Marines.[4]

The battle of Najaf cost the Marines seven killed in action and ninety-four wounded, or 14 percent of BLT 1/4's eight hundred personnel. The Eleventh MEU estimated that 1,500 of al-Sadr's Mahdi died in the fighting, and perhaps thousands were wounded. The fighting included cases of hand-to-hand combat with determined terrorists. The Marines won, but not without sustaining many serious wounds.

Vietnam combat had much in common with the warfare in Afghanistan and Iraq—security operations, patrols, snipers, and brief firefights. But with the possible exceptions of Najaf and Fallujah, nothing from the last decade matches what our Marines saw in the spring of 1968, during the Tet Offensive, on the north bank of the Cua Viet River, a few miles south of the "demilitarized zone" separating South and North Vietnam. Those engagements best illustrate the terrifying "eyeball-to-eyeball" combat that future American combatants could face.

William "Wild Bill" Weise, a retired Marine Corps brigadier general, was a lieutenant colonel then and the commanding officer of the Second Battalion, Fourth Marines, a unit that saw some of the heaviest fighting in the Vietnam War. "Most of the fighting was against well-organized, competently led, Soviet-equipped soldiers of the North Vietnamese Army (NVA) … at least six or seven times as large [as the 2/4 Marines], in well fortified positions," supported by "artillery, rockets, and an infrastructure of irregular indigenous forces native to the battle area," recalls General Weise.

The 2/4 Marines came to the fight understrength (650 Marines) and "very tired from continuous enemy contact and frequent moves. We had just completed a battalion night attack two days before," says General Weise. "In three bloody days we drove the enemy back and saved the vital Dong Ha Combat Base," but at the loss of eighty-one Marines killed and 287 seriously wounded. Among those losses were five company commanders (one killed, four wounded and evacuated), the battalion sergeant major (killed), the battalion commander and both his radio operators (wounded), and many platoon, squad, and fire-team leaders. The NVA suffered 1,368 to two thousand dead.

Bayard "Vic" Taylor, a retired lieutenant colonel, was a platoon commander of 2/4 Marines at the time, and he shared with me his experiences near the Cua Viet River in infantry combat against a professional enemy that was ruthless, brutal, and relentless. "Neither battles nor wars are won on the defense. They are not won by holding ground, by patrolling, nor by returning fire; nothing is decided by that. They are won by attacking and destroying an enemy. Infantry attack is uncivilized and uncompromising by necessity. In the assault, casualties are accepted, friendly wounded are left, enemy wounded are killed, and surrenders are rejected," Taylor says grimly. "Bayonets, rifle butts, knives, and bare hands may be in play. Beyond the line of departure, it is win or lose—no draws. If you want to win, the mission is to kill the enemy—all of them—as quickly as possible."

The following is Vic Taylor's account of the relentless three-day struggle at Dai Do, the epicenter of the Cua Viet campaign.

> The mission was protecting the Cua Viet River, the supply lifeline for all U.S. forces, from the North Vietnamese Army—which was at most only eight miles away and supported by their full range of artillery, rockets, and mortars. In a near continuous string of firefights and battles over two spring months [1968], the 2/4 Marines did just that. Then the enemy made a bold strategic move. They covertly moved an entire division [three infantry regiments] from North Vietnam, through an adjacent area of operation, into prepared fortifications just across the river from the main logistics base and Third Marine Division headquarters.

Their presence was discovered by pure accident, their intentions were unknown as was their strength. BLT 2/4 was ordered to attack. As it turned out it [the enemy] was the 320th North Vietnamese Army division with somewhere between seven and ten thousand soldiers. The 2/4's five rifle companies totaled 653 men.

I was a platoon leader in Hotel Company. As a second lieutenant my vision was pretty short and my information even shorter, but I'll tell you what I remember.

Hotel Company made the initial attack to seize a fortified riverside village named Dong Huan. It was defended by a reinforced company of NVA regulars. Hotel crawled across five hundred yards of open ground, assaulted into their defensive fires, and killed them all. There were no enemy survivors, no prisoners. Although completely successful, it was costly.

The company started with 120 men, but when our MEDEVACs were cleared there were seventy-five left. That was the price of taking a fortified position. We lost our company commander, our forward observer, all three staff NCOs, one of whom had been a platoon commander, half the sergeants, half the corporals, and a bunch of others. After the fight it was necessary to shuffle people around according to rank and experience. First Lieutenant Scotty Prescott took over the company. I took his platoon since it had no officer. Another platoon was commanded by a young buck sergeant, and he'd been a squad leader in a different platoon the day before. And so it went with the squads and teams. Essentially it was a new company. But they were all Marines, and that was enough.

Bravo Company of First Battalion, Third Marines, was loaned to 2/4. They were across the river and embarked on AMTRACSs [amphibious assault vehicles]. On order they attacked from the far bank of the Cua Viet into another enemy riverbank fortification just downstream on our side. The NVA defenders were ready. They poured devastating fires into the open hatches and onto the debarking Marines. Within minutes the senior man was a new second lieutenant. Bravo was decimated and out of the fight.

Following Hotel and Bravo attacks, Golf Company attacked the village of Dai Do. They took half the position at great cost and held it all night against continuous enemy pressure. The following morning Echo Company, with bayonets fixed, attacked and seized the remainder. Their casualties were greater than ours. Any surviving NVA fell back into a string of fortified hamlets.

Our company, Hotel, was ordered to attack and seize the next ville: Dinh To.

It was across a dry rice paddy about five hundred meters away. The ville was about eighty yards wide but deep. There was a shallow stream running down the length of its left side. We headed for it with two platoons up and one back. Mine was on the left. We were to take the lead, hang onto the creek, and the other platoons would guide on us. At a couple hundred yards the NVA opened fire. My platoon was closest. Single shots, they were accurate. One of the first rounds hit a Marine right in front of me in the belly. He kinda folded up. Next one hit my radioman in the arm. He was reaching out the handset to me. Shot his arm off at the elbow. Without orders, our Marines broke

into a run, closing the distance. We hit the first fortifica-
tions in a rush. They were unbelievable: deep trenches,
firing pits, and covered bunkers, prepared over the previous week. NVA soldiers were hard to see at first but they
were firing from all of them. Our teams and squads had
been scrambled in reorganization from the previous fight's
casualties, but they were vets of two months of the same
kind of combat and they knew what to do. Using grenades
and rifles and taking one bunker after another. As leaders
would drop, the next senior would take his place—lance
corporals relieving sergeants, privates replacing PFCs—
yard by yard.

As our numbers dwindled our frontage shrank. To keep
moving we left gaps, and probably left enemy on our flanks.

The NVA counterattacked. I didn't recognize it. At first
it was just a huge increase in incoming fire, like a big wind
in our face. We took a dozen more casualties. Then we
heard them; shouting and shooting on both right and left.
Our outside squads refused the flanks and returned fire
but it was weak. M-16s, never reliable in those days, were
jamming; half the Marines had already grabbed up enemy
weapons. Gun ammo and grenades were low; resupply
could not reach us, and there were too many casualties to
move or protect. We were losing strength while the enemy
was reinforcing and re-supplying constantly from their
rear. By that time there were between forty and fifty able-
bodied Marines left. Another counterattack was coming,
we knew it and braced—bayonets were fixed.

Somebody yelled, "Echo is coming!" I saw Captain
Livingston and a couple dozen of his men coming through

the smoke. They were dirty and bloody from their Dai Do fight—and never looked better. I could have kissed them.

About then our CO, Lieutenant Prescott, was hit and downed. We changed command on the fly. He yelled, "You got it?" I yelled back, "I got it!" We went on.

The Marines of Hotel and Echo companies were mixed together; they were also miserable and mad at everything on earth. On order they rolled over and through the NVA defenders in front and shot, stabbed, and blasted for another few yards.

When the NVA counterattacked again there was no mistaking it. It sounded like every weapon in the world had opened up. Incoming fire was shredding almost everything above ground. Leaves, twigs, branches, and whole trees were falling; old masonry hooches disintegrated. RPGs came in volleys; artillery, mortars, and rockets falling on friendly and enemy alike, and a section of heavy machine guns out on the right poured grazing fire into our flank.

The NVA infantry came right behind their fire. And that time they were easy to see. You could see more than you ever wanted. Leafy helmets and spike bayonets. They were in front, in the creek on our left and somehow back in the rear. You could hear them yelling and shooting back there; probably killing our wounded. Fair enough I guess; we would have done the same to them. Most surprising, they were coming from the right flank too. The side where the NVA gunners had been pouring heavy 12.7 fire into us all afternoon. The gunners never slackened—they were shooting through their own to get to us. Pouring on the steel.

They wanted that position and were not giving it up on the cheap.

The instances of personal initiative, selflessness, and bravery were too many to name—but not to remember. NVA soldiers charging at a run into Marine positions— machine gunner standing in the open, mowing them down; unarmed Marine snatching an NVA soldier's rifle away from him, beating him to the ground; a corpsman firing his .45 while he shielded a Marine with his own body; our company sniper, Lance Corporal Jim O'Neill, on his own initiative crawled out into the open field on our right, found the enemy machineguns and killed them all—twenty-four gunners and assistant gunners, one after the other. Only thing that slowed him down was the heat wave off the barrel distorting his sight picture.

The Second Battalion, Fourth Marines, lived up to their nickname that day [the Magnificent Bastards], and if the 320th NVA had a similar moniker they lived up to it as well. Brave young men, on both sides, inside a place not much bigger than a basketball court, were tearing each other to pieces—neither one giving an inch. For nerve, that would be hard to beat.

The Marines were outnumbered and out-gunned, but the enemy let up first. There was kind of a lull in the fire. We gathered up our wounded and fell back to a better position and held there. We were beat up, and another round would have been a toss-up, but the next push we expected never came.

Fox and Golf companies, led by "Wild Bill," passed through us and continued the attack. Their losses were heavy too, including the battalion commander and sergeant major, but they gave out worse than they took, and the next morning what was left of the NVA division was gone. I guess they had enough of old 2/4.

In the end, the essence of 2/4, and Marine combat infantry as a whole I suppose, was summed up by a fellow platoon commander: wounded himself, having lost three quarters of his men, and asked for his platoon strength, he replied, "Nine, but we're all good under fire."[5]

"By any account the Battle of Dai Do turned out to be a successful, although unplanned, spoiling attack by the 'Magnificent Bastards' of the Second Battalion, Fourth Marines," concludes General Weise. Dai Do and Najaf were tough, direct-fire, close ground combat fights, but perhaps not as tough as the fight our infantry faced in North Korea in 1950.

General Robert H. Barrow labeled the Chosin Reservoir campaign of December 1950 "probably one of the greatest epics of all time." He spoke of the extreme cold and the "constant attacking … for days, night and day … death all about." General Barrow speculated, "Suppose we had 15 percent women, 20 percent women. My supposing led me to say I wouldn't be here. I guess Kim Il Sung [the North Korean ruler at the time] would be taking care of my bones along with everyone else's in North Korea."

One of the last of the survivors, a comrade of General Barrow at Chosin, is retired Army Brigadier General Edwin L. Kennedy. Here are General Kennedy's recollections of the fateful winter of 1950–1951 in North Korea:

My class from West Point was immediately assigned to our units after graduation without the benefit of attending any officer courses. We graduated in June and the war in Korea began the same month. It was a "come as you are war." My regiment, the Fifteenth Infantry, landed in North Korea in the dead of winter after training in Japan and acquiring KATUSAs [Korean Augmentation to the U.S. Army] to fill our ranks.

Physical fitness was paramount as Korea is very mountainous, and climbing the hills and mountains is physically rigorous—exhausting. There was no way to get around it. It was not a war for the physically weak, and many of the older soldiers could not hack it. Soldiers who had successfully fought in World War II under some very difficult circumstances were not able to handle Korea. We had company commanders, experienced captains, replaced so younger men could keep up and command their units from the front.

Not only was the terrain difficult to negotiate, the conditions were primitive for infantrymen. We lived in the elements day after day. When we went to link up with the Marines withdrawing from the Chosin the temperatures were frigid. It sapped your strength trying to stay warm at night in the open. Even strong men had problems just surviving in the elements.

Returning to my platoon from the company command post one afternoon in December 1950, I accidentally ran into a North Korean patrol observing my platoon and likely preparing for an attack. They were directly between my platoon and me. Walking through snow that was making crunching noises, there was no way that I could not be noticed. I immediately yelled and fired my carbine, knocking down several North Koreans. I had to run away as they began firing their burp guns, and the rest of their unit began chasing me. As I slid down a hill into a ravine, a North Korean slid down next to me. My carbine jammed, so I used it like a ball bat and swung it as hard as I could to hit the North Korean in the head. The stock on the M-1 carbine broke, but the North Korean's neck did as well. Hand-to-hand combat was like that. It was very close, very personal, and very dependent on who was more aggressive and stronger. I was able to outrun my pursuers until I reached other soldiers from my unit.

In February 1951, when we were recapturing Seoul, I was hit in the face with a concussion grenade when attacking an objective on a steep hill. The grenade knocked me down, and when I tried to get up a North Korean soldier was standing over me with a rifle and bayonet. I quickly slid backwards down the hill, but he bayoneted me through the thigh. I wasn't a big man but I was larger than him, and I grabbed his rifle and bayonet so he could not take it. The North Korean panicked and turned to run. I was able to get up and then bayonet him with his own rifle.

This was typical infantry combat. It was very physical, very brutal. There is absolutely no woman that I have ever seen or known who could handle this kind of combat. It was tough for many men. Many of those who were not physically capable either perished or were removed because they were a detriment to the unit. They were a burden to the others and potentially placed the safety of the entire unit at risk because they could not keep up, especially the leaders.[6]

Najaf, Dai Do, and Chosin were a "bloody hell of close infantry combat" that illustrates the toughest environments our ground combat forces must train for and possibly face as they defend America in the future.

The Marines and Army warriors who fought these battles said without exception that women should not be part of such a "bloody hell," echoing what General Barrow said in his 1991 Senate testimony: "Combat is finding and closing with and killing or capturing the enemy. It's killing! It is done in an environment as difficult as you can possibly imagine; extremes of climate, brutality, death, dying. It's uncivilized and women can't do it. Nor should they even be thought of as doing it."

The Need for Congressional Action

Congressional hearings on the question of women in combat are long overdue. The House of Representatives has not hosted full hearings on women in combat since 1979, and the Senate has not done so since 1991. Article I, Section 8, of the Constitution gives Congress the responsibility to make the rules for military personnel, but past Congresses have abandoned that responsibility to the executive branch.

In the 1990s, Congress repealed the statutory barriers to sending women into combat and trusted the ground services to act reasonably. That trust was misplaced, and it is time for Congress to exercise its duty of oversight.

Congressional hearings must consider the lessons learned from recent wars in Iraq and Afghanistan and reconsider the recommendations from the 1992 Presidential Commission on the Assignment of Women in the Armed Forces. That assessment of the issues involved in assigning servicewomen to combat duty is as relevant today as when it was first presented. The intent of the hearings should be to bring law and policy in line with current realities, reflecting lessons learned from recent combat and the future needs of the all-volunteer force.

The hearings should include a panel of combat veterans who can describe their experiences in conventional close combat. Congressmen should ask them about daily life in fighting positions, strength requirements, the lack of privacy, and the loads they carried. The panelists should describe their squad, team, or platoon and how it functioned, shedding light on the importance for the unit of male bonding, which feminists are so quick to deride. And the panelists should describe the killing in detail.

The entire Joint Chiefs of Staff should also testify. Congressmen should ask each member to describe his personal experience with direct ground combat and to explain why he believes women belong in that setting. The following specific questions would be useful:

1. Do you have any personal experience of sustained conventional ground combat in which you believe that women would have performed as effectively as the same number of men?

2. How would the integration of women improve a combat unit's survivability and mission success?

3. What do your experienced warriors tell you about the plan to introduce women into ground combat units?

4. How many women must a hundred-man infantry company include to make female integration work? What effect might that integration have on the readiness of the force?

5. Describe, from a platoon leader's perspective, the three types of ground combat operations that you believe we are most likely to face in future conflicts.

6. Why does your service need women in the infantry or Special Forces?
7. Explain why you believe combat unit cohesion won't be harmed by mixing the sexes.
8. How will putting women in direct ground combat increase unit readiness?
9. Can you name any modern peer competitor military that uses women in ground combat roles such as infantry, armor, engineers, special operations, or field artillery?

Once it has collected the facts in hearings, Congress should address the defects of the armed forces' personnel policies with legislation, which would take the form of an amendment to the National Defense Authorization Act. "Congressional notification" provisions are routinely ignored. Congress must write sensible military personnel policy into law. The Pentagon's attempts to put women in combat should require legislative authorization, not mere congressional inaction. The Military Culture Coalition, an initiative of the Center for Military Readiness, has proposed legislation that would preserve the exemption of women from ground combat and the draft. Good legislation, based on that proposal, would include the following provisions:

1. Definitions
   a. Direct ground combat is engaging or attacking an enemy on the ground with individual or crew-served weapons, while being exposed to hostile fire and to a high probability of direct physical contact with personnel of the hostile force. Direct ground

combat involves locating and closing with the enemy to defeat them by fire, maneuver, or shock effect.

    b. Combat-contingent support occupations may involve incident-related attacks requiring self-defense while serving "in harm's way" in a combat theater

2. Rules
   - **a.** Service members are eligible to be assigned to all positions for which they are qualified, except that women shall not be assigned to units below the brigade level whose primary mission is to engage in direct ground combat
   - **b.** Women shall not be assigned to units below the brigade level for the following additional reasons:
     - **i.** Where the Service Secretary attests that appropriate berthing and privacy arrangements are too costly or inconsistent with mission effectiveness;
     - **ii.** Where units are engaged in long-range reconnaissance and surveillance operations and Special Operations Forces missions; and
     - **iii.** Where occupation-related physical requirements for direct ground combat operations would necessarily exclude the vast majority of women service members
   - **c.** Women shall not be required to register for Selective Service or be subject to conscription

3. Sense of Congress
   - **a.** All personnel in combat-contingent support occupations, which may involve incident-related attacks

requiring self-defense while serving in a combat theater, should receive appropriate training and career opportunities that recognize incident-related operations "in harm's way"

b. The Department of Defense should ensure that individual merit is recognized and rewarded in military occupational specialties that are open to both male and female members of the Armed Forces. No person who is best qualified should be denied access to open military occupations due to gender-based goals, ceilings, metrics, or quotas.

c. The Armed Forces of the United States may use gender-specific programs for male and female trainees in order to promote the highest level of general fitness and wellness in basic, entry-level, and pre-commissioning training, provided that

  i. Such programs do not compromise training or qualification programs for physically demanding combat or combat support MOSs; and

  ii. Policies exempting women from direct ground combat assignments are retained and codified

This exclusion of women from infantry training allows it to be as challenging as possible for average men. Physical training programs should be suitable for the majority of personnel, not the unusual few, whether male or female.

Although many assume that conscription will never return, a national emergency would be even more complicated than necessary if women were subject to Selective Service obligations. Freestanding legislation exempting women from the draft but not from combat would almost certainly be overturned by the federal courts. Combining both exemptions in one piece of legislation makes it less likely that an activist court will subject women to the draft.

Congress should also pass an amendment to the National Defense Authorization Act that requires the armed forces to establish single-sex programs for male and female trainees in order to promote the highest level of general fitness and wellness in basic, entry-level, and pre-commissioning training. Such programs, however, should not compromise training or qualification programs for physically demanding combat or combat-support specialties, and policies exempting women from direct-fire, close ground combat assignments would be retained and codified.

Reduce the Role of Politics in the Military by Adjusting the Flag and General Officer Selection System

The frequent news reports of misbehavior, double standards, and even criminal acts of senior flag and general officers, along with Army surveys of subordinate leaders, indicate that something is wrong with the system that elevates such persons to positions of leadership and great responsibility.

There is another problem, less spectacular than adulterous affairs, perhaps, but more damaging—senior officers who act more like politicians than authentic military leaders. Elected politicians must represent their constituents, and appointed officials also must support the policies of those who appointed them, but flag and general officers have an obligation to support and defend the Constitution and to look out for the welfare of the men and women serving in the ranks.

Admiral Mullen introduced the current aggressive political correctness when he decreed that diversity was a strategic imperative.

Today, the majority of the senior flag and general officers have lost sight of their responsibility. They have joined with the political appointees to do the bidding of the administration.

"Diversity" ought to be the happy result of nondiscrimination and the recognition of individual merit. But the work of the Military Leadership Diversity Committee has made it a "difficult concept to grasp" because it is not the same as the "EO [equal opportunity]-inspired mandate to be both color and gender blind."[7] The redefined concept replaces "nondiscrimination" with sex-based "diversity metrics," even without any evidence of discrimination against women.

So how does the military go about "operationalizing diversity"? In the case of the Navy, we find a clue in a leaked email message from Naval Operations dated Thursday, July 29, 2010, titled "Diversity Accountability":[8]

> CNO [Admiral Gary Roughead] is interested in who are the diverse officers with high potential and what is the plan for their career progression. He may ask what is being done within to ensure they are considered for key follow on billets within the Navy. This list must be held very closely but will provide ready reference to ensure we are carefully monitoring and supporting the careers of the best and the brightest the Navy has to offer.

The CNO's office followed up on that email:

> Consistent with CNO's Diversity Policy, the purpose of any Diversity Accountability Review is to ensure Navy leaders are involved and active in creating an environment where all Navy personnel have opportunities for personal and

professional growth. The Diversity Accountability Review calls for Navy leaders to show how they are mentoring and enabling the men and women in their commands to meet their full potential based on performance, and making sure that opportunities to reach more senior levels of leadership are available to all in an equal manner.

These messages suggest that at the highest levels of our uniformed leadership, there is a desire to hold subordinate leaders accountable if they do not rank, career-manage, and detail officers according to race, ethnicity, or sex. What started out as good intentions has turned into tragedy, then farce, and finally unvarnished discrimination.

Political correctness and non-remedial sex-consciousness have become a corrosive, demoralizing force in all branches of the military and stifled any arguments against initiatives such as the assignment of women to ground combat units. The result is a military led by senior officers who by their behavior declare, "I believe in nothing and am tolerant of everything."

A policy that is unprecedented in human history should be adopted only after careful analysis by people who know something about the subject and who are concerned above all with military effectiveness. That is not happening. It is urgent, therefore, that Congress recall General Barrow's plea from 1991: "Please, Congress of the United States, you keep this responsibility. Don't pass it to DOD. Don't pass it to the executive branch, because they come and go. You have some continuity, and you would put it in law; they put it in policy. The policy can change at a whim."[9]

As General Barrow warned, the Joint Chiefs have caved in to "the pressure." A retired Marine general agrees with that assessment.

Dempsey is "treading more PC than I would," he says. "He is out further on the limb than he needs to be."[10]

General and Flag Officers Are Failing to Protect the Military's Culture from a Smothering Atmosphere of Political Correctness

A general or flag officer who speaks out against the military's pervasive political correctness is certain to be attacked by top Pentagon officials, as Lieutenant General Benjamin Mixon learned. The commander of the U.S. Army in the Pacific, General Mixon wrote a letter to *Stars and Stripes* in March 2010 reminding the troops and their families of their right to oppose the repeal of the "Don't Ask, Don't Tell" policy on homosexuality in the forces and encouraging them "to write your elected officials and chain of command and express your views. If those of us who are in favor of retaining the current policy do not speak up, there is no chance to retain the current policy."[11]

The reaction of the Pentagon establishment was immediate. "I think that for an active-duty officer to comment on an issue like this is inappropriate," warned the secretary of defense, Robert Gates. "I feel the same way," said the chairman of the Joint Chiefs of Staff, Admiral Mullen, "and actually it is being addressed inside the chain of command in the Army." He added ominously, "I've spoken specifically to [U.S. Army chief of staff] Gen. George W. Casey Jr. about this. And General Mixon specifically is—the issue is being addressed with him."

Admiral Mullen made it clear that deviation from the approved political line is not an option. "All of us in uniform are obliged to certainly follow the direction of leadership, right up to the president.... There's an expectation that you would comply with that. And in the end, if there is either policy direction that someone in uniform disagrees with … and you feel so strongly about it the answer is not advocacy; it is in fact to vote with your feet."

The attack on General Mixon made a lasting impression on his fellow senior officers, who have generally chosen the silence of cowardice rather than risk their careers. An active-duty Army lieutenant colonel with three combat tours said the PC mania affects the entire military. "Word on the street is don't open your mouth or you'll get the axe," the colonel said. He explained that General Dempsey's lifting the combat exclusion for women was entirely political, and "it defies critical thinking because the outcome hurts combat lethality."

So what can Congress do about military political correctness? It needs to do a better job of identifying and grooming general and flag officers who demonstrate moral courage and the highest sense of personal integrity when advising political leaders and then select men like General Mixon who will protect the military's culture. Congress's goal should be to make the military as apolitical as possible in order to keep the trust of the American people.

That outcome begins by cutting the unwieldy number of general and flag officers. There were more than 950 general and flag officers on active duty as of 2012; that is one for every 1,500 officers and enlisted personnel. In August 1945, that ratio was one for every six thousand.[12] The Army has 109 major generals, the rank held to command the service's ten active divisions. The Navy has almost as many admirals as ships (245 admirals and 285 ships).[13]

A smaller cadre of top brass is easier to manage, but it also requires identifying and promoting the men and women with moral courage. The current system isn't working,[14] and the problem predates the Obama administration. Retired Army Colonel Douglas Macgregor leveled a stinging criticism back in 2006: "Today, the senior leadership of the U.S. armed forces in general and, the U.S. Army in particular, is overly bureaucratic, risk averse, professionally inadequate and, hence, unsuited to the complex military tasks entrusted to them. The Bush administration has a preference for compliant, sycophantic officers who are fatally dependent on the goodwill of the secretary of defense and the president who promoted and appointed them.... There is no political constituency for excellence in general-ship." The kind of generals we need, and aren't getting, wrote Colonel MacGregor, are "men of character and integrity, accepting risk and uncertainty as the unchanging features of war. They must also dem-onstrate a willingness to stand up and be counted, to put country before career and, if necessary to resign."[15]

Others who have taken a serious look at our flag officer system believe a major correction is past due as well. Specifically, we need officers with moral courage who provide candid military assessments and not just reports that tickle the ears of their political masters. Congress must ask the right questions and insist on the unvarnished truth. Those officers must be held accountable, and heads must roll when judgment and courage are absent.

John Nagl, a former Rhodes Scholar and retired Army lieutenant colonel, researched the flaws in the officer personnel system by ques-tioning 250 West Point graduates. He found that 93 percent of them believed that half or more of "the best officers leave the military early rather than serving a full career."[16] Only 30 percent of them agreed that the military personnel system "does a good job promoting the right officers to general," and a miniscule 7 percent agreed that it "does a good job retaining the best leaders." Most (65 percent) of the West Pointers interviewed agreed that the attrition of the best officers leaves a less competent general-officer corps, and 78 percent believe that it harms national security. That's a shattering indictment from the so-called "cream of the crop."

The fate of military reform is entirely in Congress's hands. It must assure that the U.S. armed forces keep their best leaders and promote to flag ranks only those who demonstrate the courage of General Mixon. Then those officers must be held accountable to manage the military's culture to keep it apolitical, as the Founders intended.

WHAT KIND OF COUNTRY ARE WE?

The debate over women in combat tends to focus on two questions. Proponents of the change—feminists and their allies in the government, the Pentagon, and the media—see it as a question of equality. As long as women are prohibited from engaging in the essential act of a soldier—fighting— they are condemned to second-class citizenship in the military and in civilian society. Equality, in their view, is the supreme goal of public policy. If a cost of achieving it is the diminution of the efficiency or even effectiveness of our combat forces, so be it. They won't quite come out and say this, but it is the unavoidable conclusion of their reasoning.

Opponents of opening combat units to women, when they speak up at all, stick to the pragmatic question of whether women are capable of meeting the physical demands of sustained ground combat. Since the evidence that they are not is overwhelming, the argument is that opening combat to women would compromise the primary mission of the military—fighting and defeating our enemies. This argument, however, is frequently couched in terms of regret: We all wish, obviously, that we could accommodate women's laudable ambition to serve their country in this way, but the unpleasant reality is that it's just not practicable.

The debate about sending women into combat raises other questions, however. Both sides avoid them, but they are perhaps the most important questions. What kind of society sends its women into combat? Do we want to be that kind of society? Is sending our daughters, wives, and mothers into combat good for women, for men, or for children? To a certain kind of feminist, hardened by ideology, it's repugnant even to ask these questions. We don't ask if we should send *men* into combat, so we shouldn't ask if we should send *women*. People who have blinded themselves to the profound and wonderful differences between the sexes are not open to a discussion about the consequences of those differences, and perhaps there is nothing more to say to them. But those people should not set the terms of the public debate. The American people need to stop pretending that sending women into combat involves questions no deeper than how far they can carry a seventy-pound rucksack.

Between September 11, 2001, and May 2013, 154 American servicewomen were killed in the line of duty in Afghanistan and Iraq. Nineteen of those women were mothers of children aged eighteen and younger. By comparison, sixteen women were killed during the Vietnam War, and six were killed in the first Persian Gulf War.[1]

Now women will be asked to shoulder a much heavier burden. More mothers of young children will be killed and wounded in war than ever before. And all young women will eventually be subject to the draft. This radical policy change erases the boundaries of sex and normalizes the exposure of women to lethal violence. Meet the real "war on women."

Two consequences of the Obama administration's new policy reveal its savagery with special clarity. The first is the moral certainty that female prisoners of war will be subjected to sexual crimes that will make their captivity even more horrifying than men's. The same people who decry sexual harassment in the barracks shrug their shoulders at the prospect of American servicewomen's falling into the hands of the world's most depraved misogynists.

The other savage consequence of sending women into combat is the forced separation for months on end—and perhaps forever—of mothers from their young children. This already happens, of course, when mothers are deployed to support positions on the other side of the globe. But now the pain of separation will be amplified by the anxiety that comes with combat duty. It drives feminists crazy to suggest that sending a two-year-old's mother to war is worse than sending the child's father, but it is. The two-year-old knows this, and so does everyone else—even Barack Obama, Leon Panetta, and Martin Dempsey.

The decision to put women in combat bespeaks our deep confusion over manhood and womanhood. C. S. Lewis, who fought in the trenches of World War I, instructed children that "battles are ugly when women fight." People who know less about battle and less about man than Lewis did scoff at that unfashionable notion.

The pastor and theologian John Piper speaks for a remnant of American men for whom this issue is about more than career opportunities in Today's Army:

> If I were the last man on the planet to think so, I would
> want the honor of saying no woman should go before me

into combat to defend my country. A man who endorses women in combat is not pro-woman; he's a wimp. He should be ashamed. For most of history, in most cultures, he would have been utterly scorned as a coward to promote such an idea. Part of the meaning of manhood as God created us is the sense of responsibility for the safety and welfare of our women.[2]

President Obama is betting that ideas like this are already incomprehensible to most Americans. We shall soon see if he's right.

ACKNOWLEDGMENTS

t is impossible to thank all of those who have been so generous with their time. But I would like to mention: Tom Spence, my Regnery editor, for his encouragement, insights, and skillful assistance building the arguments; Elaine Donnelly, president of the Center for Military Readiness, for her leadership, friendship, and guidance on this tough issue; and Rear Admiral Hugh Scott, MC, U.S. Navy (Ret.), for his valuable help addressing the complex medical science and for his cultural insights and edits. Special thanks to the many Marine and Army warriors who unearthed painful combat memories to present the reader with an unvarnished battlefield perspective, to the anonymous patriots who were frank about their experiences but feared retribution if their names were exposed, to the women service members past and present who provided a critical perspective, and to my friends and family for putting up with this labor of love.

Above all, I acknowledge my heavenly Father, without whom this book could never have been written.

—Robert L. Maginnis, Woodbridge, Virginia

NOTES

Chapter 1

1. "Gen Robert H. Barrow on Women in Combat," *Leatherneck*, http://www. mca-marines.org/leatherneck/gen-robert-h-barrow-women-combat.
2. Matt Smith, "How America's Top General Came to Endorse Women in Combat," CNN, January 26, 2013, http://www.cnn.com/2013/01/24/us/ military-women.
3. "Gen. Dempsey's Interview with Ted Koppel for 'Rock Center,'" JCS Speech, January 24, 2013, http://www.jcs.mil/speech.aspx?id=1747.
4. Cheryl Pellerin, "Dempsey: Allowing Women in Combat Strengthens Joint Force," American Forces Press Service, January 24, 2013, http:// www.defense.gov/news/newsarticle.aspx?id=119100.
5. Lieutenant General Jerry Boykin (USA Ret.), interview by author, March 20, 2013.
6. Heather Mac Donald, interview by author, March 25, 2013.
7. Tom Bowman, "Air Force Chief Resigns over Disputes '97 Terrorist Bombing Was Source of Division," *Baltimore Sun*, July 29, 1997, http:// articles.baltimoresun.com/1997-07-29/news/1997210031_1_air-force-fogleman-force-chief.
8. General Carl Mundy (USMC Ret.), interview by author, March 30, 2013.

9.   "Generals v. Presidents," *The Week*, November 29, 2009, http://theweek. com/article/index/102748/generals-vs-presidents.

10.   *Wikipedia*, s.v. "John K. Singlaub" http://www.ask.com/wiki/John_K._ Singlaub?o=2801&qsrc=999.

11.   "Obama Relieves McChrystal of Command," NBC News, June 23, 2010, http://www.nbcnews.com/id/37866754/ns/us_news-military/.

12.   Retired Marine Corps general, interview by author, March 27, 2013.

13.   General Carl Mundy (USMC Ret.), interview by author, March 30, 2013.

14.   Ryan Riley et al., "2011 Center for Army Leadership Annual Survey of Army Leadership," The Center for Army Leadership, May 21, 2012, http:// usacac.army.mil/cac2/repository/CASAL_TechReport2012-2_Army Civilians.pdf.

15.   C. B. Johnson, "1992 Survey of Retired Flag and General Officers," Staff Summary Report, Presidential Commission on the Assignment of Women in the Armed Forces, October 1992.

16.   Note: this retired Marine general officer asked for anonymity.

17.   Major General Paul Vallely (USA Ret.), interview by author, March 2013.

18.   Robert L. Maginnis, "The Future of Women in the Army," *Military Review* 72, no. 7 (July 1992): 24.

19.   Jone Johnson Lewis, "Boudicca (Boadicea)," Women's History, About. com, http://womenshistory.about.com/od/boudicca/p/boudicca.htm.

20.   Invictus, "Zenobia, Queen of the East," All Empires, Online History Community, June 2006, http://www.allempires.com/article/index. php?q=zenobia.

21.   Maginnis, "The Future of Women in the Army," 24.

22.   Ibid.

23.   Ibid.

24.   Ibid.

25.   Ibid.

26.   Ibid.

27.   Ibid.

28.   Richard Bray and Chris MacLean, "Infantry Women," *Frontline Defence* 9, no. 5 (2012), http://www.frontline-canada.com/Defence/index_ archives.php?page=2026.

29. Barbara A. Goodno, "American Women in the Military," Command-information product of Army Public Affairs, November 11, 1993, http://gos.sbc.edu/g/goodno.html.

30. "Early Women Soldiers," Women in the U.S. Army, The Official Homepage of the U.S. Army, http://www.army.mil/women/history.html.

31. Jennie Wood, "A History of Women in the U.S. Army," Information Please Database, last modified 2007, http://www.infoplease.com/us/military/women-history.html#ixzz2PD5uPJYN.

32. "Highlights in the History of Military Women," Women in the Military Service for America Memorial Foundation, Inc., http://www.womens memorial.org/Press/highlights.html.

33. Goodno, "American Women in the Military."

34. "Early Women Soldiers," Women in the U.S. Army, The Official Homepage of the U.S. Army.

35. Jone Johnson Lewis, "Dr. Mary E. Walker," Women's History, About.com, http://womenshistory.about.com/od/physicians/a/Mary-Edwards-Walker.htm.

36. Mercedes Graf, *A Woman of Honor: Dr. Mary E. Walker and the Civil War* (Gettysburg, PA: Thomas Publications, 2001); as cited in "Dr. Mary Walker, Surgeon, Civil War," Women in Military Service for America Memorial Foundation Inc., http://www.womensmemorial.org/H&C/History/walker.html.

37. Ibid.

38. Mattie E. Treadwell, *The Women's Army Corps*, Office of the Chief of Military History: 1954. Reprinted 1995. Center of Military History, U.S. Army e-book, http://www.history.army.mil/books/ wwii/Wac/ch01.htm. See also "Early Women Soldiers."

39. Goodno, "American Women in the Military."

40. Ibid.

41. Ibid.

42. Ibid.

43. Ibid.

44. Ibid.

45. "History of Women in the Military," Defense Equal Opportunity Management Institute, https://www.deomi.org/EOAdvisorToolkit/documents/Sexism_History_Of_Women_In_The_Military.pdf.

46. "First Woman to Lead Troops in Battle Praised," *Kansas City Star*, January 4, 1990, A-1.

47. Ibid.

48. These numbers come from the Department of Defense's Defense Casualty Analysis System, accessed June 2013, https://www.dmdc.osd.mil/dcas/pages/report_oif_woundall.xhtml.

49. Establishment of Navy Nurse Corps, Pub. L. No. 115, 35 Stat. 146 (1908). Available online at http://www.fas.org/sgp/crs/natsec/R42075.pdf.

50. Treadwell, *The Women's Army Corps.*

51. *Conservapedia*, s.v. "American Expeditionary Forces," http://www.conservapedia.com/American_Expeditionary_Forces.

52. "Women Pilots of World War II," Women in the U.S. Army, The Official Homepage of the U.S. Army, http://www.army.mil/women/pilots.html.

53. Ibid.

54. "A New Era: Post World War II (1945-1950)," Women in the U.S. Army, The Official Homepage of the U.S. Army, http://www.army.mil/women/newera.html.

55. Ibid.

56. "Title 10: Armed Forces," 10 U.S.C. § 8549 (1956). Repealed 1991. Available online at http://codes.lp.findlaw .com/uscode/10/D/II/843/8549.

57. "History and Accomplishments," Defense Advisory Committee on Women in the Services, http://dacowits.defense.gov/History/.

58. Anne W. Chapman, *Mixed-Gender Basic Training: The U.S. Army Experience, 1973–2004* (Fort Monroe, VA: U.S. Army Training and Doctrine Command, 2008), 72f, http://www.tradoc.army.mil/historian/pubs/mixed%20gender.pdf.

59. David F. Burrelli, *Women in Combat: Issues for Congress*, Congressional Research Service, April 5, 2012, 3, http://www.fas.org/sgp/crs/natsec/R42075.pdf.

60. Carolyn Becraft, "Facts about Women in the Military, 1980-1990," Women's Research and Education Institute, Washington, D.C., June 1990, http://mith.umd.edu/WomensStudies/GovernmentPolitics/Military/factsheet.

61. "Title 10: Armed Forces," 10 U.S.C. § 8549 (1951). Repealed. Pub. L. 102-190, Div. A, Title V, §531(a)(1), Dec. 5, 1991, 105 Stat. 1365. Available online at http://www.gpo.gov/fdsys/granule/USCODE-2006-title10/USCODE-2006-title10-subtitleD-partII-chap843-sec8549/content-detail.html.

62. "Title 10: Armed Forces," 10 U.S.C. § 6015. Repealed. Pub. L. 103-160, Div. A, Title V, §541(a), Nov. 30, 1993, 107 Stat. 1659. Available online at http://www.gpo.gov/fdsys/granule/USCODE-2006-title10/USCODE-2006-title10-subtitleC-partII-chap555-sec6015/content-detail.html.

63. Lana Obradovic, "Being All She Can Be: Gender Integration in NATO Military Forces" (Ph.D. diss., City University of New York, 2010), http://udini.proquest.com/view/being-all-she-can-be-gender-goid:305193577/.

64. "Secretary of Defense Aspin Expects to Open New Opportunities for Women with new Direct Ground Combat Rule," Office of Assistant Secretary of Defense, news release, January 13, 1994.

65. Togo D. West Jr., "Recommendations for Opening Additional Positions for Women Under the DOD Assignment Policy–Decision Memorandum," Memorandum for the Secretary of Defense, June 1, 1994.

66. Ibid.

67. "Title 10: Armed Forces," 10 USC § 3062 (Policy; composition; organized peace establishment) (1956). Available online at http://www.law.cornell.edu/uscode/text/10/3062.

68. Testimony before the Presidential Commission on the Assignment of Women in the Armed Forces, June 8, 1992 (statement of Binford Peay, Lieutenant General, Army Deputy Chief of Staff for Operations and Plans).

69. Testimony before the Presidential Commission on the Assignment of Women in the Armed Forces, August 27, 1992 (statement of Raymond Smith, Jr., Rear Admiral, Commander, Naval Special Warfare Command); and Testimony before the Presidential Commission on the Assignment of Women in the Armed Forces, August 27, 1992, Dallas, TX. See "Alternative Views" of the *Report to the President*, 76–77.

70. Office of Assistant Secretary of Defense, "Secretary of Defense Perry Approves Plans to Open New Jobs for Women in the Military," news release, Washington, DC, July 29, 1994.

71. William J. Perry, letter to Honorable Sam Nunn, Chairman, Committee on Armed Services U.S. Senate, July 28, 1994.

72. Ibid.

73. Rostker v. Goldberg, 453 U.S. 57 (1981). Available online at http://law2. umkc.edu/faculty/projects/ftrials/conlaw/RostkervGoldberg.html.

74. Office of Assistant Secretary of Defense, "Secretary of Defense Perry Approves Plans to Open New Jobs for Women in the Military."

75. Ibid.

76. Ibid.

77. Ed O'Keefe, "Live Blog: 'Don't Ask, Don't Tell' Senate Hearing," *Washington Post*, February 2, 2010, http://voices.washingtonpost.com/federal-eye/2010/02/live_blog_dont_ask_dont_tell_s.html.

78. U.S. Department of Defense, Office of the Assistant Secretary of Defense (Public Affairs), "Press Briefing by Secretary Panetta and General Dempsey from the Pentagon," January 24, 2013, http://www.defense.gov/transcripts/transcript.aspx?transcriptid=5183.

79. David Horowitz, "The Feminist Assault on the Military," FrontPageMag.com, January 28, 2013, http://frontpagemag.com/2013/david-horowitz/the-feminist-assault-on-the-military/.

80. John Garvey, "Why We're Going Back to Single-Sex Dorms," *Wall Street Journal*, June 13, 2011, http://online.wsj.com/article/SB1000142405270 2304432304576369843592242356.html.

81. Ibid.

82. Horowitz, "The Feminist Assault on the Military."

83. "U.S. Military Casualties—Operation Iraqi Freedom (OIF) Wounded in Action—All," Defense Casualty Analysis System, Department of Defense https://www.dmdc.osd.mil/dcas/pages/report_oif_woundall.xhtml.

84. Hank Pellissier, "Women-Only Leadership: Would it Prevent War?," Institute for Emerging Ethics and Technologies, February 15, 2011, http://ieet.org/index.php/IEET/more/pellissier20110215.

85. Ibid.

86. Carey Roberts, "Men and Women Are Interchangeable? Silly Feminists," The New Media Alliance, August 17, 2006, http://www.getbig.com/boards/index.php?topic=89646.0;wap2.

87. Stephen Baskerville, "Sexual Politics" (unpublished manuscript, April 2013).

88.   "Allen West Slams Women in Combat: 'Another Misconceived Lib Vision of Fairness and Equality,'" Fox News, January 25, 2013, http://nation. foxnews.com/allen-west/2013/01/25/allen-west-slams-women-combat-another-misconceived-lib-vision-fairness-and-equality.

89.   Michael Moore, "In Defense of Zero Dark Thirty," Facebook, January 24, 2013, https://www.facebook.com/mmflint/posts/10151199285611857.

90.   *Aliens*, directed by James Cameron (Century City, CA: 20th Century Fox), 1986. Clip available online: http://www.youtube.com/watch?v=eycDq4 NW88o&feature=youtu.be.

91.   Marcia Rock, "Women in … Military Documentaries," NYWIFT-35, November 3, 2011, http://www.nywift.org/article.aspx?id=3429.

92.   David Martin, "Panetta to Lift Ban on Women in Combat," CBS News, January 23, 2013, http://www.cbsnews.com/2102-18563_162-57565479. html.

93.   David Martin, "Female Veteran Lauds New Policy on Women in Combat," CBS News, January 25, 2013, http://www.cbsnews.com/2102-18563_162-57565970.html.

94.   "Pentagon Lifts Ban on Women in Combat," NBC News, January 23, 2013, http://www.nbcnews.com/video/nightly-news/50567232# 50567232.

95.   Chris Lawrence, "Military to Open Combat Jobs to Women," with Barbara Starr, CNN, January 23, 2013, http://security.blogs.cnn. com/2013/01/23/military-to-open-combat-jobs-to-women/.

96.   Chelsea J. Carter and Steve Almasy, "Former Troops Say Time Has Come for Women in Combat Units," CNN, January 24, 2013, http://www.cnn. com/2013/01/23/us/women-combat-troop-reaction.

97.   Bill Briggs, "Female Vets Cheer New Era for Women in Combat: 'It's About Time!,'" NBC News, January 23, 2013, http://usnews.nbcnews. com/_news/2013/01/23/16665551-female-vets-cheer-new-era-for-women-in-combat-its-about-time?lite; "Defense Secretary Leon Panetta Lifts Armed Services Ban on Women in Combat," interview by James Kitfield, PBS *NewsHour*, January 23, 2013, http://www.pbs.org/newshour/ bb/military/jan-june13/womencombat_01-23.html?print.

98.   Justin Fishel and the Associated Press, "Military Leaders Lift Ban on Women in Combat Roles," Fox News, January 24, 2013, http://www. foxnews.com/politics/2013/01/24/panetta-opens-combat-roles-to-

women/print#ixzz2N5L48fr5; Barnini Chakraborty, "Decision to Allow Women in Combat Roles Raises Questions about Draft," Fox News, January 24, 2013, http://www.foxnews.com/politics/2013/01/24/decision-to-allow-women-in-combat-roles-raises-questions-about-draft/print#ixzz2N5MDzk2g.

99.   Editorial, "Women in the Battlefield," *New York Times*, January 24, 2013, http://www.nytimes.com/2013/01/25/opinion/women-in-the-battlefield.html?pagewanted=print.

100. Editorial Board, "Women in Combat," *Washington Post*, January 24, 2013, http://articles.washingtonpost.com/2013-01-24/opinions/36527548_1_thousands-of-front-line-jobs-female-service-members-martin-dempsey.

101. Doug Mataconis, "Poll: 75% of Americans Support Women in Combat," Outside the Beltway, February 7, 2013, http://www.outsidethebeltway.com/poll-75-of-americans-support-women-in-combat/.

102. Alyssa Brown, "Americans Favor Allowing Women in Combat," Gallup, January 25, 2013, http://www.gallup.com/poll/160124/americans-favor-allowing-women-combat.aspx?version=print.

103. "Statement by the President on the Opening of Combat Units to Women," White House Office of the Press Secretary, news release, January 24, 2013, http://www.whitehouse.gov/the-press-office/2013/01/24/statement-president-opening-combat-units-women.

104. Retired Marine Corps general, interview by author, March 30, 2013.

105. Reid J. Epstein, "No Culture War over Women in Combat," *Politico*, January 23, 2013, http://dyn.politico.com/printstory.cfm?uuid=D46773CE-53E0-4853-B053-F8E4CEA07793.

106. Ibid.

107. Pellerin, "Dempsey: Allowing Women in Combat Strengthens Joint Force."

108. Epstein, "No Culture War over Women in Combat."

109. Ibid.

110. Brad J. Bushman and Craig A. Anderson, "Comfortably Numb: Desensitizing Effects of Violent Media on Helping Others," *Psychological Science* 20, no. 3 (2009): 277.

111. Neil M. Malamuth and James V.P. Check, "The Effects of Mass Media Exposure on Acceptance of Violence," *Journal of Research in Personality* 15, no. 4 (1981): 436.

112. "72 Percent of Black Kids Raised by Single Parent, 25% Overall in U.S.," NewsOne, April 27, 2011, http://newsone.com/1195075/children-single-parents-u-s-american/.

113. "Violence Against Women in the United States: Statistics," National Organization for Women, http://www.now.org/issues/violence/stats.html.

114. "Fatherless Homes Breed Violence," *Getting Men Involved: The Newsletter of the Bay Area Male Involvement Network*, FatherMag.com, spring 1997, http://www.fathermag.com/news/2778-stats.shtml.

115. Ibid.

116. Skip Burzumato, "Delayed Marriage on Rise: Good for College Educated, Tough on Middle America," National Marriage Project, March 15, 2013, http://nationalmarriageproject.org/wp-content/uploads/2013/03/KnotYetPressRelease-Final.pdf.

Chapter 2

1. Active-duty infantry Army major, interview by author, April 9, 2013.

2. A representative statement of this argument is Megan H. MacKenzie, "Overdue: Why It's Time to End the U.S. Military's Female Combat Ban," Daily Beast, October 26, 2012, http://www.thedailybeast.com/articles/2012/10/26/overdue-why-it-s-time-to-end-the-u-s-military-s-female-combat-ban.html.

3. Exec. Order No. 9,981, 3 C.F.R. (1943–48). Available at http://www.ourdocuments.gov/doc.php?flash=true&doc=84&page=transcript.

4. William P. Snyder and Kenneth L. Nyberg, "Gays and the Military: An Emerging Policy Issue," policy paper, *Journal of Political and Military Sociology* 8, no. 1 (Spring 1980): 74.

5. "Policy Concerning Homosexuality in the Armed Forces," 10 USC § 654 (2010). Available at http://www.gpo.gov/fdsys/pkg/USCODE-2010-title10/pdf/USCODE-2010-title10-subtitleA-partII-chap37-sec654.pdf.

6. Active-duty combat arms Army officer, interview by author, March 25, 2013.

7. "Why Women Leave the Military," militarywomen.org, last updated June 2004, http://www.militarywoman.org/whyleave.htm.

8. Testimony before the Presidential Commission on the Assignment of Women in the Armed Forces, June 26, 1992, Washington, D.C. (statement

of John W. Ripley), http://www.tfp.org/tfp-home/fighting-for-our-culture/testimony-of-col-john-w-ripley-to-the-presidential-commission-on-the-assignment-of-women-in-the-armed-forces.html.

9. Standards of Medical Fitness, Army Regulation 40-501 (Washington, D.C.: Department of the Army, December 14, 2007), http://www.apd.army.mil/pdffiles/r40_501.pdf.

10. Former U.S. Air Force commander, interview by author, March 21, 2013.

11. Desiree Maxwell (U.S. Army), interview by author, February 18, 2013.

12. Richard Sisk, "Panetta: Women in Combat Strengthens US Military," Military.com, January 24, 2013, http://www.military.com/daily-news/2013/01/24/panetta-women-in-combat-strengthens-us-military.html.

Chapter 3

1. Jane Blair, "Five Myths about Women in Combat," *Washington Post*, May 27, 2011, http://articles.washingtonpost.com/2011-05-27/opinions/35232036_1_combat-units-gender-integration-military-women.

2. Michael Cohen, "Counterinsurgency Trap: Future of the US Military," Atlantic Council, March 23, 2009, http://www.acus.org/new_atlanticist/counterinsurgency-trap-future-us-military.

3. Joint Chiefs of Staff, *Joint Operations: Joint Publication 3-0*, U.S. Department of Defense, August 11, 2011, V-1, http://www.dtic.mil/doctrine/new_pubs/jp3_0.pdf.

4. Gian P. Gentile, "Is the U.S. Army Ready for Conventional War?," *Christian Science Monitor*, September 2, 2008, http://www.csmonitor.com/Commentary/Opinion/2008/0902/p09s01-coop.html?nav=topic-tag_topic_page-storyList.

5. Retired combat arms officer who participated in a U.S. Army study with the IDF after the 2006 war with Hezbollah, interview by author.

6. Ray Odierno, "The Force of Tomorrow," *Foreign Policy*, February 4, 2013, http://www.foreignpolicy.com/articles/2013/02/04/the_force_of_tomorrow.

7. *National Security Strategy for the United States of America*, White House, (Washington, D.C.: May 2010), http://www.whitehouse.gov/sites/default/files/rss_viewer/national_security_strategy.pdf.

8. *Sustaining U.S. Global Leadership: Priorities for 21st Century Defense*, U.S. Department of Defense, January 2013, http://www.defense.gov/news/Defense_Strategic_Guidance.pdf.

9. *The National Military Strategy of the United States of America*, U.S. Department of Defense, 2011, http://www.jcs.mil//content/files/2011-02/020811084800_2011_NMS_-_08_FEB_2011.pdf.

10. "Broad Support for Combat Roles for Women," Pew Research Center for the People and the Press, Washington, D.C., January 29, 2013, http://www.people-press.org/2013/01/29/broad-support-for-combat-roles-for-women/.

11. "Americans Back Women In Combat 3-1," Quinnipiac University, February 7, 2013, http://www.quinnipiac.edu/institutes-centers/polling-institute/national/release-detail/?ReleaseID=1847.

12. Elaine Donnelly, "Constructing the Co-Ed Military," *Duke Journal of Gender Law & Policy* 14, no. 2 (2007): 854–55, http://scholarship.law.duke.edu/cgi/viewcontent.cgi?article=1130&context=djglp.

13. Adam Kredo, "Women in Combat Hurt Retention, Marine Study Suggests," Washington Free Beacon, February 14, 2013, http://freebeacon.com/wpcontent/uploads/2013/02/CNA-WISRR-Survey-ExSum-without-cover.pdf.

14. Female Marine officer, interview by author, April 8, 2013.

15. Ibid.

16. Kristina Wong, "Few Female Marines Step Forward for Infantry," *Washington Times*, November 25, 2012, http://www.washingtontimes.com/news/2012/nov/25/few-female-marines-step-forward-for-infantry/#ixzz2MTUKbxj4.

17. Pauline Jelinek, "Women in Military No Rush to Join Infantry," Huffington Post, April 1, 2013, http://www.huffingtonpost.com/2013/01/05/women-in-military_n_2415748.html.

18. Ibid.

19. Eileen Patten and Kim Parker, "Women in the U.S. Military: Growing Share, Distinctive Profiles," Pew Research, December 22, 2011, http://www.pewsocialtrends.org/2011/12/22/women-in-the-u-s-military-growing-share-distinctive-profile/.

20.   Matt Cover, "Unemployment Rises for Women, African Americans in December," CNS News, January 4, 2013, http://cnsnews.com/news/article/unemployment-rises-women-african-americans-december.

21.   Presidential Commission on the Assignment of Women in the Armed Forces, *Report to the President*, "Section II: Alternative Views," 50.

22.   Matthew D. Laplante, "Military Recruiters Tailor Message for Women, but Numbers Still Fall," *Salt Lake Tribune*, July 28, 2008, http://www.sltrib.com/news/ci_10009008.

23.   Richard Buddin, "Success of First-Term Soldiers," RAND Monograph, document number MG-262-A, 2005, http://www.rand.org/pubs/monographs/MG262.html.

24.   Sara Wood, "Woman Soldier Receives Silver Star for Valor in Iraq," American Forces Press Service, June 16, 2005, http://www.defense.gov/news/newsarticle.aspx?id=16391.

25.   Micah E. Clare, "Face of Defense: Woman Soldier Receives Silver Star," March 24, 2008, American Forces Press Service, http://www.defense.gov/news/newsarticle.aspx?id=49348.

26.   Alexandra Zavis, "New U.S. Combat Policy Affirms Role Women Already Play," *Los Angeles Times*, February 18, 2013, http://articles.latimes.com/2013/feb/18/world/la-fg-us-women-combat-20130219.

27.   Ibid.

28.   Ibid.

29.   Active-duty combat arms officer, interview by author, March 25, 2013.

30.   NPRST Survey and NNS130104-05: Coalition of Sailors Against Destructive Decisions (CSADD), 1/4/2013.

31.   "Sex Runs Wild in U.S. Military," Newsmax.com, October 12, 2005, http://archive.newsmax.com/archives/ic/2005/10/12/171046.shtml.

32.   Lolita C. Baldor, "Sex Is Major Reason Military Commanders Are Fired," Associated Press, January 21, 2013, http://news.yahoo.com/sex-major-reason-military-commanders-fired-123720150.html.

33.   Jennifer Steinhauer, "Sexual Assaults in Military Raise Alarm in Washington," *New York Times*, May 7, 2013, http://www.nytimes.com/2013/05/08/us/politics/pentagon-study-sees-sharp-rise-in-sexual-assaults.html?pagewanted=all&_r=2&.

34.   "2012 Workplace and Gender Relations Survey of Active Duty Members," Human Resources Strategic Assessment Program, March 15, 2013, http://

www.sapr.mil/media/pdf/research/2012_Workplace_and_Gender_Relations_Survey_of_Active_Duty_Members-Survey_Note_and_Briefing.pdf.

35. Lindsay L. Rodman, "The Pentagon's Bad Math on Sexual Assault," May 19, 2013, *Wall Street Journal*, http://online.wsj.com/article/SB10001424127887323582904578484941173658754.html.

36. *Annual Report on Sexual Harassment and Violence at the Military Service Academies: Academic Year 2011-2012*, Department of Defense, December 2012, http://www.sapr.mil/media/pdf/reports/FINAL_APY_11-12_MSA_Report.pdf.

37. "Dempsey: Combat Ban Contributed to Sexual Assault Problem," Washington Free Beacon, January 24, 2013, http://freebeacon.com/dempsey-combat-ban-contributed-to-sexual-assault-problem/.

38. Heather Mac Donald, interview by author, March 25, 2013.

39. "Sexual Assaults and Cultural Confusion in the Military's New Gender Order," June 2, 2013, Center for Millitary Readiness, http://www.cmrlink.org/content/home/37028/sexual_assaults_and_cultural_confusion_in_the_military_s_new_gender_order.

40. Military Leadership Diversity Commission, *From Representation to Inclusion: Diversity Leadership for the 21st-Century* (Arlington, VA: March 15, 2011), 47, https://www.hsdl.org/?abstract&did=11390.

41. Joseph Knapik and Katy Reynolds, "Load Carriage in Military Operations," Borden Institute Walter Reed Army Medical Center, U.S. Army Medical Department Center & School (Aberdeen Proving Ground, MD), 11, http://www.scribd.com/doc/124549874/Soldier-s-Load-Carriage.

42. Knapik and Reynolds, "Load Carriage in Military Operations."

43. Arthur C. Guyton and John Edward Hall, *Textbook of Medical Physiology*, 11th ed. (New York: Elsevier Saunders, 2006) 80:1003.

44. Rear Admiral Hugh Scott, interview by author.

45. Presidential Commission on the Assignment of Women in the Armed Forces, *Report to the President*, (Washington, D.C.: 1992).

46. The Presidential Commission on the Assignment of Women in the Armed Forces, *Report to the President*.

47. Knapik and Reynolds "Load Carriage in Military Operations," 31.

48. Michael Giladi et al., "External Rotation of the Hip: A Predictor of Risk for Stress Fractures," *Clinical Orthopaedics and Related Research*, 216

(1987): 131–34; and Michael Giladi et al., "Stress Fractures: Identifiable Risk Factors," *American Journal of Sports Medicine* 19 (1991): 647–52.

49. P. F. Hill et al., "Stress Fracture of the Pubic Ramus in Female Recruits," *Journal of Bone Joint Surgery* 78 (1996): 383–86, http://www.bjj.bone andjoint.org.uk/content/78-B/3/383.full.pdf.

50. D. W. Trone et al., "Negative First-Term Outcomes Associated with Lower Extremity Injury during Recruit Training among Female Marine Corps Graduates," *Military Medicine* 172, 1:83 (2007), http://www.dtic.mil/dtic/tr/fulltext/u2/a496952.pdf.

51. Philip J. Belmont Jr. et al., "Disease and Nonbattle Injuries Sustained by a U.S. Army Brigade Combat Team During Operation Iraqi Freedom," *Military Medicine* 7:469 (2010): 175, http://www.dtic.mil/cgi-bin/GetTRDoc?AD=ADA535873.

52. Larry Tye, "Exercise Your Judgment," *Boston Globe*, March 7, 1995, 63.

53. Ira Dreybuss. "Too Much Exercise, Too Little Eating May Hurt Reproductive Ability," Associated Press, November 5, 1995.

54. Force System Directorate, "Valuation of the Military Entrance Physical Strength Capacity Test (E-MEPSCAT)" (Bethesda, MD: US Army Concepts Analysis Agency, October 1985), http://www.dtic.mil/docs/citations/ADA166582.

55. "Physically Demanding Jobs: Services Have Little Data on Ability of Personnel to Perform," United States General Accounting Office, GAO/NSIAD-96-169, July 1996, http://www.gao.gov/assets/230/222816.pdf.

56. Everett Harman et al., *Effects of a Specifically Designed Physical Conditioning Program on the Load Carriage and Lifting Performance of Female Soldiers*, preliminary report, U.S. Army Medical Research and Material Command (Fort Detrick, MD: U.S. Army Research Institute of Environmental Medicine, January 26, 1996).

57. Rowan Scarborough, "Why Can't a Woman Be More like a Man?" *Washington Times*, February 14, 1995, A-1.

58. Robin Estrin, "Study Shows Most Women Can Do Heavy Army Tasks," *Philadelphia Inquirer*, January 30, 1996.

59. Soraya S. Nelson, "Training Program Toughens Women to Handle Army's Men-Only Jobs," *Army Times*, February 12, 1996, 3.

60. Hannah Wahlig, "How Much More Muscle Mass Does a Male Have Than a Female?," *Healthy Living*, http://healthyliving.azcentral.com/much-muscle-mass-male-female-1709.html.

61. April Holladay, "Women's Sizes by Country: The Age Group with the Best Memory," *USA Today*, December 12, 2006, http://usatoday30.usa-today.com/tech/columnist /aprilholladay/2006-12-04-size-age_x.htm.

62. The Presidential Commission on the Assignment of Women in the Armed Forces, *Report to the President*.

63. William J. Gregor, "Why Can't Anything Be Done? Measuring Physical Readiness of Women for Military Occupations," paper presented at the 2011 International Biennial Conference of the Inter-University Seminar on Armed Forces and Society, October 21–23, 2011, http://www.thelizlibrary.org/undelete/1110-GregorW.pdf.

64. E. J. Marcinik et al., "Gender Differences in Emergency Shipboard Damage Control Task Performance: Human Factors Solutions," Naval Medical Research Institute, Bethesda, MD, September 1, 1995, http://www.dtic.mil/cgibin/GetTRDoc?Location=U2&doc=GetTRDoc.pdf&AD=ADA299996.

65. Kirsten Scharnberg, "A Mile in Their ... : A Woman Goes to War in a Man's World," *Chicago Tribune*, May 18, 2003, http://articles.chicagotribune.com/2003-0518/news/0305180483_1_shower-chemical-suits-humvee.

66. Anna Mulrine, "8 Other Nations That Send Women to Combat," *National Geographic*, January 24, 2013, http://news.nationalgeographic.com/news/2013/13/130125-women-combat-world-australia-israel-canada-norway/.

67. Ibid.

68. Jonathan Pearlman, "Aussie Women Can Try Out Military Life," *Singapore Straits Times*, September 8, 2012, 28.

69. Hanna Helene Syse, senior advisor, Norweigan Ministry of Defense, email message to author, March 12, 2013.

70. Ibid.

71. Mulrine, "8 Other Nations That Send Women to Combat."

72. Ibid.

73. "Normalität: Frauen in der Bundeswehr," Bundeswehr, October 1, 2012, http://www.bundeswehr.de/portal/a/bwde/!ut/p/c4/DcLBDYAgDADAWVyg_

ftzC-VDihTSQKqpRdbX3GHAn9IrlVwupY47HqesaUKameFxY_
FmxMUZqg3NnSorFKPBGkVjZotp4t225QMCZ4Gb/.

74. Stefan Theil, "German Soldiers Can't Shoot," Daily Beast, June 26, 2011,
http://www.thedailybeast.com/articles/2011/06/26/german-soldiers-can-
t-shoot.html.

75. Nancy Loring Goldman, *The Utilization of Women in Combat: An His-
torical and Social Analysis of Twentieth-Century Wartime and Peacetime
Experience*, U.S. Army Research Institute for the Behavioral and Social
Sciences, Technical Report 563, January 1982, 2.

76. Goldman, *The Utilization of Women in Combat*, 3.

77. Ibid.

78. "Women in the Russian Armed Forces: The Secret Weapon?," The Dutch
Eye, February 25, 2011, http://www.thedutcheye.com/interests/history/
women-in-the-russian-armed-forces-the-secret-weapon-.html.

79. "Russian Military Cuts Female Staff by Two-Thirds," Mangalore Media
Company, March 6, 2013, http://www.mangalorean.com/news.php?ne
wstype=local&newsid=382070#.

80. Ibid.

81. "Women Should Bring Up Children: Russia's Only Female General,"
Mangalore Media Company, March 7, 2013, http://www.mangalorean.
com/news.php?newstype=local&newsid=382400#.

82. Paul D. Shinkman, "Former IDF Chief: Women Will 'Surprise' the U.S.
Military," *U.S. News & World Report*, January 25, 2013, http://www.
usnews.com/news/articles/2013/01/25/former-idf-chief-women-will-
surprise-the-us-military_print.html.

83. Fay Voshell and Jacqueline Hamilton, "'Equality' on the Battlefield,"
American Thinker, February 1, 2013, http://www.americanthinker.
com/2013/02/equality_on_the_battlefield.html.

84. Goldman, *The Utilization of Women in Combat*, 9.

85. U.S. Army officer who attended the Israeli Armored Corps course, interview by author, March 9, 2013.

86. "Integration of Women in the IDF," *Jewish Daily News*, March 9, 2009,
http://groups.yahoo.com/group/Jewish_Daily_News/message/6748.

87. Julie Sergel, "Redefining the Israeli Defense Force's Feminine Side," *Jewish Post*, http://www.jewishpost.com/news/Redefining-the-Israeli-
Defense-Forces-Feminine-side.html.

88. Gil Ronen, "General Who Supported Women in Combat Says: 'No More!'" *Arutz Sheva 7*, July 23, 2011, http://www.israelnationalnews.com/News/News.aspx/146001.

89. "Canadian Millitary Strength," Global Fire Power, October 29, 2012, http://www.globalfirepower.com/country-military-strength-detail.asp?country_id=Canada.

90. Stewart Bell, "Women Filled 8.3 Percent of Canada's Combat Positions in Afghanistan: Study," *National Post*, November 11, 2001, http://news.nationalpost.com/2011/10/25/women-filled-8-3-of-canadas-combat-positions-in-afghanistan-study/.

91. Alistair MacDonald, "Canada Offers Lessons on Women in Combat," *Wall Street Journal*, January 24, 2013, http://online.wsj.com/article/SB10001424127887323539804578262002928698208.html.

92. Valerie Fortney, *Sunray: The Death and Life of Captain Nichola Goddard* (Toronto: Key Porter Books, 2010); quoted in Sandra, "Presentation by Tamara Lorincz, 'Canada's Invisible War: Exposing Violence against Women in the Canadian Military,'" *Canadian Voice of Women for Peace* (blog), March 27, 2013, http://vowpeace.org/presentation-by-tamara-lorincz-canadas-invisible-war-exposing-violence-against-women-in-the-canadian-military/.

93. MacDonald, "Canada Offers Lessons on Women in Combat."

Chapter 4

1. *Wikipedia*, s.v. "Battlestar Galactica," last modified May 15, 2013, http://en.wikipedia.org/wiki/Battlestar_Galactica.

2. Ellen Willis, "Radical Feminism and Feminist Radicalism," in *No More Nice Girls: Countercultural Essays* (Middletown, CT: Wesleyan University Press, 1992), 117–50.

3. George Neumayr, *The American Spectator*, May 1, 2005.

4. Martin van Creveld, *Men, Women, and War* (London: Cassell, 2001), 43, 193.

5. "AF to Open Remaining Combat Positions to Women," Official Web Site of the U.S. Air Force, January 24, 2013, http://www.af.mil/news/story.asp?id=123333783.

6.   Donna Mills, "Commission to Recommend Lifting Ban on Women in Combat," *American Forces Press Service*, January 18, 2011, http://www.defense.gov/News/NewsArticle.aspx?ID=62483.

7.   Kingsley R. Browne, "The Report of the Military Leadership Diversity Commission: An Inadequate Basis for Lifting the Exclusion of Women from Direct Ground Combat," Wayne State University Law School Research Paper, No. 2012–13, April 2012, http://www.ssrn.com/link/Wayne-State-U-LEG.html.

8.   Ibid.

9.   Elaine Donnelly, "Seven Reasons Why Women-in-Combat Diversity Will Degrade Tough Training Standards," Center for Military Readiness, January 29, 2013, http://www.cmrlink.org/content/home/36488/seven_reasons_why_women_in_combat_diversity_will_degrade_tough_training_standards.

10.   Ibid.

11.   Ibid.

12.   Ibid.

13.   Mindy Belz, "Command Performance," *World*, August 12–19, 1995, 15.

14.   Kristin Moorefield, "Online Update," *American Spectator*, October 28–November 3, 1997.

15.   Moorefield, "Online Update."

16.   Presidential Commission on the Assignment of Women to the Armed Forces, *Report to the President*, C-78.

17.   Helen Rogan, *Mixed Company: Women in the Modern Army* (New York: Putnam, 1981), 104.

18.   "Army Historical Summary, FY 1982," *Army Times*, May 17, 1982, cited in Anne W. Chapman, *Mixed-Gender Basic Training: The U.S. Army Experience, 1973–2004* (Fort Monroe, VA: U.S. Army Training and Doctrine Command, 2008), 61, http://www.tradoc.army.mil/historian/pubs/mixed%20gender.pdf.

19.   Federal Advisory Committee on Gender-Integrated Training and Related Issues, *Report of the Federal Advisory Committee on Gender-Integrated Training and Related Issues to the Secretary of Defense* (December 16, 1997), cited in Elaine Donnelly, "Constructing the Co-Ed Military," *Duke Journal of Gender Law & Policy*, 14 (May 2007): 884, http://scholarship.law.duke.edu/cgi/viewcontent.cgi?article=1130&context=djglp.

20. Congressional Commission on Military Training and Gender-Related Issues, supra note 290, at 11 (alteration added), cited in Donnelly, "Constructing the Co-Ed Military."

21. See generally *Senior Review Panel Report on Sexual Harassment*, July 1997; and *Report of the Federal Advisory Committee on Gender-Integrated Training and Related Issues to the Secretary of Defense: Congressional Commission on Military Training and Gender-Related Issues* (July 1999), as cited in Donnelly, "Constructing the Co-Ed Military."

22. Chapman, *Mixed-Gender Basic Training*, 66.

23. Ibid.

24. Office of Assistant Secretary of Defense (Public Affairs), "Secretary of Defense Aspin Expects to Open New Opportunities for Women with New Direct Ground Combat Rule," press release, January 13, 1994.

25. Memorandum by Togo D. West Jr. to the under secretary of defense (personnel and readiness), "Increasing Opportunities for Women in the Army," July 27, 1994.

26. *Gender Integration in Basic Training: The Services Are Using a Variety of Approaches, Before Senate Subcommittee on Personnel, Committee on Armed Services*, 105th Cong. (1997) (Statement for the Record of Mark E. Gebicke). Available online at http://www.dtic.mil/cgi-bin/GetTRDoc?AD=ADA327323.

27. "Candidate Fitness Assessment Instructions," United States Military Academy Admissions, http://www.westpoint.edu/admissions/Shared%20Documents/CFA_Instructions.pdf.

28. Kelly Schloesser, "The First Women of West Point," Official Homepage of the United States Army, October 27, 2010, http://www.army.mil/article/47238/the-first-women-of-west-point/.

29. Ibid.

30. Ibid.

31. *Military Academy: Gender and Racial Disparities*, report to congressional requesters, U.S. General Accounting Office, GAO/NSIAD-94-95, March 1994, http://www.gao.gov/assets/160/154159.pdf.

32. John Nettles, "USMC Women in the Service Restrictions Review WISRR," brief to DACOWITS, September 22, 2011, 10, http://dacowits.defense.gov/Reports/2011/Documents/DACOWITS%20September%20

2011%20Committee%20Meeting/16%20USMC%20WISR%20 DACOWITS%20Brief.pdf.

33. Donnelly, "Seven Reasons Why Women-in-Combat Diversity Will Degrade Tough Training Standards."

34. James Dao, "Women (and Men) Face Big Hurdles in Training for Marine Infantry Units," *New York Times*, March 29, 2013, http://www.nytimes. com/2013/03/30/us/marines-test-women-for-infantry-roles.html.

35. Laura Boussy, "No Women in Ground Combat," *U.S. Naval Institute Proceedings* 122 (November 1996): 43; and Molly Moore, "Canada Puts Women on Front Line," *Los Angeles Times*, November 23, 1989.

36. Boussy, "No Women in Ground Combat," 43.

37. Patrick Brady, "Warriors with Wombs: Women in Foxholes," WND.com, February 18, 2013, http://www.wnd.com/2013/02/women-in-foxholes/.

38. Ibid.

39. Katie Petronio, "Get Over It! We Are Not All Created Equal," *Marine Corps Gazette*, July 2012, https://www.mca-marines.org/gazette/article/ get-over-it-we-are-not-all-created-equal.

40. David A. Patten, "Ex-SEAL Zinke: 'Nearly Certain' Women in Combat Will Cost Lives," Newsmax.com, January 25, 2013, http://www.newsmax. com/Headline/zinke-women-combat-panetta/2013/01/23/id/472695.

41. James R. Webb, "Women in the Infantry?," www.jameswebb.com, February 11, 2013, http://www.jamesrwebb.com/2013/02/women-in-infantry. html.

42. Webb, "Women in the Infantry?"

43. Ibid.

44. Ibid.

45. "FM 7-22: Army Physical Readiness Training," Department of the Army, October 2012, A-1, http://armypubs.army.mil/doctrine/DR_pubs/dr_a/ pdf/fm7_22.pdf.

46. Cheryl Pellerin, "Dempsey: Allowing Women in Combat Strengthens Joint Force," American Forces Press Service, January 24, 2013, http:// www.defense.gov/news/newsarticle.aspx?id=119100.

47. Rick Maze, "Hunter Fears Lax Standards for Women in Combat," *Marine Times*, March 8, 2013, http://www.marinecorpstimes.com/news/2013/03/ military-lawmaker-hunter-fears-lax-standards-for-women-in-combat- 030813w/.

48. John Leo, "A for Effort, Or for Showing Up," *U.S. News and World Report*, October 10, 1993, http://www.usnews.com/usnews/opinion/articles/931018/archive_015927.htm.

49. "Dempsey Considers Lowering Standards for Women in Combat," *This Ain't Hell* (blog), January 26, 2013, http://thisainthell.us/blog/?p=33817.

50. Pellerin, "Dempsey: Allowing Women in Combat Strengthens Joint Force."

51. "How to Prepare: Initial Strength Test," U.S. Marine Corps, http://www.marines.com/becoming-a-marine/how-to-prepare.

52. "Job Opportunities for Women in the Military: Progress and Problems," GAO Report FPCD-76-26, May 1976, 13.

53. Chapman, *Mixed-Gender Basic Training*, 66.

54. Kathryn M. Hodges, "Women in the Army Policy Review: An Exclusive Interview with Lt Gen Maxwell R. Thurman, Vice Chief of Staff of the Army," *Minerva*, June 22, 1983, 86–89.

55. *Army Budget Overview: Hearing before the Senate Appropriations Committee, Subcommittee on Defense*, 98th Cong., 2d sess. (1983) (exchange between Sen William Proxmire and Gen Meyer).

56. Interview by author's wife, March 19, 2013.

57. Michael Shaffstall, interview by author, February 20, 2013.

58. W. K. Prusaczyk et al., "Physical Demands of U.S. Navy Sea-Air-Land (SEAL) Operations," Naval Health Research Center, Report No. 95-24, October 1998, San Diego, CA.

59. Active-duty combat Army officer, interview by author, March 25, 2013.

60. Petronio, "Get Over it! We Are Not All Created Equal."

61. Author interview with Admiral Scott, who provided the following sources: K. A. Beals and M. M. Manore, "Disorders of the Female Athlete Triad among Collegiate Athletes," *International Journal of Sport Nutrition and Exercise Metabolism* 12, no. 3 (2002), 281–93, http://www.ncbi.nlm.nih.gov/pubmed/12432173; C. L. Otis, B. Drinkwater, and M. Johnson, "American College of Sports Medicine Position Stand: The Female Athlete Triad," *Medicine and Science in Sports Exercise* 29, no. 5 (1997), i–ix; J. Sundgot-Borgen and M. K. Torstveit, "Prevalence of Eating Disorders in Elite Athletes Is Higher Than in the General Population," *Clinical Journal of Sport Medicine* 14, no. 1 (2003), 25–32; M. Yannakoulia, M. Sitara, and A. L. Matalas, "Reported Eating Behaviour and Attitudes

Improvement after a Nutrition Intervention Program in a Group of Young Female Dancers," *International Journal of Sport Nutrition and Exercise Metabolism* 12, no. 1 (2002), 24–32; K. K. Miller, "Mechanisms by Which Nutritional Disorders Cause Reduced Bone Mass in Adults," *Journal of Women's Health* 12, no. 2 (2003), 145–50.

62. D. E. Gwinn et al., "The Relative Incidence of Anterior Cruciate Ligament Injury in Men and Women at the United States Naval Academy," *American Journal of Sports Medicine* 28, no. 1 (2000): 98–102, http://www.ncbi.nlm.nih.gov/pubmed/10653551.

63. Elaine Donnelly, "Diversity for Women in Land Combat," Center for Military Readiness, http://www.cmrlink.org/content/essential-resources/34584/diversity_for_women_in_land_combat.

64. Michael Evans, "Women Pay Painful Price for Equal Military Training," *Times* (London), March 22, 2005.

65. Ian M. M. Gemmell, "Injuries among Female Army Recruits: A Conflict of Legislation," *Journal of Royal Society Medicine* 95, no. 1 (2002): 23–27, http://www.ncbi.nlm.nih.gov/pmc/articles/PMC1279143/.

66. Elaine Donnelly, "British Study Finds Soldiers 'Too Weak' for Land Combat," Center for Military Readiness, January 14, 2002, http://cmrlink.org/content/women-in-combat/page-2/34433/british_study_finds_female_soldiers_too_weak_for_landcombat?year=2002.

67. "Report on the Review of the Exclusion of Women from Ground Close-Combat Roles," Center for Military Readiness, November 2010, http://cmrlink.org/data/sites/85/CMRDocuments/RptOnReviewOfExclusOfWomenFromGrndClose-CombatRoles-Nov2010.pdf.

68. Rowan Scarborough, "Army May Train Women for Rigor of Front Lines," *Washington Times*, July 30, 2012, http://www.washingtontimes.com/news/2012/jul/30/army-may-train-women-for-rigor-of-front-lines/?page=all.

69. "General Order Number 1: Prohibited Activities for Multi-National Division-North," 3rd Infantry Division, Task Force Marne, Iraq, November 4, 2009, http://documents.nytimes.com/general-order-no-1-prohibited-activities-for-soldiers.

70. Andrew Tilghman, "Report Outlines Pregnancy Policy Concerns," *Navy Times*, October 17, 2009, http://www.navytimes.com/article/20091017/NEWS/910170304/Report-outlines-pregnancy-policy-concerns.

71. Presidential Commission on the Assignment of Women in the Armed Forces, *Report to the President*, "Section II: Alternative Views," 57.

72. Ibid., 58.

73. Master Sergeant Sally Kennedy, telephone interview with author, February 23, 2013.

74. Cristina Silva, "Navy Seeks to Combat Unplanned Pregnancies," *Stars and Stripes*, January 7, 2013.

75. *Military Personnel: DOD Has Taken Steps to Meet the Health Needs of Deployed Servicewomen, but Actions Are Needed to Enhance Care for Sexual Assault Victims*, U.S. Government Accountability Office, report to congressional addressees, GAO-13-182, January 29, 2013, 10, http://www.gao.gov/assets/660/651624.pdf.

76. Ibid., 11.

77. *Sustaining Female Soldiers' Health Performance During Deployment: Guidance for Small Unit Leaders*, U.S. Army Medical Research & Material Command, U.S. Army Research Institute of Environmental Medicine, July 1996.

78. Viktor Frankel and Margareta Nordin, *Basic Biomechanics of the Skeletal System* (Philadelphia: Lea & Febiger, 1980).

79. Beth L. English, "Most Women Realize Combat Is a Man's Arena," *Navy Times*, February 13, 1995, 29.

80. Diane W. Wardell and Barbara Czerwinski, "A Military Challenge to Managing Feminine and Personal Hygiene," *Journal of the American Academy of Nurse Practitioners* 13, no. 4 (2001).

81. Hugh Mulligan and Gary Davis, "Collaborative Research and Support of Fitzsimmons Army Medical Center and Research Program Projects: Evaluation of the Performance Impact and Treatment of Exercise Induced Urinary Incontinence among Female Soldiers," http://www.stormingmedia.us/95/9559/A955923.html.

82. Wardell and Czerwinski, "A Military Challenge to Managing Feminine and Personal Hygiene."

83. Ibid.

84. Ibid.

85. Gregg Zoroya, "Female Soldiers' Suicide Rate Triples When at War," *USA Today*, March 18, 2011, http://usatoday30.usatoday.com/printedition/news/20110318/1asuicides18_st.art.htm.

86.   Julia Savacool, "Military Women: Home Safe but Not Sound," *Women's Health*, http://www.womenshealthmag.com/life/military-families.

87.   Ibid.

88.   Mona P. Ternus, "Military Women's Perceptions of the Effect of Deployment on their Role as Mothers and on Adolescents' Health," study presented at 12th Annual Force Health Protection Conference, Albuquerque, NM, 2009.

89.   Anita Chandra et al., "Children on the Homefront: The Experience of Children from Military Families," *Pediatrics* 125, no. 1 (January 1, 2010), http://pediatrics.aappublications.org/content/125/1/16.abstract.

90.   "Women, Trauma and PTSD," U.S. Department of Veterans Affairs, January 1, 2007, http://www.ptsd.va.gov/public/pages/women-trauma-and-ptsd.asp.

91.   *Military Personnel: DOD Has Taken Steps to Meet the Health Needs of Deployed Servicewomen.*

92.   Quoted in Frank M. Richardson, *Fighting Spirit: A Study of Psychological Factors in War* (London: Leo Cooper, 1978), 3.

93.   Kingsley R. Browne, "Band of Brothers or Band of Siblings? An Evolutionary Perspective on Sexual Integration of Combat Forces," in *Oxford Handbook of Evolutionary Perspectives on Violence, Homicide, and War*, eds. T. K. Shackelford and V. Weekes-Shackelford (New York: Oxford University Press, 2012), 372–92.

94.   Ibid.

95.   Ibid.

96.   "Homicide Trends in the United States, 1980–2008: Annual Rates for 2009 and 2010," Bureau of Justice Statistics, NCJ 236018, November 16, 2011, http://bjs.ojp.usdoj.gov/index.cfm?ty=pbse&sid=31.

97.   Wiley-Blackwell, "Men Respond More Aggressively Than Women to Stress and It's All Down to a Single Gene," ScienceDaily.com, March 7, 2012, http://www.sciencedaily.com/releases/2012/03/120308071058.htm.

98.   Browne, "Band of Brothers or Band of Siblings?"

99.   Cited by Browne; and Samuel A. Stouffer et al., *The American Soldier: Combat and Its Aftermath*, vol. 2 (Princeton: Princeton University Press, 1949).

100. Monika Jansen Drake, "Ambivalence at the Academies: Attitudes toward Women in the Military at the Federal Service Academies," *Social Thought*

and Research 27 (2006): 43–68, http://kuscholarworks.ku.edu/dspace/bitstream/1808/5209/1/STARV27A3.pdf.

101. Madeline Morris, "By Force of Arms: Rape, War, and Military Culture," *Duke Law Journal* 45 (1996): 651–781, cited in Drake, "Ambivalence at the Academies," 60.

102. Browne, "Band of Brothers or Band of Siblings?"

103. John Piper, "Co-Ed Combat and Cultural Cowardice," desiringGod.com, November 2, 2007, http://www.desiringgod.org/resource-library/taste-see-articles/co-ed-combat-and-cultural-cowardice.

104. Ryan Smith, "The Reality That Awaits Women in Combat," *Wall Street Journal*, January 23, 2013, http://online.wsj.com/article/SB10001424127887323535980457826013211473150.html.

105. Presidential Commission on the Assignment of Women in the Armed Forces, *Report to the President*, "Section II: Alternative Views," 65.

106. Ibid., 71.

107. Heather Mac Donald, "Women in Combat and Sexual Assault," *The Corner* (blog), National Review Online, January 27, 2013, http://www.nationalreview.com/corner/338942/women-combat-and-sexual-assault-heather-mac-donald.

108. Liz Trotta interview with Eric Shawn, Fox News, February 13, 2012, http://www.youtube.com/watch?v=4ooMMue-qwQ.

109. Anna Mulrine, "Pentagon Report: Sexual Assault in the Military Up Dramatically," *Christian Science Monitor*, January 19, 2013, http://www.csmonitor.com/USA/Military/2012/0119/Pentagon-report-Sexual-assault-in-the-military-up-dramatically.

110. "2012 US Military Suicides Hit Record High of 349," Fox News, January 14, 2013, http://www.foxnews.com/politics/2013/01/14/2012-us-military-suicides-hit-record-high-34/.

111. Anna Mulrine, "Women in Combat Units: Could It Reduce Sexual Assault in the Military?," *Christian Science Monitor*, January 25, 2013, http://www.csmonitor.com/USA/Military/2013/0125/Women-in-combat-units-Could-it-reduce-sexual-assault-in-the-military.

112. Mark Thompson, "Covert Combat Sex," *Time*, November 26, 2012, http://nation.time.com/2012/11/26/covert-combat-sex/.

113. CW2 Brady Greer, interview by author, February 21, 2013.

114. *World*, August 12–19, 1995, 15.

115. Presidential Commission on the Assignment of Women in the Armed Forces, *Report to the President*, "Section II: Alternative Views," 60.

116. "A Woman's Burden," *Time*, March 28, 2003, http://www.time.com/time/nation/article/0,8599,438760,00.html.

117. Dianna Lynn, "Jessica Lynch: I Was Raped," WND.com, November 6, 2003, http://www.wnd.com/2003/11/21645/

118. Department of Defense, "Conflict Casualties," Defense Casualty Analysis System as of June 2013, https://www.dmdc.osd.mil/dcas/pages/casualties.xhtml.

119. As cited in Anita Ramasastry, "What Happens When GI Jane Is Captured? Women Prisoners of War and the Geneva Conventions," FindLaw.com, April 2, 2003, http://writ.news.findlaw.com/ramasastry/20030402.html.

120. Presidential Commission on the Assignment of Women in the Armed Forces, *Report to the President*, "Section II: Alternative Views," 70.

121. Ibid.

122. Testimony before the Presidential Commission on the Assignment of Women in the Armed Forces, June 26, 1992, Washington, D.C. (testimony of John W. Ripley), http://www.tfp.org/tfp-home/fighting-for-our-culture/testimony-of-col-john-w-ripley-to-the-presidential-commission-on-the-assignment-of-women-in-the-armed-forces.html.

123. Testimony before the Presidential Commission on the Assignment of Women in the Armed Forces (testimony of John W. Ripley).

124. Dara Kay Cohen et al., *Wartime Sexual Violence: Misconceptions, Implications, and Ways Forward*, United States Institute of Peace, February 2013, http://www.usip.org/publications/wartime-sexual-violence-misconceptions-implications-and-ways.

125. Svetlana Alexievich, *The War's Unwomanly Face* (Moscow: Progress Publishers, 1988). Excerpt available online at http://www.dursthoff.de/book.php?m=3&PHPSESSID=bb99c3d42ce637a826936fbe2c46fdcd&aid=40&bid=66.

126. Jeffrey Burds, "Sexual Violence in Europe in World War II, 1939-1945," *Politics and Society* 37, no. 1 (March 2009): 45, http://pas.sagepub.com/cgi/content/abstract/37/1/35.

127. Anne Leland and Mari-Jana Oboroceanu, *American War and Military Operations, Casualties: Lists and Statistics*, CRS report for Congress, February 26, 2010.

128. Department of Defense, "Conflict Casualties," Defense Casualty Analysis System, https://www.dmdc.osd.mil/dcas/pages/casualties.xhtml.

129. Kristina Wong, "Women Fighting and Dying in War, Despite Combat Exclusion Policy," ABC News, May 30, 2011, http://abcnews.go.com/US/women-fight-iraq-afghanistan-preclusion-ground-combat/story?id=13716419&page=3.

130. Sergeant Hester's military police squad was ambushed in Iraq in 2005. She was awarded the Silver Star for valor in fighting off the attackers.

131. Ray Odierno, "The Force of Tomorrow," *Foreign Policy*, February 4, 2013, http://www.foreignpolicy.com/articles/2013/02/04/the_force_of_tomorrow.

132. General Martin E. Dempsey, "CJCS Info Memo for Secretary of Defense, Subject: Women in the Service Implementation Plan," CM-0017-13, January 9, 2013.

133. Wong, "Women Fighting and Dying in War."

134. Adam Kredo, "Women in Combat Hurt Retention, Marine Study Suggests," Washington Free Beacon, February 14, 2013, http://freebeacon.com/women-in-combat-could-hurt-retention-marines-study-suggests/.

135. Andrew Tilghman, "2013 Military Times Poll: Officers Much Happier Than Enlisted Members," *Military Times*, March 26, 2013, http://militarytimes.com/static/projects/pages/military-poll-2013.pdf.

136. "Background of Selective Service," History and Records, Selective Service System, April 30, 2002, http://www.sss.gov/backgr.htm.

137. The Military Selective Service Act, 50 U.S.C. App. 451 et seq. (2003). Available online at http://www.sss.gov/pdfs/mssa-2003.pdf.

138. The Military Selective Service Act, 50 U.S.C. App. 451 et seq. (2003). Available online at http://www.sss.gov/pdfs/mssa-2003.pdf.

139. "How the Draft Has Changed Since Vietnam," History and Records, Selective Service System, 2007, http://www.sss.gov/viet.htm.

140. "Rostker v. Goldberg, 448 U.S. 1306 (1980). Available online at http://laws.lp.findlaw.com/getcase/US/448/1306.html. "Briefly, the procedural history of this case is as follows: The original complaint was filed in June 1971 by male citizens subject to registration and induction who argued

that the Selective Service Act violated several of their constitutional rights, including the right to equal protection of the laws guaranteed by the Fifth Amendment. Application to the United States District Court for the Eastern District of Pennsylvania for the convening of a three-judge court under the then applicable statute, 28 U.S.C. 2282 (1970 ed.), was denied, and the suit was dismissed. On review, the United States Court of Appeals for the Third Circuit upheld the dismissal of all claims except that founded upon the failure to conscript females. The Court of Appeals remanded the case to the District Court for a determination of the substantiality of the equal protection claim, and of plaintiffs' standing to raise that issue. On remand, the District Court found that plaintiffs had standing, and convened a three-judge court."

141. Rostker v. Goldberg, 453 U.S. 57 (1981). Available online at http://law2. umkc.edu/faculty/projects/ftrials/conlaw/RostkervGoldberg.html.

142. National Coalition for Men et al. v. Selective Service System et al., CV13-02391 (California Central District Court, 2013).

143. Robert Fenn, "Robert Gates Says Health Care Costs Hurt Defense Budget," *U.S. News & World Report*, February 24, 2011, http://www.usnews.com/ opinion/blogs/Peter-/Fenn/2011/02/24/robert-/gates-/says/healthcare-/ costs-/hurt-/defense-/budget; Department of Defense Office of the Actuary, *Statistical Report on the Military Retirement System, Fiscal Year 2011*, May 2012, 20, http://actuary.defense.gov/Portals/15/Documents/ statbook11.pdf.

144. U.S. Office of Management and Budget, *Historical Tables: Budget of the U.S. Government Fiscal Year 2011* (Washington, DC: Government Printing Office, 2010), 84, 89, 127, 132, http://www.whitehouse.gov/sites/ default/files/omb/budget/fy2011/assets/hist.pdf.

145. Karl W. Eikenberry, "Reassessing the All-Volunteer Force," *Washington Quarterly*, (Winter 2013): 11, http://iis-db.stanford.edu/pubs/23958/ TWQ_13Winter_Eikenberry.pdf.

Chapter 5

1. David F. Burrelli, *Women in Combat: Issues for Congress*, U.S. Library of Congress, Congressional Research Service, CRS Report R42075 (Washington, D.C.: Office of Congressional Information and Publishing, May 9, 2013).

2. Another instructive description of recent ground combat is found in Dakota Meyer and Bing West, *Into the Fire: A Firsthand Account of the Most Extraordinary Battle in the Afghan War* (New York: Random House, 2012). Meyer is a former Marine who was awarded the Medal of Honor for actions during the Battle of Ganjgal, Afghanistan.

3. The details of that fight are chronicled in an outstanding "battle study" published by the Marine Corps, *U.S. Marines in Battle an-Najaf* (Washington, D.C.: U.S. Government Printing Office, 2004).

4. Active-duty Marine, interview by author.

5. Bayard "Vic" Taylor, USMC Lt. Col. (Ret.), interview by author.

6. Edwin L. Kennedy, USA Brig. Gen. (Ret.), interview by author.

7. Military Leadership Diversity Commission, *From Representation to Inclusion: Diversity Leadership for the 21st Century Military,* final report, 2011.

8. "Operationalizing Diversity," U.S. Navy, July 2010, http://cdrsalamander. blogspot.com/2010/07/diversity-thursday_29.html; and Editorial, "High Seas Segregation," *Washington Times,* July 30, 2010, http://www. washingtontimes.com/news/2010/jul/30/high-seas-segregation/.

9. "Gen Robert H. Barrow on Women in Combat," *Leatherneck,* http://www. mca-marines.org/leatherneck/gen-robert-h-barrow-women-combat.

10. Retired U.S. Marine Corps general, interview by author, March 30, 2013.

11. Kevin Baron, "Pentagon Rebukes General for Opposing Repeal of 'Don't Ask, Don't Tell' Law," *Stars and Stripes,* March 25, 2010, http://www. stripes.com/news/pentagon-rebukes-general-for-opposing-repeal-of-don-t-ask-don-t-tell-law-1.100302.

12. William H. McMichael, "Webb Wants Officer-to-Enlisted Ratio Explained," *Navy Times,* May 16, 2010, http://www.navytimes.com/ news/2010/05/airforce_military _officers_051710w/; and Richard Sisk, "Panetta Promises to Cut Military Brass," Military.com, December 18, 2012, http://www.military.com/daily-news/2012/12/18/panetta-promises-cuts-to-military-brass.html.

13. Carlton Meyer, "Tenure Flag Officers," G2Mil, 2009, http://www.g2mil. com/tenured.htm.

14. See the criticism leveled at general and flag officers by Thomas Ricks, "General Failure," *Atlantic,* October 24, 2012, http://www.theatlantic.

com/magazine/archive/2012/11/general-failure/309148/; and Paul Yin-
gling, "A Failure in Generalship," *Armed Forces Journal*, May 2007, http://
www.armedforcesjournal.com/2007/05/2635198.

15. Douglas A. MacGregor, "The Failure of Military Leadership in Iraq: Fire the
Generals!," Counterpunch, May 26–28, 2006, http://www.counterpunch.
org/2006/05/26/fire-the-generals/.

16. Tim Kane, "West Point Graduates: Why Our Best Officers Are Leaving
Early," *Christian Science Monitor*, January 5, 2011, http://www.csmonitor.
com/Business/Growthology/2011/0105/West-Point-graduates-Why-our-
best-officers-are-leaving-early.

Conclusion

1. "Grim Toll of Military Women Killed in War," Center for Military Readiness, April 1, 2013, http://www.cmrlink.org/content/home/35891/
grim_toll_of_military_women_killed_in_war.

2. John Piper, "Combat and Cowardice: Men Were Not Wired to Follow
Women into Danger," *World*, November 10, 2007, http://www.worldmag.
com/2007/11/combat_and_cowardice.

INDEX

617th Military Police Company, 65

737th Training Group, 142

2011 Military Leadership Diversity Commission (MLDC), 75, 101, 112, 154, 164

A

Aberdeen Proving Ground, 73, 106

Afghanistan, 74, 76, 146, 157, 160. *See also* War in Afghanistan

women in, 18, 29, 40, 64–71, 94–95, 98–99, 143–44, 150–51, 194

Africa, 149

Air Force Combat Controllers, 25

Aliens, 33

Allen, Mary, 15

All Kinds of Families, 133

all-volunteer force (AVF), x, 3, 88–89, 159–62, 181

al-Sadr, Muqtada, 166, 170

Altman, Robert, 34

"Amanda," 4

American Academy of Nurse Practitioners, 131

American Academy of Pediatrics, 133

American Civil Liberties Union, 35

American Expeditionary Force, 16, 19

American Family Association, 38

Amidror, Yaakov, 93

Amos, James, 38

Anderson, Thomas, 67

Andrews Air Force Base, 37

Annual Report on Sexual Harassment and Violence at the Military Service Academies, 73–74
Apache helicopters, 32
Arab Spring, 10
Army Command, 8
Army Engineer Corps, 43
    Sapper School of, 43–44
Army Medical Department, 126
Army Physical Fitness Test (APFT), 83–84, 115
Army Rangers, 25, 43–44
Army Research Institute, 61, 90
Army Research Institute of Environmental Medicine, 82–83
Army Special Forces, 24, 182
Arnold, Henry H., 20
Art of War, The, 27
Ashton, Kimberly, 94
Asia, 12, 86
Aspin, Les, 22, 26, 108
Associated Press, 63, 70, 93
Australia, 29
    Defense Force of, 86–87

B

Bacevich, Andrew, Jr., 56
Bailey, "Mad Ann," 15
Balkans, 119, 149
Barrow, Robert H., 1–3, 177, 180, 187–88
Basic School, 110

Baskerville, Stephen K., 31
Battle of Monmouth, 14
Battleship, 33
Battlestar Galactica, 97
Bell, Catherine, 34
Bell-Johnson, Katrina L., 98
Bhagwati, 143
Bild, 89
bin Laden, Osama, 33
Black Hawk helicopters, 17, 35, 146
Blair, Anita, 105
Blair, Jane, 55–56
Boehner, John, 37
Boston University, 56
Boudicca, 12
Boxer, Barbara, 103
Boykin, Jerry, 7–8, 12
Brady, Patrick, 111–12
Bray, Linda, 17
Britain, 12
Broadwell, Paula, 70
Browne, Kingsley R., 101, 136–38
Brown, Melissa, 64, 66
Brown, Monica Lin, 18
Bundeswehr, 88–89. *See also* Germany, army of
Bureau of Justice Statistics, 137
Burns, Patrick, 104
Burrelli, David, 116
Bush administration, 25–26, 190
Bush, George W., 7, 26, 59
Buzzatto, Charles, 119–120

C

C-17 aircraft, 119
"cadet respect officers," 103
Canada, 14, 153
    army of, 94–95, 110–11
Cannon, Laura, 43–44, 144
Capitol Hill, 10, 12, 29
Caracal Battalion (Israel), 93
Carnegie Hero Fund Commission, 136
Carter, Jimmy, 9, 16, 157–58
Casey, George W., Jr., 166, 188
Catwoman, 33
Cawvey, Jessica L., 98
CBS News, 22, 34
Center for Army Leadership, 11
Center for Military Readiness, the, 38, 75, 104–6, 182–84
Centers for Disease Control and Prevention, 128
Central Intelligence Agency (CIA), 33, 70
CHEN (Israeli women's corps), 92
Cheney, Dick, 11
Cherry, Fred, 147–48
Chicago, 85, 92
Chicago Tribune, 85
China, 9, 59
China Beach, 34
Chosin, 40, 177–180
Christian Coalition, 38
Christian Science Monitor, 143

City University of New York, 64
Civil War (United States), 14–15, 45, 156
Clark, Mark, 16
Clark, William, 107
Clinical Psychology Review, 136
Clinton administration, 24–26, 107–8
Clinton, Bill, 8–9, 22, 26, 107
CNN, 35
Cobra helicopters, 32
Cohen, William, 105
Cold War, 59, 88, 156
Colorado, 73, 82
Combat Action Badge, 73
Combat Endurance Test, 110
Combat Related Employment for Women (CREW), 14
"Comfortably Numb: Desensitizing Effects of Violent Media on Helping Others," 39
Command and General Staff College, 8
Concerned Women for America, 38
Cone, Robert, 102–3
Confederates, 9, 15
Congressional Budget Office (CBO), 160
Congressional Commission on Military Training and Gender-Related Issues, 105
Congressional Research Service, 116, 164

conscription, 3, 25, 60–61, 88–89, 92, 100, 156–59, 161–62, 183–84. *See also* Selective Service System
Con-Tien, 148
Continental Army, 45
Cornum, Rhonda, 146, 150
counterinsurgency, 40, 50, 56–59, 66–67, 147, 151–53, 165–66
counterterrorism, 57, 59, 166
Cuba, 13
Czechoslovakia, 13

D

Dai Do, 171–77, 179
Danish military, 111
Darby, Rosie, 68
Dark Knight Rises, The, 33
David, Ann Simpson, 14
Decatur, Stephen, 15
Defense Advisory Committee on Women in the Services, 110, 153
Democratic Republic of Congo, 149
Democrats, 4, 22, 24, 35, 82, 149
Dempsey, Martin E., 152–53, 156, 164, 188–89, 195
Department of Veterans Affairs, 160
Desgrosseilliers, Todd, 110
direct combat probability coding (DCPC) system, 21
Distinguished Service Cross, 8
Dong Ha Combat Base, 170
Dong Huan, Vietnam, 172
Donnelly, Elaine, 105–7

"Don't Ask, Don't Tell" policy, 26, 188
Downing, Tom, 141
Duckworth, Tammy, 35
Duma, the, 91

E

Edmonds, Sarah, 15
"Effects of Mass Media Exposure on Acceptance of Violence against Women, The," 39
Egypt, 12, 93
Eikenberry, Karl, 161
Eisenhower, Dwight D., 20
El Salvador, 149
England, 13, 16
English, Beth, 130
European Court of Justice, 88
Executive Order 9981, 44

F

F-14 Tomcats, 104
Facebook, 69
Family Research Council, 38
female engagement team (FET), 67–68
feminism, feminists, 28, 32, 98–99
Feminist Majority, 38
Fitzsimmons Army Medical Center, 130
Flynt, Larry, 69
Fogleman, Ronald, 8–9
Foreign Policy, 58, 152
Fort Bliss, 105
Fort Bragg, 17, 119, 144

Fort Carson, 73
Fort Dix, 105
Fort Jackson, 105
Fort Leavenworth, 15, 83
Fort Leonard Wood, 105, 119
Fort McClellan, 105
Fort Sill, 105
Founders, the, 165, 191
Fox News, 35
France, 13–14, 16
Fredericksburg, 15
French Indochina War, 14
Friends of the IDF, 91–93
Fulton, Sarah, 15

G

Gallup, 36
Gannett, Deborah Sampson ("Robert Shurtleff"), 15
Gates, Robert, 26, 188
"gender-norming," 30, 109, 116, 163–64
General Accounting Office, 81–82, 117–18. *See also* Government Accountability Office (GAO)
General Order No. 1, 74–75, 144
George Mason University, 132
Germany, 13, 33, 88
    army of, 89–90. *See also* Bundeswehr
Gershon, Yitzhak, 91
G.I. Jane, 32–33, 40
Gilstrap, Lori, 82
Gjerde, Ingrid, 88

"glass ceiling," 36, 98–99, 103
Goddard, Nichola, 95
Good-Bye Painting, The, 133
Government Accountability Office (GAO), 81–82, 108–9, 128, 132–35. *See also* General Accounting Office
"Great Patriotic War," 89
Greer, Bradley, 144
Gregor, William, 83
Grenada, 17
Grey, James. *See* Snell, Hannah
Guadalcanal, 40
Guidance for the Employment of the Force, 59
Gulf War. *See* Persian Gulf War
Gutmann, David, 92

H

Haiti, 139
Hampton Roads, 127
Hanoi Hilton, 37
Harman, Everett, 82
Hasselman, Kelly, 67
Hawn, Goldie, 34
"Hello Girls," 16
Hero of the Soviet Union award, 90
Hester, Leigh Ann, 18, 65–66, 151
Hezbollah, 57–58
Hobart, Melissa J., 98
Houlihan, Margaret J., 34
Hue, 40
Hultgreen, Kara, 104
Hundred Years' War, 13

Hungary, 13
Hunger Games, The, 33
"hypermasculinity," 138–40

I

Ia Drang, the, 40
Iceni, 12
Imam Ali Mosque, 166–67
improvised explosive devices (IEDs), 40, 66, 151, 168
Independent Women's Forum, 105
Infantry Officer Course (IOC), 110
initial strength test (IST), 117–18
Iran, 10, 57–59
Iraq, 18, 29, 35, 40, 98, 119, 122–28, 140–47, 180, 194
Iraq War, 43–44, 47, 51, 55–59, 64–65, 68–69, 80, 85, 150–53, 160, 166. *See also* Operation Iraqi Freedom
    Battalion Landing Team, First Battalion, Fourth Marines (BLT 1/4), 166–67, 169–70, 176–77
    Fallujah, 166, 170
    "March Up," 167
    Najaf, 166–67, 169–70, 177
Ireland, Mary Lloyd, 80
"Islamic Terror and Sexual Mutilation" (symposium), 92
Israel, 91–93
    512th Brigade, 93
    Armored Corps Commander's Course of, 92–93
    army of, 14, 57. *See also* Israel Defense Forces (IDF)
    Military Service Law of, 91
    Southern Command, 93
Israel Defense Forces (IDF), 57, 91–93. *See also* Israel, army of

J

JAG, 34
Japan, 146, 149, 178
Jelinek, Pauline, 63
Joan of Arc, 13
Johnson, Harold K., 8
Johnson, Lyndon B., 8–9
Joint Chiefs of Staff, 1, 4–5, 7, 142, 164, 181, 188
Joint Strategic Capabilities Plan, 59
Journal of the Royal Society of Medicine, 125–26

K

Kandahar, 69–70
    Kandahar FOB, 70, 94
Kansas, 15, 83, 105
Kaplan, Mark, 132
Kassebaum, Nancy Landon, 105
Kennedy, Edwin L., 177–80
Kennedy, Sally, 69, 73, 128
Knyazeva, Yelena, 90–91
Kober, Avi, 57
Konovalenko, Maria, 30
Korean War, 9, 59

Chosin Reservoir campaign, 40, 177–79

   Korea Augmentation to the U.S. Army (KATUSA), 178–79

   U.S. Fifteenth Infantry, 178–79

L

Lackland Air Force Base, 72–73, 142

Lainez, Eileen, 151

Las Vegas, 103

Lee, Joohyung, 137–38

LeMay, Curtis, 9

Leo, John, 116

Lepowsky, Maria, 28–29

Lewis, C. S., 195

Lewis, Debra, 109

Libya, 33

Lincoln, Abraham, 9

Lioness, 34

Load Carriage in Military Operations, 79

Long Binh, 17

Los Angeles Times, 67

Loucks, Anne, 80

Love, Nancy Harkness, 20

Lyles, Lester L., 154

Lynch, Jessica, 146, 148

M

M1A2 Abrams tanks, 120

M203 grenades, 65

MacArthur, Douglas, 9

Macdonald, Anne, 109

Mac Donald, Heather, 7, 75, 142

Macgregor, Douglas, 189–90

Mackenzie, Sarah ("Mac"), 34

Mahdi militia, 166–68, 170

Manassas, 15

Manhattan Institute, 7, 75

Marshall, Mary, 15

M*A*S*H, 34

Massachusetts, 15

Mattis, James ("Mad Dog"), 10

Maxwell, Desiree, 51, 73

McCain, John, 37

McCall's, 22

McCauley, Mary Hays, 14

McChrystal, Stanley, 10

McClellan, George, 9

McDaniel, Norman, 148

McKeon, Buck, 37

McKinley, Steve, 44

McSally, Martha, 32

Medal of Honor, 15–16

Mexican War, 15

Mexico, 15

   army of, 13

Meyer, Edward, 118

Miklaszewski, Jim, 35

Military Culture Coalition, 182

Military Enlistment Physical Strength Capacity Test (MEPSCAT), 80–81, 118–19

military occupational specialty (MOS), 21, 61–62, 118, 120, 184

Military Selective Service Act (MSSA), 157

Military Times, 156

"Miranda," 119

Missouri, 119

mixed-sex basic training, 104–6, 108

Mixon, Benjamin, 188–89, 191

"Molly Pitcher." *See* McCauley, Mary Hays

Moman, Katie, 94

Monash University, 29

Moore, Demi, 34–33, 113

Moscow, 30

Mosul, 70

MSNBC, 35

Mulan, 33

Mullen, Michael, 26, 164, 185, 188

Mundy, Carl, 9–11, 166

N

Nagl, John, 190–91

Najaf, 166–70, 177, 179

Nasiriya, 146

National Coalition of Men (NCM), 158

National Defense Authorization Act, 1992–1993 version, 23
1994 version, 24
2012 version, 134–35
proposed amendments to, 182, 185

National Geographic, 88

National Institute of Mental Health, 132

National Marriage Project, 29

National Military Strategy of the United States of America, The, 59

National Organization for Women, 38

Naval Health Research Center, 121

Navy Nurse Corps, 19

Navy SEALs,
combat exclusion and, 24,
G.I. Jane and, 33
standards of, 37, 113, 120–22

New Castle Army Air Base, 20

Newcom, Elizabeth C., 15

New York Times, 35
New York Times–CBS News poll, 22

New Zealand, 87

New Zealand Defense Force, 87

Nixon, Richard, 157

North Atlantic Treaty Organization (NATO), 87

North Carolina, 17, 119, 144

North Korea, 9, 177–79

North Vietnam, 9, 147–48, 170–71

North Vietnamese Army (NVA), 170–77

Northwestern University, 92

Norway, 87–88

Norwegian Ministry of Defense, 87–88

Nunn, Sam, 24–25

O

Obama administration, ix, 25, 26, 38, 101, 156, 159, 161–63, 189, 195

Obama, Barack
Congress and, 26, 37, 160
"Don't Ask, Don't Tell" and, 26
James "Mad Dog" Mattis and, 10
lifting the combat exclusion of women and, 4, 6–7, 10, 12, 36–38, 195–96
National Security Strategy of the United States, 2010, and, 59
Stanley McChrystal and, 10
unemployment and, 161

Odierno, Raymond, 38, 58, 103, 115, 152

OH-58 helicopters, 144

Ohio University, 80

O'Neill, Jim, 176

Operation Anaconda, 76

Operation Desert Shield, 127–29. *See also* Persian Gulf War

Operation Desert Storm, 17, 127–29. *See also* Persian Gulf War

Operation Iraqi Freedom, 80, 166–69. *See also* Iraq War

Operation Just Cause, 17

Operation Petticoat, 34

O'Rear, Valerie, 5

Osbourne, Pamela, 98

P

Panama, 17, 22

Panetta, Leon, ix, 6, 26–27, 36, 53, 75, 101, 143, 195

Patrick Henry College, 31

Patton, George, 164

Peay, J. H. Binford, III, 24

Pennsylvania, 14–15, 226

Pentagon
1994 rule of, 24–25, 66, 101
2011 Military Leadership Diversity Commission, 75–76
budget of, 132, 142, 159–60
civilian hierarchy of, 2, 76, 159
Congress and, 2, 22, 24–25, 163–64, 182
female employees of, 63
feminists and, 76, 99, 193
leaders of, 7, 75–76, 100–1, 188
lifting the combat exclusion of women by, 3–4, 6, 34–36, 38, 75, 123, 150–51, 155–56, 193
Office of Sexual Assault Prevention and Response, 71
readiness and, 100–1, 104, 116
risk rule and, 146
surveys on sexual harassment conducted by, 71–72, 142

Perry, William, 24–25

Pershing, John J., 16

Persian Gulf War, 128, 139–140, 146, 194. *See also* Operation Desert Shield and Operation Desert Storm

Petraeus, David, 70

Petronio, Katie, 112–13, 123–24, 132,
    155
Pew Research Center, 63
Pew Research Center–*Washington
    Post* national survey, 60
Philippines, 13, 16, 146
Piestewa, Lori Ann, 98
Piper, John, 139, 195
Plymouth, 15
political correctness, 4, 11, 18–19, 38,
    103, 115, 164–65, 185–93
Powell, Colin, 11
Prescott, Scotty, 172, 175
Presidential Commission on the
    Assignment of Women in the
    Armed Forces,
    findings of, 11–12, 23, 30, 63–64,
        78–79, 83, 104–5, 110, 128, 145,
        180
    testimonies before, 28–29, 111,
        140–41, 147–49
Psychiatric Services, 123, 132
Psychological Science, 39
Public Broadcasting Service (PBS),
    34–35
Pudil, Charles ("Chuck"), 53
Purple Heart, 16

Q

Quantico, 62, 110
Queen Isabella of Spain, 13
Quinnipiac University national poll,
    60–61

R

RAND Corporation, 46, 64
Ranger School, 43–44
rape. *See also* sexual harassment, assault
    by captors, 145–47, 149
    in foreign militaries, 95, 149
    hypermasculinity and, 138
    in the U.S. military, 73, 142–45
Red Cross,
    American Red Cross, 16
    International Red Cross, 147
Reed, Ralph, 38
*Report of the Joint Service Administrative
    Discharge Study Group*, 45
Republicans, 4, 37, 81
Reserve Officers' Training Corps
    (ROTC), 53, 84
    Advanced Camp, 83
    Leader Development Assessment
        Course, 83
Revolutionary War, 14–15
Richmond (KY), 65
Richmond (VA), 15
Ripley, John W., 49, 148–49
"risk rule," 21–22, 146
Riyadh, 18
Rolling Stone, 10
Ron-Tal, Yiftach, 93–94
"roofies," 73
Rostker v. Goldberg, 25, 158
ROTC. *See* Reserve Officers' Training
    Corps
Roughead, Gary, 186–87

Russia. *See also* Soviet Union
  122nd Air Group of, 90
  as antagonist of the United States, 59
  army of, 13, 52, 89–91
  Central Sniper Training Center for Women, 90
  revolution of, 13
  Women's Reserve Rifle Regiment (Russia), 90

S

Salt Lake City, 64
Salt Lake Tribune, 64
Santo Tomas camp, 16
Saudi Arabia, 8–9, 18, 71
Scharnberg, Kristen, 85–86
School of Advanced Military Studies, 83
School of Infantry (Marine Corps), 117
Schroeder, Patricia, 82
Schwarzkopf, H. Norman, 18
Scott, Hugh, 75–76
Selective Service System. *See also* conscription
  court cases regarding the, 25, 157, 158
  laws regarding the, 25, 157
  registration for the, 25, 100, 183–4
Seoul, 179
September 11, 2001, 59, 150, 161, 194
Service: When Women Come Marching Home, 34

Service Women's Action Network, 143
sexual harassment, assault. *See also* rape
  by captors, 145–50, 195
  in foreign militaries, 92, 95, 149
  in the media, 39
  in the U.S. military, x, 28–29, 31, 62, 70–75, 100, 103, 134, 138, 142–149, 155, 195
Shaffstall, Michael, 119
Sierra Leone, 149
Silver Star award, 18, 65–66
Sinclair, Jeffrey, 70
Singlaub, John K., 9
Smeal, Eleanor, 38
Smith, Raymond C., Jr., 24
Smith, Ryan, 140
Smith, Stephen, 140–41
Snell, Hannah (James Grey), 13
Snow White and the Huntsman, 33
Sobieck, Tom, 104
Somalia, 139
South Carolina, 104–5
South Vietnam, 8, 170
Soviet Union. *See also* Russia
  Cold War and, 59
  invasion of Afghanistan, 157
  Josef Stalin and, 18
  sexual assault and, 149
  Vietnam War and, 170
  women fighting for, 18, 52, 89–90, 136

Spanish-American War, 45

Sparacino, Marietta, 64

Sparrow, Rob, 29–30

SPARS (Coast Guard Women's Reserve), 19–20

SRY gene, 137–38

Standards of Medical Fitness (U.S. Army), 50

Stand Up America, 12

Stark, Christine, 34–35

Stars and Stripes, 188

Stepanova, Yelena, 90

"Success of First-Term Soldiers" (RAND Corporation study), 64

Sung, Kim Il, 177

Sun Tzu, 27

survival, evasion, resistance, and escape (SERE) training, 145

Sustaining Female Soldiers' Health and Performance During Deployment, 129–30

Sustaining U.S. Global Leadership: Priorities for 21st Century Defense, 58–59

Sweat, Cherry, 62–63

Syria, 12

T

Tailhook Association Symposium, 103

Taylor, Bayard ("Vic"), 171–77

Ternus, Mona, 132

Texas, 72–73, 142

Textbook of Medical Physiology, 76

Third Reich, 149

Thurman, Maxwell, 118

Tompkins, Sally, 15

Training and Doctrine Command (TRADOC), 102, 105, 118

Triangle Institute for Security Studies Project on the Gap between Military and Civilian Society, 13

Trooper Mary, 13

Truman, Harry, 9, 20, 44–45

U

United Service Organizations, 16

University of Arkansas (Razorbacks), 53

University of Virginia, 29

University of Wisconsin, 28

U.S. 146th Transportation Company, 70

U.S. 187th Regiment, 76

U.S. 782nd Brigade Support Battalion, 66

U.S. Air Force
jobs in, 48
leadership of, 8, 9, 147–48, 154
pregnancy policies in, 126,
sexual assaults in, 72–74, 142,
women in, 5, 20–22, 24–25, 32, 37, 50–51, 104

U.S. Army Delta Force, 7

U.S. Army First Armored Division, 4

U.S. Army General Staff, 19

U.S. Central Command, 10

U.S. Coast Guard, 19

U.S. Code,
Title 10, Section 6015, 21–22, 108
Title 10, Section 8549, 21–22

U.S. Congress,
and conscription, 157–59, 161, 163
and defense spending, 160
and military experience, 39–40
and military oversight, ix, 2–3,
10–11, 19, 21– 23, 25–27, 45, 99,
108, 135, 157, 161, 163–65
proposed action for, 180–85, 187,
189–91

U.S. Constitution, 185
Article 1, Section 8, 25, 180

U.S. Department of Defense
*Annual Report on Sexual Harass-
ment and Violence at the Military
Service Academies*, 73
appropriations and, 160
policies of, 2, 48, 132, 134, 151, 184
RAND Corporation study and, 46
"risk rule," and, 21
Sexual Assault and Response
Office, 142–43

U.S. Eighty-Second Airborne Division, 6, 70–71, 76

U.S. Eleventh Marine Expeditionary
Unit (MEU), 166–70

U.S. House of Representatives, 180
House Armed Services Committee,
37

U.S. Institute of Peace (USIP), 149

U.S. Marine Corps
combat experiences of, 148, 166–80
Congress and, 10–11
desegregation of, 44–45
mixed-sex basic training, 105
officers of, 1, 8–10, 12
physical fitness standards in, 65,
110–13, 117, 154–55
pregnancy in, 126–27, 154
women in, 19–22, 25, 49, 61–62, 80,
154–55

U.S. military
battle casualties in the, 150
Congress and, ix, 1–3, 10–11,
19–23, 25–27, 99, 105, 108, 116,
146, 157–59, 161, 163–65, 180–
187, 189–91
effectiveness of, 1–2, 25, 44, 53, 60,
84, 90, 99, 101, 107, 114, 125–26,
141, 164–65, 187, 193
feminists and, 7, 28–30, 36, 38,
97–98, 112, 115, 153–54, 164,
194
future conflicts of, 57–59, 151
"gender-norming" and, 30, 98, 106,
109, 116, 114, 163
homosexuals in, 6, 9, 44–45, 51, 107
job placements in, 117–121, 183–
84
leadership of, 3–7, 10–11, 19, 31,
37, 68–70, 73, 112–13, 164–165,
185–91

physical fitness standards of, 30–31,
    75–85, 103, 106, 107–9, 112,
    116–121
political correctness and, 4, 11, 18,
    38, 103, 115, 164–65, 185, 187–
    91
pregnancy in, 126–28
public understanding of, 32, 39–40,
    60–61, 159, 165
recruitment and, 52, 60, 62–64,
    100, 107, 122, 136, 141–42, 154–
    62
sexual assault in, 29, 71–75, 100,
    142–45
size of, 50, 86, 100
warrior culture of, lx, 63, 100, 109,
    135–42, 164
women serving in, 4–5, 13–27,
    33–37, 45–50, 60–66, 75, 79, 107,
    112, 129–32, 145
U.S. Military Academy's candidate fit-
    ness assessment, 109
U.S. National Guard, 65, 86, 127,
    159
U.S. Olympic Committee, 82
USS *Abraham Lincoln*, 104
U.S. Senate, 180
    Senate Appropriations Committee,
    118–19,
    Senate Armed Services Committee,
    1–2, 24, 107, 180
USS *John Paul Jones*, 33
USS *United States*, 15

U.S. Supreme Court, 25, 156, 158–59,
    161
U.S. Third Infantry Division, 43
U.S. V Corps, 16

V

Vallely, Paul, 12
van Creveld, Martin, 98–99
Vietnam, 9, 14, 148
    Cua Viet River, 170–73
    Dinh To, 173
Vietnam Veterans Memorial, 17
Vietnam War, 3, 8, 34, 160
    casualties of, 16–17, 150, 194
    Tet Offensive of, 170–77
    U.S. First Battalion, First Marines,
    173–77
    U.S. Second Battalion, Fourth
    Marines (2/4 Marines) ("Mag-
    nificent Bastards"), 170–77
    U.S. Third Marine Division, 171–77
Virginia, 15, 62, 110, 114, 127

W

Wadi-us-Salaam cemetery, 166–69
Walker, Mary Edwards, 15–16
"Wall, the," 17
Wall Street Journal, 94, 140
Walter Reed Army Medical Center, 79
War of 1812, 15, 45
War in Afghanistan, 10, 40, 58, 59, 67,
    76, 124, 130, 144, 146, 161, 166,
    170, 194. *See also* Afghanistan

casualties of, 98, 143, 150, 153

contractors in, 160

foreign forces in, 88, 94–95

women serving in, 18, 29, 56, 64–65, 67–70, 74, 119, 128, 150–52

War Department, 19

War of Independence (Israel), 14, 91–92

warrior spirit, warrior culture, ix, 109, 112, 63, 100, 135–42

Washington, D.C., 4, 17

Washington, George, 14, 45

Washington Post, 11, 35, 55, 60, 144

Weaver, Sigourney, 33

Webb, James, 114–15

Webb, Jim, 114

Weise, William ("Wild Bill"), 8, 170, 177

Welsh, Kit, 13

West, Allen, 32

West Point, 43, 63, 70, 103, 109, 177–78, 190

West, Togo, Jr., 23, 108

White House, 7–10, 99

Wieker, Volker, 89–90

Wilcox, W. Bradford, 29

Wilson, Lou, 10–11

women

    awards given to, 65–66

    children of, 132–34, 194–95

    combat exclusion of, lx, 3–5, 21, 24–5, 27, 34–36, 43, 45, 48, 101, 180, 182

"comfort women" system of Japan, 149

conscription and, 3, 25, 158–59, 161–63, 183–84

"critical mass" of, 102–3, 152–55

differences between men and, 24, 28–30, 48–53, 55, 64, 67, 75–81, 83–86, 97, 99, 101, 105, 112–5, 134–42, 180

"direct combat" and, x, 1–4, 7–8, 10, 12, 23, 26–29, 31, 36, 39–40, 57–61, 152, 165, 183–85

equality and rights of, 1, 28, 36, 40, 45–46, 50

injuries and, 122–27, 129–32, 154–56

media portrayal of, 5, 32–36, 40

military job assignments and, 115–22, 181–82, 186–87

other countries and, 12–13, 18, 86–95, 110–111, 124–26

performance standards and, 103–4, 106–8, 115–17, 164

physical fitness standards and, 24, 30–1, 38, 43, 62, 65, 67–68, 75–76, 78–86, 90, 101–3, 105, 108–110, 112–22, 140, 194

pregnancy and, 126–28

retention and, 47–48, 61, 64, 154–56

sexual assault of, 5, 31, 39, 71–74, 92, 95, 103, 142–49

sexual relationships and, 24, 28–29, 67–71, 74–75, 143–45

in the U.S. armed services, 4–5, 13–27, 45, 47, 52, 56–58, 62–64, 67, 86

wounded and killed, 29, 40, 98, 146–47, 150–51, 153–54, 194–95

Women Accepted for Volunteer Emergency Service (WAVES), 19

Women Air Force Service Pilots (WASPs), 20

Women's Armed Services Integration Act (1948), 20–21

Women's Army Auxiliary Corps (WAAC), 19. *See also* Women's Army Corps (WAC)

Women's Army Corps (WAC), 17, 19–20. *See also* Women's Army Auxiliary Corps (WAAC)

Women's Auxiliary Ferrying Squadron (WAFS), 20

Women's Reserve (U.S. Marine Corps), 20

Women, War & Peace, 34

World War I, 45, 146, 156, 195
women and, 16, 19, 89

World War II, 2, 8, 40, 45, 59, 83, 138, 149, 178
Japan and, 156
Pacific theater, 16
warfare since, 40, 59, 147
women in, 13–14, 16, 52, 89–90, 146

X

Xenophon, 135
"X-Factor" test, 118

Y

Yugoslavia, 13

Z

Zenobia, 12
Zero Dark Thirty, 33
Zinke, Ryan, 113–14